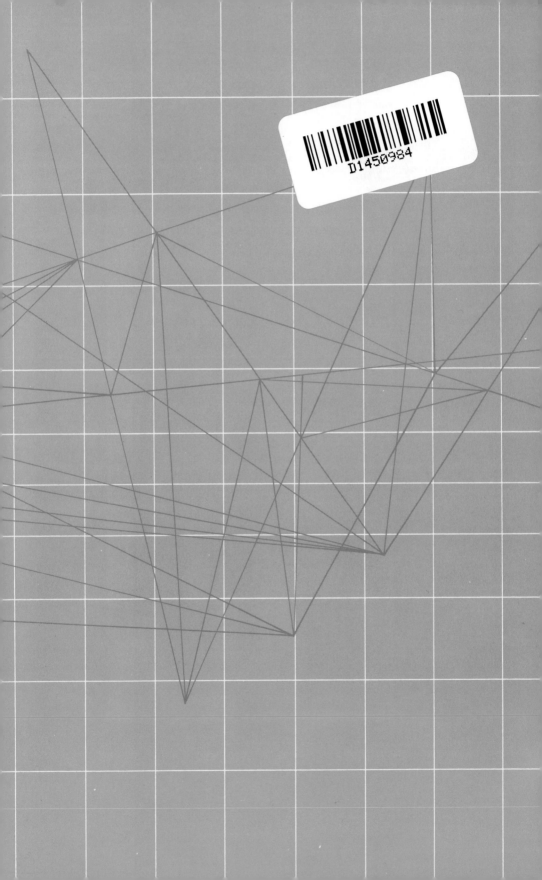

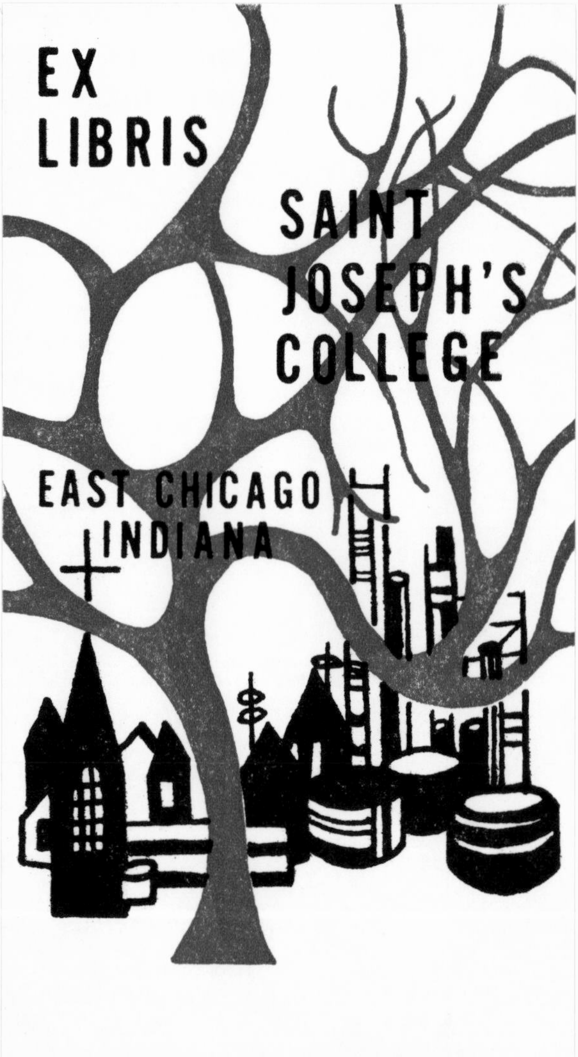
EX
LIBRIS
SAINT
JOSEPH'S
COLLEGE
EAST CHICAGO
INDIANA

WORLD BUSINESS

STUDIES OF THE MODERN CORPORATION
Columbia University Graduate School of Business

FRANCIS JOSEPH AGUILAR
Scanning the Business Environment

HERMAN W. BEVIS
Corporate Financial Reporting in a Competitive Economy

COURTNEY C. BROWN
World Business: Promise and Problems

RICHARD EELLS
The Corporation and the Arts

RICHARD EELLS *and* CLARENCE WALTON
Man in the City of the Future

JAY W. LORSCH
Product Innovation and Organization

KENNETH G. PATRICK *and* RICHARD EELLS
Education and the Business Dollar

IRVING PFEFFER
The Financing of Small Business

GEORGE A. STEINER
Top Management Planning

GEORGE A. STEINER *and* WARREN M. CANNON
Multinational Corporate Planning

GEORGE A. STEINER *and* WILLIAM G. RYAN
Industrial Project Management

GUS TYLER
The Political Imperative

CLARENCE WALTON *and* RICHARD EELLS
The Business System (3 volumes)

W O R

B U S

PROMISE AND

EDITED BY

AN ARKVILLE PRESS BOOK

L D

I N E S S

PROBLEMS

COURTNEY C. BROWN

THE MACMILLAN COMPANY, NEW YORK
COLLIER-MACMILLAN LIMITED, LONDON

STUDIES OF THE MODERN CORPORATION
Columbia University Graduate School of Business

The Program for Studies of the Modern Corporation is devoted to the advancement and dissemination of knowledge about the corporation. Its publications are designed to stimulate inquiry, research, criticism, and reflection. They fall into four categories: works by outstanding businessmen, scholars, and professional men from a variety of backgrounds and academic disciplines; prizewinning doctoral dissertations relating to the corporation; annotated and edited selections of business literature; and business classics that merit republication. The studies are supported by outside grants from private business, professional, and philanthropic institutions interested in the program's objectives.

RICHARD EELLS
Editor of the Studies

Contents

PART IV

THE ROLE OF EQUITY

PART V

AMBIGUITIES OF THE LAWS

CONTRIBUTORS

ARTHUR B. TOURTELLOT

Vice President, Columbia Broadcasting System, Inc., ARTHUR B. TOURTELLOT was for many years a partner and chairman of Earl Newsom and Company. A writer and associate producer of March of Time films at Time, Inc., he produced the two series "Crusade in Europe" and "Crusade in the Pacific." Mr. Tourtellot is the author and editor of many books and articles and a trustee of several historical societies. He is Chairman of the Editorial Board of the *Columbia Journal of World Business*.

COURTNEY C. BROWN

Business, government and education have all been the scenes of COURTNEY C. BROWN's career. He served as Dean of the Columbia Graduate School of Business for fifteen years and continues as Professor of Business Policy, Chairman of the Board of the American Assembly and Editor of the *Columbia Journal of World Business*. During World War II Dr. Brown served with the Department of State and the Commodity Credit Corporation in negotiations with other countries to procure exportable surpluses of needed supplies. Following the war, he was associated with the Standard Oil Company (N.J.) as Economist, Assistant to the Chairman of the Board and a director of Esso Standard Oil Company. He now serves on the Boards of the American Electric Power Company, Associated Dry Goods Corporation, Borden Company, Columbia Broadcasting System, Union Pacific Railroad, and Uris Buildings Corporation.

EMILE BENOIT

Professor of International Business at Columbia in the Schools of Business and of International Affairs, EMILE BENOIT is a specialist on the economics of defense and disarmament. Formerly Senior Economist in the Department of Labor and a Foreign Service Reserve Officer in London and Vienna, he has served as consultant to the United Nations Secretariat, the U.S. Departments of State and Defense, the Arms Control and Disarmament Agency, and the Asian Development Bank. Dr. Benoit has written widely on economics, business, and international relations.

GILBERT H. CLEE

Chairman of McKinsey & Company, Inc., international management consultants, the late GILBERT H. CLEE served as an adviser on finance and organization to many international companies. He helped expand the international operations of McKinsey, beginning with the opening of the London office in 1959 and continuing with offices in Zurich, Paris, Amsterdam, Düsseldorf, and Melbourne. Prior to joining McKinsey Mr. Clee was a loan officer for Latin America of the World Bank. At the time of his death in 1968 he was President of the Board of Trustees of Wesleyan University.

KENNETH SIMMONDS

Professor of Marketing at the London Graduate School of Business Studies, KENNETH SIMMONDS is a native of New Zealand and has had many years of industrial and consulting experience. His chief research interests are in the fields of international business strategy and cultural differences in purchasing behavior. Professor Simmonds has directed advanced management programs and seminars for a wide range of multinational corporations. He is marketing adviser to International Publishing Corporation and serves on the Textile Council and several editorial boards.

DAVID B. ZENOFF

Associate Professor at the Columbia Graduate School of Business, DAVID B. ZENOFF specializes in foreign direct investment, policy and strategy formulation in multinational companies, management of foreign licensing agreements, foreign environmental analysis and international financial management. He has conducted research on business problems in the Philippines and Mexico and is a consultant to the U.N. Industrial Development Organization, the U.S. Tariff Commission, and several multinational corporations. Professor Zenoff is the author of *Private Enterprise in the Developing Countries* and co-author of *International Financial Management*.

HOWARD V. PERLMUTTER

Trained as an engineer and a psychologist, HOWARD V. PERLMUTTER is now Professor of Industry at the Wharton School and Director of Research and Development of Worldwide Institutions at the University of Pennsylvania. He spent eight years at MIT's Center for International Studies and five years on the faculty of IMEDE, the Management Development Institute at the University of Lausanne, Switzerland. Professor Perlmutter's main interests are in the theory and practice of institution building, particularly worldwide enterprises.

JOHN FAYERWEATHER

Professor of International Business at the Graduate School of Business Administration of New York University, JOHN FAYERWEATHER is also Managing Editor of the *International Executive*. He is a consultant and lecturer for the multinational executive program of CETI, a French organization, Director of Workshops for Professors of International Business at N.Y.U., and a former member of the faculty of the Columbia Graduate School of Business. Professor Fayerweather is the author of many books, including *The Executive Overseas, Management of International Operations* and *International Business Management: A Conceptual Framework.*

CHARLES P. KINDLEBERGER

Professor of Economics at the Massachusetts Institute of Technology, CHARLES P. KINDLEBERGER is well known as an author and government adviser. Immediately after World War II he was Chief, Division of German and Austrian Affairs, Department of State, and Adviser, European Recovery Program. More recently Professor Kindleberger was a member of President Johnson's Advisory Committee on International Monetary Arrangements. He is the author of *International Economics, American Business Abroad: Six Lectures on Direct Investment,* and many other books.

JACK N. BEHRMAN

Professor of International Business at the Graduate School of Business Administration of the University of North Carolina, JACK N. BEHRMAN is engaged in research on the multinational enterprise and the role of foreign investment in economic development. For nearly four years Dr. Behrman was Assistant Secretary of Commerce for Domestic and International Business. His critique on investment controls, "Direct Manufacturing Investment, Exports and the Balance of Payments," prepared for the National Foreign Trade Council, was published in 1968.

ISAIAH A. LITVAK

Professor of International Business at McMaster University in Canada, ISAIAH A. LITVAK has served as consultant to government and industry in the field of international business. He has participated in a number of executive development programs sponsored by multinational corporations in North America, Europe, and Africa. Professor Litvak is the author of a number of books and articles. His latest book (with Christopher Maule) is *Foreign Investment: The Experience of Host Countries.*

CHRISTOPHER MAULE

Assistant Professor of Economics at McMaster University, CHRISTOPHER MAULE has a continuing research interest in industrial organization and foreign investment. He has served as a consultant to government and business and is the author of numerous articles. Professor Maule spent the summer of 1969 researching the topic of foreign investment and the multinational corporation in Europe.

RICHARD EELLS

Director and Editor of the Program for Studies of the Modern Corporation at the Graduate School of Business, Columbia University, RICHARD EELLS is also Adjunct Professor of Business. He is President of the Arkville Press, an adviser to the Committee for Economic Development, a trustee of several foundations, and a consultant to various business corporations. Professor Eells has published widely on the emerging role of the modern corporation in our society. His books include *Conceptual Foundations of Business* (with Clarence Walton), *The Government of Corporations,* and *The Corporation and the Arts.*

FRANK TANNENBAUM

Professor emeritus of Latin-American history and Director of University Seminars at Columbia at the time of his death in 1969, FRANK TANNENBAUM was a newspaper correspondent in Mexico in the 1920s and crossed the country on muleback. His thirty years of teaching included a weekly seminar on Latin America that attracted chiefs of state as well as political exiles to Columbia. Professor Tannenbaum also promoted interdisciplinary dialogues by starting the University Seminars in 1945, bringing together businessmen and government leaders from all countries. His many books included *Ten Keys to Latin America* and *The Balance of Power in Society.*

WARREN J. KEEGAN

Associate Professor at the Columbia Graduate School of Business, WARREN J. KEEGAN specializes in international business, strategic planning, marketing, and organization studies. He has served on the research staff of IMEDE, the Management Development Institute in Lausanne, Switzerland, and, under the auspices of the MIT Fellows in Africa Program, as Assistant Secretary in the Ministry of Development Planning in Tanzania. Dr. Keegan is a consulting instructor at the General Electric Manager Development Program and numerous other executive programs.

THEODORE L. WILKINSON

A frequent delegate to international accounting conferences, THEODORE L. WILKINSON joined Price Waterhouse & Co. in 1937 and opened the firm's Bogotá, Colombia, office in 1944. Mr. Wilkinson joined the International Department in New York in 1948 and was made a partner in 1954. He is a member of the AICPA, U.S. delegate to the International Study Group (joint committee of British, Canadian, and U.S. institutes of accountants) and Chairman of the International Committee for Accounting Cooperation.

BURT NANUS

A member of the faculties of the Graduate Schools of Business Administration and Public Administration at the University of Southern California, BURT NANUS has had over twelve years of managerial and long-range planning experience. Firms with which he has been associated include Sperry Rand Univac, Operations Research, Inc., System Development Corporation, and his own consulting firm, Planning Technology, Inc. He is the author of a book on management games and articles on simulation, systems analysis, and management information systems.

FREDERICK HELDRING

Senior Vice President of the Philadelphia National Bank, FREDERICK HELDRING is responsible for the Bank's international division. He is also President of The Philadelphia International Bank in New York. Born in Holland, Mr. Heldring studied economics at the University of Amsterdam and was graduated from the Wharton School of the University of Pennsylvania. He is Chairman of the Philadelphia Regional Export Expansion Council, Chairman of the Advisory Committee for International Banking and Finance to the Comptroller of the Currency in Washington, and Chairman of the International Affairs Committee of the Chamber of Commerce of Greater Philadelphia.

SIR RICHARD COSTAIN

Chairman of the Costain Group of Companies, the late SIR RICHARD COSTAIN guided its fortunes for 39 years. He joined the small building business founded by his grandfather in Liverpool in 1865 and built it into a public company with assets of about £25 million at the time of Sir Richard's death in 1966. His first overseas venture was the construction of a difficult section of the Trans-Iranian Railway in 1935-36. After World War II offices were set up in West and Central Africa, Pakistan, Australia, Canada, and Western Europe. Sir Richard was knighted in 1954.

DONALD M. BARRETT

Director—Air Agreements in the Executive Department of Pan American World Airways, DONALD M. BARRETT negotiates bilateral air transport agreements and operating permits with foreign governments on behalf of the company. He also represents the airline before the Civil Aeronautics Board and the Department of State in traffic rights matters. Mr. Barrett is a graduate of the School of Law of the University of California at Los Angeles and the Institute of Air Law at McGill University.

WILLIAM H. HANNUM

Associate Professor of Business Economics and Statistics at the College of Business Administration, Syracuse University, WILLIAM H. HANNUM has also served as a consultant to business and government organizations, both in the United States and overseas. He is the author of papers and articles in managerial economics and statistics. The insights and information for his article for the *Columbia Journal of World Business,* published in this book, were developed while he served as a research economist for the Maxwell Graduate School of Syracuse University.

DONALD M. KENDALL

President and chief executive of PepsiCo, DONALD M. KENDALL has spent virtually his entire business career with that company. Pepsi's international growth under his leadership has been dramatic. Sales in the United States and 115 overseas countries are approaching $1 billion annually. President Nixon appointed Mr. Kendall chairman of the National Alliance of Businessmen, and he is also chairman of the Emergency Committee for American Trade. Mr. Kendall is a director of Atlantic Richfield, McCulloch Oil Corporation, Prudential Lines, Inc., Daytona International Speedway, and Investors Diversified Services.

RICHARD D. ROBINSON

Senior Lecturer at the Sloan School of Management at the Massachusetts Institute of Technology, RICHARD D. ROBINSON's fields are international business and Middle Eastern development. Dr. Robinson is also a lecturer in the Department of History at Harvard and the author of several articles and books. Among the latter are *The First Turkish Republic: A Case Study in National Development, International Business Policy,* and *International Management.*

HENRY P. de VRIES

Professor of Law, Associate Director of the Parker School of Foreign and Comparative Law, and Director of the Inter-American Law Center of Columbia University, HENRY P. DE VRIES is also special counsel on foreign and international legal matters to the firm of Baker & McKenzie. He has served as Professor of Private International Law at The Hague

Academy of International Law and as Professor of Inter-American Law at several Brazilian law schools. Professor de Vries is presently working on a new edition of his book *Foreign Law and the American Lawyer*.

CORWIN D. EDWARDS

Professor of Economics at the University of Oregon, CORWIN D. EDWARDS has written extensively in the field of cartels, monopolies, and restrictive trade practices. He was a consultant on cartels to the Department of State during World War II and headed the Mission on Japanese Combines in 1946. More recently Professor Edwards has been a consultant to the President's Assistant for Consumer Affairs and a member of the Consumers Advisory Council. Among his many publications are *Trade Regulations Overseas: The National Laws* and *Control of Cartels and Monopolies: An International Comparison*.

GEORGE W. BALL

A senior partner of the international investment banking firm of Lehman Brothers, GEORGE W. BALL was formerly Under Secretary of State and U.S. Ambassador to the United Nations. During World War II he served as General Counsel of the Foreign Economic Administration and as a director of the U.S. Strategic Bombing Survey based in London. After the war Mr. Ball became a founding partner of a law firm with offices in New York, Washington, Paris, and Brussels, now known as Cleary, Gottlieb, Steen and Hamilton, to which he is presently Counsel. He is the author of the recent book *The Discipline of Power*.

Foreword

EVER SINCE THE DAWN OF HISTORY, the primary effort of man has been the organization of his energies to provide for the material basis of life. When this activity ceased to be a solitary one and commerce was born, the two central themes of the human experience had their beginnings: the fact of civilization and the idea of freedom. The ancient societies of the Middle East and the Orient, the classical societies of Greece and Rome, the modern societies of Elizabethan England and the American republic became rich in the arts and the humanities—in all that we prize in civilizations—not in spite of their being successful in commerce, but because of it; for it is the wealth that surpasses basic needs that makes way for all that is achieved beyond those needs. And the idea of freedom is neither born nor realized among peoples the span of whose days and the reach of whose years are wholly absorbed in the simple sustaining of life. There is more than a persistent afterglow of Puritan orthodoxy, despite the styptic adjectives, to Emerson's "The greatest meliorator of the world is selfish, huckstering trade."

Because it has been a prerequisite to the civilized state, business has played a major role in the growth and spread of civilizations and has thus formed a major content of the histories of nations, regions and empires from the beginning. Since the Second World War, however, and to some extent even before, old national, regional and imperial boundaries have been breaking down as frontiers of business activity. The new frontier is the world, even though, as Professor Fayerweather points out in this symposium, this new awareness of world dimensions by business, looking to the future, can often run head-on into such basically anachronistic survivals as the spirit of nationalism, which, whatever the sources of its pride or the objects of its aspirations, looks essentially to the past. These new dimensions, moreover, in response to new needs, new realities and new capacities, have implications that go far beyond the economic. Some of the more significant of these, so far as the developing countries are concerned, are discussed in these pages by Professor Hannum in "Profit Maker by Design, Educator by Circumstance."

Dean Brown's thoughtful and provocative speculations in "Prologue to a New World Symphony?" press the case and suggest that the new world enterprise, characterized today by the multinational corporation, can provide the most powerful impetus toward world accord that we are likely to see in our time. The doyen's insight seems to me realistic and its inference, unless I misread history altogether, incontrovertible. Unless man can organize himself so as to develop, manage and distribute the world's resources, he is not likely, by way either of mood or of purpose, to organize himself politically or socially—nor, for that matter, is he apt to be free to do so.

Consequently, the whole subject of this vastly promising but still incipient force is a matter of very grave importance, not only for the historic effects to which it can give rise in the future, but for the sweep and depths of its significance for the present. One could go further: unless we come to understand this force—what it is, the climate in which it is emerging, the counterforces that it must resist, the conditions both internal and external to itself that it must recognize and cope with, and the complex issues which it generates—then we may have lost, in Dean Brown's heartening phrase, "an unmatched force for peace."

The task of understanding involves much. In my judgment, we have in America suffered very gravely over the years from a failure to construct an adequate theory even of the largely domestic corporation—let alone of the multinational corporation. And yet everyone knows that corporate action is far from being either a passing or an incidental phenomenon: it is lasting, and it is central, simply because, in the intricacy and sophistication of affairs today, there is no alternative to the corporation, however much you might change its structure, its government, its methods, its lexicon, or even its name. The construction of a sound theory of the corporation is not merely an intellectual desideratum, stimulating as that might be; it is absolutely essential in a practical sense not only to the most effective use of the corporation, national or multinational, in advancing the human situation, but also to the accommodation of the corporation to general human values.

The absence of an adequate theory of the corporation, on the other hand, has unquestionably been a contributing factor to the absence, too, for example, of a suitable body of law relating to its activities, with the result that the corporation almost every day has to fight its way through a tangle of contradictory, redundant, outmoded and unserviceable statutes and regulations that have simply accumulated over the years, often having been enacted or promulgated in response to some passing felt but undefined uneasiness and without regard to the fundamental broad purposes of the corporation. And although I am aware of the dangers in causal oversimplifications, I nevertheless think that there can be found persuasive historical evidence that this legal chaos has, in turn, led to the failure of any real form of corporate constitutionalism to develop—to the detriment, I think, of the fullest development of the corporation.

If this lack of a theory of the domestic corporation has been a constant harassment, insufficient theoretical inquiry into the nature, as it emerges, of the multinational corporation, with all the sensitivities it must cope with, all the misconceptions it must contend with, and all the inevitable hostilities it must face—not to mention the staggering day-to-day problems of diverse accounting systems, varying ethical concepts and disparate corporate-governmental relationships—will be far more hazardous.

Under the prescient guidance of Courtney Brown, who brought to the deanship many years of administrative experience in the life of the corporation as a world entity, the Graduate School of Business of Columbia University recognized this need to understand world business in reforming the School's curricula and reorienting its emphases some years ago. As a further move in this direction, the School established the *Columbia Journal of World Business*, in 1965, to help provide a forum for the exchange of ideas, the proliferation of a literature and the application of specific cases to general propositions. This book is a compendium of some of the most thoughtful and perceptive contributions to that publication by distinguished scholars and businessmen, many of whom have also served in public service agencies of national or international jurisdiction. As such, the volume offers a stimulating and absorbing point of departure for further exploration of some of the major aspects of world business.

Among the most immediate of these is the transitional state in which global business now finds itself. Dean Brown clearly articulates the promise, and there seems to me also in his views an insistent strain of that essential ingredient in democratic outlook that no progressive social order has ever been wholly without: faith. Yet it is a knowing faith, and the Dean warns that the path ahead is not easy. The succeeding papers in the first part of this symposium illumine both the grounds for great expectations and the curve of the ordeal implicit in the early evolution of any emerging social force.

But there is an affirmative inevitability, too, in all evolutionary processes—probably, along with the accidental rise of great men, one of the few genuine mystiques in history. And this book's strength is that it seeks to fall in with that evolution rather than to dispute it. Robert Frost, when asked once what constituted a "great" century, said quite simply that it was a century that made its point. It seems clear now—after the bleak desperation of two world wars, and despite the abortion of the League of Nations and present barrenness of the United Nations—that the chief point of this century must be the consolidation, on a worldwide basis, of the efforts of mankind to provide its sustenance and enrich its leisure—to master its environment, in other words, and to elevate its destiny. The common ground of the authors represented in this collection is that they all take a positive, though not an uncritical and certainly not a relaxed, position on this challenge and opportunity that time has dealt us. Their approaches, however, are from quite different concerns, and their perspectives from different points.

The observations and reflections in Part II of this book on phases of the confrontation between multinational business and nationalism seem to me, on the whole, quite hopeful, although—as Mr. Behrman points out—there are some issues that have not yet been fully faced. It is interesting, however, to note that, throughout the pages of this section, there is a strength of substance in the position of the multinational corporation that does not exist in the case of the sometimes frantic tenacity of nationalism. Even that austere image of resurrected nationalism, Charles de Gaulle, saw some uses in continental economic boundaries—provided, of course, that they were Francocentric.

That world business has unique features—characteristics either not present at all in businesses functioning solely within national boundaries or else present in such different degrees as to be wholly different in their impact—is, of course, inevitable. But some of these which are harassments need not always be so, and the important thing here is that thoughtful attention is being given the major problem areas. Accounting, the language of business, for example, must obviously clarify rather than mystify management, investors and everyone else having an interest in the multinational corporation, if it is to serve as the same kind of constructive adjunct to the growth of world business as it has to national business. Mr. Wilkinson's discussion of this in "International Accounting: Harmony or Disharmony" takes an expert and candid look at the situation, and in the same section there are equally informed and no less forthright observations on other special aspects of business activity as they apply particularly to such activity when it is undertaken on a world scale.

Some of the larger questions—basically conceptual but of profound importance—are just beginning to surface; and in many respects, they represent intellectually, as well as economically and socially, some of the most absorbing as well as demanding problems confronting us. Two of these—perhaps the most difficult and certainly the most fundamental—are centered in the idea of equity and in a legal framework for world business activity. It is especially significant that they are given treatment here each in its own context. And it is strikingly symptomatic of the whole spirit of this volume that it concludes with the eloquent and, I am quite convinced, soundly prophetic utterance of George W. Ball at the end of his exhilarating probing into "the importance of being stateless."

It is easy, of course, to read into any area of activity that one's life has touched upon more meaning and greater essentiality than time will prove to have been justified. Nevertheless, I am struck, when I ponder what I believe to be the vital importance of the multinational corporation, by a fragment of evidence now in hand. The most recent version of utopia that has been visited upon the American people, as I write, was the descent of some 300,000 of the beautiful and liberated upon a tiny farm community in New York State. All those products of life that can be made, and long have been in the past, by individual workmen—seemly garb, for example, and simple soap—were dispensed with. But two products that cannot possibly be made except by large corporations, many of them multinational, were absolutely essential—the transistor radio and the automobile. Trivial grounds for prediction, perhaps, but surely as revealing of the times as one could find.

ARTHUR B. TOURTELLOT

WORLD BUSINESS
IN TRANSITION

CHAPTER 1

COURTNEY C. BROWN

A new and powerful influence has emerged as communication and transportation technology has facilitated rapid multiplication of global contacts of businessmen.

Prologue to a New World Symphony?

SELDOM IN THE ANNALS OF MAN has there been a time when the unusual has become so commonplace. Change is ubiquitous in the environment. Change is to man today as water to a fish; it surrounds him, he cannot escape. It presses in on him from all directions: technological change, economic change, political change, societal change, and change in the ordering of life's values. Among the most significant are changes that extend the geographical range of his awareness and the dimensions of his expectations.

Change in all of these matters is too rapid to be fully understood. One of its expressions is a restiveness that has bestirred the youth of all lands. In some vague way it is felt, indeed deeply believed, that so much change must have meaning for the quality of life for all men everywhere.

But the vision of a golden future loses its luster in a tarnished present. The tragic asymmetry of the world is an enlarged reflection of the condition of local populations in the cities and rural regions of most nations. The difficulties of the present are amplified and made more intractable by disparate population growth, racial dissension and what seems to be a growing acceptance of group violence as the only effective means of protest. Even if all of the surplus resources available to man might be assigned to the alleviation or eradication of present social ills, the task would still be enormous. With military conflict and the preparation for conflict the priority claimant, it may be impossible.

In the meantime, change proceeds at its dizzy pace and expectations for the halcyon future rise still further. Instant sound and sight via satellite make the expressions of change globally apparent. The marvels of information storage, retrieval and computation, alarming advances in molecular biology, transplants of human organs, adventures in space—all underscore by sharply contrasting with some of the lagging attitudes, programs and policies needed to relieve our unbalanced world. Is there any wonder that the youth of the world are impatient and in revolt against the existing order even though they do not seem able to offer identifiable substitutes?

Change itself may be the catalyst, for it is compelling a more realistic and compassionate reappraisal of disparities, both locally and globally. That inimitable phrasemaker, James Reston, recently put these seminal issues succinctly: "In short, there is now a cry in the world, not so much for new personalities—but for a new philosophy, for the priorities of life rather than the priorities of death, for some unity of purpose and common control of human affairs, not only for a League of Nations, but for a League of Minds."

Looked at from the broad perspective of time, the world may be in the midst of one of those historical periods when a groundswell of change occurs in attitudes that has major significance for the entire human condition. This has happened before. It occurred when the spiritualism of the medieval world gave way to more material interests. It occurred as the exquisite artistry of the Renaissance was replaced by preoccupation with science.

The world's politicians for several centuries have had as their major concern the question of which nation or nations would dominate other nations or possess the undeveloped regions of the world. Today, they continue to whet the emotions of nationalism and seem to be primarily concerned with these same considerations, although they are typically presented in terms of defense against external enemies, or the exercise of hegemony in regions of "vital" interest. The unpleasant rumblings of youth are a crescendo of vivid and visible protest against these preoccupations of contemporary political leaders.

Another and, in the long run, perhaps more effective constraint to the extremes of nationalistic ambitions is of a quieter nature. It is in the incentives, the pressures and the compulsions to eliminate poverty, both locally and globally. National prestige and sovereignty, even tribal ambitions, are still very much in evidence, as a determinant of human behavior. More humanitarian impulses, however, have begun to assert themselves with increasing insistence and to capture public interest and attention. There is now an abrasiveness that will not go away in the global desire to alleviate conditions of life for those who are deprived of the opportunity of full personal development. These include a majority of the world's population. This impulse will insistently influence the accommodation of political policy among nations. It will continue to make subtle encroachments on the sanctity of sovereignty. The relative weight of politics and economics seems slowly but surely to be shifting in favor of the latter.

The contest has only begun. The roots of nationalistic emotion run deep. They have long been nourished with large dosages of resources and public commitment. The confluence of two new forces, however, may now begin to compel a shift. The amount of resources required to support a nation's "position" in the world has increased alarmingly in recent decades. Aggregate expenditures of all nations for "defense" have been estimated to exceed 150 billion dollars annually. At the same time the technology that has made these expenditures so high is providing the potential of abundance on which rising expectations have been based.

In the maelstrom of debate, it is too often overlooked that the priorities of life for those that are deprived are not an illusive political security but greater physical comforts and personal security. The provision of material abundance is the business of business. Whether publicly or privately owned, or local or global

in nature, business organizations are the instruments of society
that have demonstrated the capability and adaptability to pour
forth an ever-increasing flow of the goods and services that make
possible, but do not necessarily assure, the "good" life.

Two decades after the 1945 meeting of the world's politicians
in San Francisco to create the United Nations, an event that may
be ultimately of comparable significance occurred in the same city.
This time it was not the world's political leaders who met to
discuss global matters but an assembly of more than 500 business
leaders from more than sixty nations. And though they discussed
the usual topics that emerge when businessmen from different
countries convene—trade barriers, foreign investment, currency
and payments arrangements and price movements—the delibera-
tions of the delegates to this, the third meeting of the International
Industrial Conference, were not confined to these subjects.

Indeed, there was widespread recognition that to so limit themselves would be self-defeating. Underlying the important business
issues of our time is the question of world peace. And so, like the
politicians who preceded them twenty years ago, these men also
talked of peace—not a peace of national alliances, of international police forces, of a balance of terror; but of world order
resulting from the spread of interlocking channels of commerce
and finance. They spoke of a businessman's peace, fostered by
industry for the sake of industry, if you will; but collaterally for
the sake of mankind everywhere. When existing curtains are
parted, said Crawford Greenewalt of the Du Pont Company, we
may find that business leaders have become a peace corps of
enormous and lasting effectiveness.

The role of business in promoting world peace is properly connected with the idea of trade. In expanding his markets, the
trader necessarily forges ties of mutual respect, understanding and
support. He teaches mankind that, as the late Wroe Alderson so
sagely observed, it is far less profitable "to cleave skulls than to
insinuate ideas into them."

But the contribution of the businessman to international comity
goes beyond his status as trader. A new role for business is beginning to take shape as a consequence of far-reaching changes in the
structure of world commerce. The most significant of these developments is that comparative advantage is now less a matter of

geography than of superior technical knowledge and service efficiency. As the importance of resource endowment diminishes and that of knowledge and service increases, the logic of localized production and marketing becomes inescapable. The stage is set for the emergence of business organizations that, ideally, are dedicated to pursuing profits anywhere in the world and are not necessarily limited by identification with a given national home or particular operational headquarters. In close proximity to their customers and supported by international research and development facilities, such enterprises are admirably fitted to the new requirements of today's world markets that are everywhere expanding. Traditional labels, such as manufacturer or mining company, no longer serve as a precise fit for these organizations. Today, many firms have no choice but to transform themselves into "problem solvers."

Thus at a faster pace than is sometimes realized, great manufacturing and trading companies, with home offices in many advanced nations, are becoming what has come to be known as multinational organizations. There has developed a vast interwoven network of reciprocal interests, of open communications for exchange of technology and commercial intelligence, of personnel and cultural patterns—yes, even of new friendships and loyalties that cut across national boundaries. This is a powerful unifying influence in the affairs of mankind that has not yet been fully recognized, but which must inevitably make itself more felt in the years to come.

The multinational company thereby becomes a major vehicle to carry the have-nots toward "take-off" and the haves into frontier fields. As such it is an unmatched force for peace. Yet despite the benefits they promise, these new world enterprises have not had an easy time of it. Part of the problem is that the multinational executive must still learn much about the unique problems of shaping and administering a worldwide enterprise. The major difficulties arise from the continued strength of nationalistic commitments, traditional attitudes inherited from a feudalistic past, and political distrust of private motivations in many areas of the globe. No uniform global regulatory machinery has been devised, and it is hardly conceivable that a few marginal businessmen will fail to take advantage of situations, unprotected by competition, local laws, or established habits of rectitude. They always have. Yet, the emergence of the multinational corporation in the post-war period has brought a new and profoundly important influence to bear in world affairs. The numbers have become many and their size enormous. The annual sales of some exceed the total gross national product of many nations.

Unlike the typical situation of a political settlement, global companies operate in an environment in which their negotiations do not carry a heavy baggage of emotional commitment, but in which the resolutions are most often mutually beneficial to both parties to the transaction. They provide a network of interconnected conduits that facilitate the optimum utilization of financial and technical resources. There are those who have expressed the view that these multinational corporations which have developed so quietly, but so suddenly, may be the hoped-for force that will provide a means of unifying and reconciling the aspirations of mankind: a task which all the politicians have utterly failed to achieve.

While such optimistic and imaginative thinking may prove to be realistic in the long run, there can be no doubt of the difficult hurdles that obstruct the immediate realization of these sanguine expectations. It is still the nation that is sovereign, not the corporation. What is a corporation? Who gives it sanction? Its charter is granted by a political state, the laws of which may give it the protection of a citizen. But which laws shall govern in the case of the multinational corporation—the laws of the parent-home government or the laws of the host governments of affiliated organizations, or perhaps even the internal administrative rulings of its own management? Is there a clear definition of which laws will serve whose public interest; and how can a management, convinced that its ultimate sanction is related to its service of the public interest, adapt itself to the heterogeneous milieu in which it lives?

Should the multinational corporation be used and treated as an expression of national prestige by the parent government? Is the host government justified in treating an "imported" organization as an instrument of its own national political policy, a policy that may differ from that of the parent government? What are the available means of protection, if any, from discriminatory treatment by host governments relative to taxes, labor laws and ownership? To what extent must the management attempt to collaborate with the purposes and policies of international political instrumentalities dealing with world payments, world development and other such matters?

These and other issues are just beginning to emerge in sharp focus. Their resolution will undoubtedly require many years of study, experience and adjustment. Meanwhile, what are the criteria that should guide the managers of multinational corporations? Only partial answers are now possible. Multinational management may withdraw from a nation or it may refuse to make new commitments if circumstances deny the opportunity of sound business judgment. It can always discuss in frank and open fashion the qualifications imposed on normal business practice by political considerations. It can explore with parent and with host governments the accuracy of the interpretation of public desires as expressed in given political policies and programs. It may even raise the question of whether national political purposes narrowly conceived necessarily serve in the long term "the greatest good of the greatest number."

As might be expected, the entry of more and more of these international affiliates into national markets has not always been welcomed by their national rivals, who sometimes resent their highly effective competition for markets and for scarce resources of labor and capital. Moreover, governments tend to dislike the increased difficulty of controlling such units, which can shift their capital, management and markets to affiliated production units in other countries if dissatisfied, and whose decisions taken on the basis of centralized worldwide corporate policy may not always be in accordance with the balance of payments, monetary, tax, antitrust, or industrial plans and aspirations of the countries in which the affiliates are located, or of the governments of the countries of the parent corporation.

One consequence of this emerging pattern of world business is that it tends to confuse political policies of a nation designed to help its own nationals. The old, simple and direct means of trade subsidies or restrictions may not get the results expected. As an example, in recent years the industrialized nations have been urged to provide preferential tariffs for imported manufactures from the less developed parts of the world, presumably to encourage the nationals of the LDCs to develop a manufacturing industry. One of the most plausible consequences in the present situation, however, could be that a foreign affiliate of a multinational corporation, located in an LDC, might be used by the home office to manufacture components or finished products for export into the industrialized world, in-

cluding the home country. This is not necessarily bad; indeed, it
may be the most effective means of achieving the long-sought development of manufacturing industries in the LDCs, but it is not
what the political negotiators typically have in mind.

In other words, whether willed or not, the managers of multinational corporations are being forced to accept some of the responsibilities of world statesmanship. As their organizations and
influence grow, their opportunities and challenges to serve mankind
will correspondingly expand.

The Greek god Proteus was a hard man to get hold of. When
seized or cornered, he disengaged simply by changing shape. Proteus conjures up two quite distinct images to modern man: one, that
of the mercurial changeling; the other, that of the supple innovator.

It is in the second sense that the modern corporation has proven
a worthy inheritor of the protean tradition. Its capacity to adapt
its structure, procedures and commitments to the requirements of
evolving circumstances has confounded its critics, amazed and delighted its supporters. Cast in the role of world developer, yet
hemmed in by a wide array of political, financial or military obstacles, the corporation has had to pioneer or pull out. It has elected to
pioneer—and in ways that some would have thought unworkable,
radical, or simply absurd a half century ago.

The earliest modification of traditional corporate foreign investment practices was the joint venture, in which equity ownership is
shared in varying proportions with citizens of the receiving countries
or with the host government. In the area of natural resource industries—oil and minerals—novel modifications of the joint venture have
been developed to give recognition to both the home country's
inherent property rights and the contributions of foreign enterprises.

A nonequity form of joint venture is the service contract under
which the "investing" company agrees with a host representative—
again either the government or private groups—to provide services
for a fixed fee. When the "service" includes the creation and management of a previously non-existent enterprise, the arrangement
goes by the name "management contract." A variant of the management contract as applied particularly to Soviet-bloc countries is the
co-production scheme. The corporate partner in this setup may
supply machinery, technology, management and perhaps a market
outlet; whereas the host may furnish the plant, the workers and the

raw materials. Compensation for the foreign partner may be by fee or, more typically, by a predetermined share of the end product.

All of these arrangements are supplementary to the more traditional form of foreign investment—the overseas affiliate that holds indefinite tenure in the country of operation. Whether these practices represent transitional steps in the development of regional or global arrangements that would in turn diminish their necessity or desirability is a question that cannot now be answered. It is sufficient to observe that, in the aggregate, they represent a significant enlargement of the opportunity of the modern corporation to adapt itself to a world of political disparities.

The imaginative means by which the multinational corporation has spread its commitments around the globe are an interesting part, but only a part, of the story. The complexities associated with its daily operation require comparable initiatives, adaptability and sensitivity.

A variety of trade policies and practices have developed throughout the world regarding monopoly and competition. Adaptations to a host country's customs and attitudes may, and frequently do, run afoul of the position of a home country jurisdiction; yet competitive disadvantages with local firms may be incurred through failure to adapt. A whole host of financial problems with novel features emerges in the acquisition of new capital, the transfer of funds, yes, and even in the wide variety of accounting requirements and practices in different countries. Intracompany transactions become international transactions.

New concepts of organizational structure and management control must be designed. Personnel policies relating to both management and labor, adjusted to personal needs as well as local custom and legislation, must be developed. The question of to whom management is accountable becomes even more ambiguous in the world setting: to employees and customers? to the local community as represented by the indigenous government? to stockholders? and who should the stockholders be, the people back home, the local citizens, or scattered investors throughout the world?

Clearly, there is no shortage of problems ahead for the world business organization. Yet despite its newness as a world influence and its vast reservoir of unsolved tasks, it is pregnant with great promise. There is now an urgent need for a vast creative effort in the affairs of mankind. To the surprise of many, and the satisfaction of some, political efforts by themselves have proved insufficiently creative, and in many instances misdirected. Mankind's insistence on action and its impatience with conventional political nostrums combine to provide the setting in which business organizations and their far-flung activities have been brought to the center of interest on the global stage. In the afternoon of the 20th century, the people of the world are awakening to the realization that they must look to the day-to-day, no-nonsense activities of practical men of affairs to help achieve release from grinding drudgery.

CHAPTER 2

EMILE BENOIT

The "one world" that men have so long dreamt of seems almost possible as two revolutions—one military, the other economic—spur challenging new forms of cooperation among nations.

Interdependence on a Small Planet

WE NOW LIVE IN A WORLD in which all men are so close that only a few minutes' communicating, orbiting, or shooting time separates them—a world which is only a tiny footstool for the beginning of man's exploration of the universe. Yet we are still trying to make do with a system of international relations based on a much earlier order, one that could accommodate scores of "independent" self-centered nation-states, each claiming the absolute rights of a Machiavellian "sovereign" to do what its own interest appeared to dictate, to withdraw from (or ignore) prior agreements when inconvenient, and to be bound solely by its own judgment in international disputes—including disputes about the meaning of its promises and agreements.

The tension between these two worlds—the vast one of petty "independent" quarreling human groups and the small one inextricably linked for good or for ill by modern technology—is the central drama of our era; it is unimaginable that these two concepts of the world can coexist for long. One or the other—or both—must go. It is the writer's belief that the universe of seemingly sovereign political entities will gradually disappear as mankind grows to understand the basic facts of its interdependence and learns to fashion political tools more consistent with them. This interdependence is both military and nonmilitary. The first variety has been accorded greater publicity, but even in this area the nature and strength of the ties that bind mankind are but imperfectly understood.

Few truly comprehend that we are now in the strange position of being militarily dependent upon our opponents. This paradoxical situation has arisen out of the contemporary revolution in military technologies. Contrary to Alfred Marshall's soothing adage, nature does make jumps; they are rare, but when they occur, a new system emerges and that new system is no longer understandable and predictable by the laws that governed the old one.

Anatomy of a Quantum Jump

The main features of the current military revolution need no detailed exposition here. As every modern schoolboy now unfortunately knows, the Hiroshima bomb was thousands of times more powerful than earlier weapons, and the first hydrogen bomb a thousand times stronger than that. These nuclear explosives, of continuously improving efficiency, were then incorporated into missiles capable of delivering havoc at least forty times more quickly than World War II planes. Their effectiveness was again raised by another large factor with the development of inertial guidance systems that can direct the missiles to their targets with fantastic precision. When the possibility of an active antimissile defense arose, decoys and jamming devices were quickly installed on the incoming missiles to make the chance of intercepting any significant percentage of them exceedingly remote. As a final step, missile launchers have been hardened, dispersed, concealed, or kept in motion beneath the oceans or in the air so that there is little hope of preventing any decisive proportion of them from functioning by means of a preclusive attack.

All this adds up to a true quantum jump of the order of hundreds, or thousands, of millions. Changes of that magnitude are comparatively rare in cosmic experience: they may be likened to the gathering of forces behind the explosion of stars, or the mutation which led to the emergence of the human brain in the evolutionary process. Certainly the magnitude of the present weapons revolution completely dwarfs that of the invention of gunpowder, cannons, and muskets which in its time destroyed the viability of feudalism. It is surprising that, in the light of these developments, so many people can expect a political system based on war as the means of settling major disputes to go on much as before.

In effect, what has occurred is a *mass exchange of hostages,* leaving the population of the world's major cities subject to sudden slaughter by hostile governments. This is interdependence on a new plane of intensity: to an unbelievable and gruesome degree we now depend on each other's leaders to be rational, to be predictable, to be sane. One has only to imagine for a moment what the situation would be like today if Hitler and the Nazi Party were in charge of a military force like that of the U.S. or the USSR to appreciate how desperately we now depend on each other's leaders to be relatively free of paranoia and endowed with humane qualities.

Breaking the Language Barrier

It would be a mistake, however, to overemphasize military interdependence to the exclusion of other types. Military interdependence is simply one facet of the technological revolution which, by overcoming the obstacles of distance and time, is in an operational sense "shrinking" our planet. Already the jet plane and modern electronics have greatly reduced the girth of our globe: electronic advances can transmit the essential raw material of human intercourse—exchanges of thought—as well as the impulses for aiming weapons. The presence of Telstar in the sky is a reassuring omen, preparing us for a day in the near future when international communication, and indeed when television and facsimile pictures—which are so much more readily comprehended across linguistic boundaries than are mere words—will flow easily over national boundaries, enlarging the community of experience out of which the community of feeling and of trust needed for political cooperation must grow. But this will require cooperation; hostile use of such facilities could quickly create chaos in the airwaves.

Geographic and physical aspects of human interdependence will increasingly obtrude on our attention and demand solutions. Recognition has gradually emerged that nuclear fission explosions in the air raise the radioactivity of the atmosphere and can spread malignancy and death far from where they initially were set off. We are now becoming more aware that the atmosphere is also subject to gradual deterioration from the effects of the wastes dumped into it by a rapidly growing industrial civilization. The world's rivers and seas may be similarly affected, especially if better technical solutions are not found for disposal of nuclear wastes before there is large-scale use of nuclear fission for electric power generation. Already the conservation of ocean food resources poses an acute problem for international cooperation.

Dealing with Overpopulation

Another serious danger arises from the unchecked growth of population which not only imperils living standards in the over-populated countries themselves but raises intractable long-term problems for their neighbors—which as a minimum will have to continue raising larger and larger food surpluses for relief programs or accept the horror of large-scale famine in the world community. Further, all too soon in the time scale of human history, nations will probably be able to modify their own climate, and—intentionally or unintentionally—the climate of their neighbors. We have already seen how diversion of river water can threaten to become a *casus belli*. Imagine the implications of changing a neighbor's mean temperature by, say, 15 or 20 degrees, or lowering the average rainfall by several inches! Finally the exploration of space is emotionally felt by most people as a generically human rather than as a merely national enterprise. Increasingly, it will provide a perspective against which national divisions will appear secondary and irrelevant to man's highest ambitions.

Nor are the triumphs of understanding and invention in the twentieth century by any means confined to the realm of physical realities. Our knowledge of how to create and distribute goods and services has also taken giant steps forward. This includes not only the vast progress in applying physical technology to production, but also—and not less significant for man's welfare, I think—the tremendous progress in economic theory, policy and administration. It is only within my adult lifetime that national accounts and related statistical series have provided the market economies with a reasonably clear picture of what was going on, and that Keynesian insights and neo-Keynesian techniques have enabled us to avoid the depressions that made the *laissez-faire* economy violently and dangerously unstable, unbearably wasteful, and morally unsupportable.

The centrally planned economies also are improving their knowledge of aspects of economic reality and performance (such as standards of quality and the preferences of consumers) hitherto undeservedly ignored. They are reconstructing their planning methods to make better use of such information, and also to liberate the creative power of individual incentive and inventiveness—which can never be entirely pre-planned, but which add so much to the quality of a society's output, if only the plans are flexible enough to accommodate them.

At the same time, great improvements in the techniques of managing the individual production unit have been developing both in the market and the centrally planned economies. Examples are the use of computers to solve technically difficult problems of inventory management as well as production layout and sequencing; the precise identification of the skill requirements of different categories of jobs; the effective matching of such requirements with employee capabilities; the use of programmed learning and simulation techniques for industrial training and retraining; the precise measurement and accounting analysis of elements in the cost structure and their variation with scale of production; the influence of worker morale on production, and the factors affecting such morale, etc.

This vast progress in economic understanding and management has greatly enhanced the possibilities of cooperation. In the first place, it has so enormously increased the potential output of goods and services through the normal processes of economic activity that it makes any possible gains from the use of force seem trivial by comparison. Not only wars, but colonialism and other forms of exploitation through political power fade in attractiveness, even to the least humanitarian spirit, as the human contribution to production becomes less and less a matter of simple repetitive physical effort (which can easily be measured and coerced) and more and more a positive, creative expression of skill and imagination, within a complex and subtle team activity in which the individual's contribution is hard to isolate and measure, let alone impose by force.

Moreover, the outpouring of material benefits available in this way is so vast that the struggle over the division of these benefits should subside, with a concomitant softening of class hostility. Even if injustices in distribution are slower to be eliminated than our consciences desire, it is easier to bear them if there is enough so that even the poorest of the world receive what is essential for human dignity and development.

Secondly, the improvements being made both in the market economies and in the centrally planned economies are gradually drawing the two systems together. In essence this "depolarization" may be characterized as a movement toward centralization in the West, and away from it in the East. The convergence of the two systems may help to weaken the widespread ideological illusion of total opposition and conflict between the two types of economy, which is so dangerous a feature of contemporary life—distorting and exaggerating as it does the inevitable conflicts of power politics between national states.

With convergence arises a greater possibility of fruitful economic cooperation. So long as the two economic types are viewed as deadly rivals locked in a blind struggle for survival, cooperation is difficult. Even mutually beneficial activities are suspect, since they will almost invariably be (or seem to be) more helpful to one side than to the other, and will therefore be opposed by the other side. Indeed, even a willingness of one side to accept a given agreement is likely to arouse the suspicions of the other that there must be some asymmetry in the benefits—even if it cannot be readily identified.

But the process of convergence will not merely enhance the possibility of routine economic cooperation; of perhaps even greater significance, it will open vast geographic areas to a relatively new type of business association—one that is proving increasingly valuable in the West. Hopes of improved economic cooperation among Western nations had hitherto centered mainly on the possibility of a balanced expansion of commodity imports and exports. I would like to register my conviction, however, that trade in the conventional sense of a balanced two-way flow of goods is now being displaced in importance by a different, though little noticed, mode of economic cooperation.

Investment Displacing Trade

Essentially, what seems to be happening is that conventional international trade, involving autonomous "untied" exchange of exports and imports, has been rapidly losing in importance to a type of international economic activity dependent on private or public investment or grants. Thus, of the $21.9 billion of U.S. nonmilitary exports in 1963, a third were either financed by government loans or grants ($2.7 billion) or involved sales to U.S. foreign affiliates (estimated at $5 billion) and were thus to a degree dependent on earlier investment. Only $14.2 billion were balanced exports of the conventional autonomous sort, not the result of prior investment or aid-giving decisions.

Moreover, even the total export figure is completely dwarfed by *production abroad by American-owned enterprises.* U.S.-owned foreign manufacturing enterprises alone showed sales of $31.3 billion for 1963. My own rough estimate (based on the ratio of foreign investment and earnings in manufacturing to total foreign investment and earnings) suggests that total 1963 sales of goods and services produced abroad by American-controlled companies were of the order of $60-$70 billion, which is about the size of the national income of France, the United Kingdom, or Germany. (Value added by these companies would, of course, be less than sales. On the other hand, a substantial additional amount of output was obtained as a result of technical and managerial assistance by U.S. companies under licensing and management contract agreements, and is not reflected in the above foreign investment and earnings estimates.) Incidentally, this foreign production of American-owned companies is not only much larger than U.S. exports, but seems to be growing twice as fast.

Why is this so? What has happened to give such growing emphasis to producing abroad in place of exporting? I suspect that this trend reflects a fundamental change now occurring in the determinants of comparative advantage and specialization. Conventional economic analysis lays great stress on differences in factor endowments as the source of international division of labor. Particularly emphasized were gross geographic differences of climate, soil and mineral or other natural resources. The tropics would, in this view, export tropical fruits, coffee and tea, petroleum, rubber, silk, tin, etc., because their climate and raw material endowments gave them a unique ability to produce such items at low cost. Similarly, it was thought that the industrial countries had the capacity to produce and export steel because of the availability, in close proximity, of high quality deposits of coal and iron ore.

While this concept may have been adequate to explain trade patterns in agriculture or basic metals, it never shed much light on the pattern of trade in manufactures. It could not, for example, explain why the three leading producers and exporters of machinery, the U.S., U.K., and Germany, also bought such a large quantity of machinery *from each other*. It is becoming even less useful as manufactures grow to constitute a far larger share of world trade. This process is the inevitable result of the displacement by synthetics of tree rubber, silk, wood and other natural products, as well as continued technical improvements reducing the amount of raw materials per unit of output and permitting the use of lower-grade material. The industrialized countries have also insisted on developing their own agriculture and reserves of oil, gas and other natural resources, even when adequate imported supplies at low cost were available. Thus, the explanation of trade in terms of gross geographic advantage applies satisfactorily to an ever smaller part of the world's commerce.

Triumph of the Superior Firm

Competitive advantage in manufactures is only indirectly and partially dependent on possession of the required raw materials or other strictly geographic advantage. Rather it is now primarily an attribute of *particular firms, or even particular product lines.* It

rests on the capability of a given company, establishment or production unit to produce a superior bundle of goods and services—
including such services as speedy delivery, favorable terms of
payment, availability of spare parts, technical advice on using the
product and technical servicing to keep it operating efficiently
during its normal life period. Such advantage is the fruit of superior
technical knowledge, new products, and better product specification
resulting from past research and development activities, and from
greater efficiency in meeting the varied needs of customers. Sometimes, this is accompanied by lower prices, but often it is not, since
the buyer may be more concerned with the dependability of the
product, or the quality of the services provided, than with marginal
savings on the original price.

To provide such services reliably, a company must command
resources that will enable it to extend meaningful service guarantees
far into the future and a vast organization which can offer a variety
of personnel opportunities for a lifetime career. Such enormous,
virtually permanent, worldwide organizations as General Motors,
Jersey Standard, Unilever, Philips' Gloeilampen, etc., with assets
and life expectations paralleling those of nation-states, completely
transcend the competitive-market assumptions of classical economics.

As the key competitive advantages become essentially matters
of skill, knowledge and organization rather than of climate or natural resource location, the economies of scale are altered. It becomes less advantageous to complete a production operation in one
central place and ship bulky goods for long distances to where they
will be used. Opportunities will increasingly be found to sell or rent
the superior knowledge or skills and ideas that convey the crucial
competitive advantages. Alternatively, efforts will be made to establish new production affiliates close to where the goods and services
will eventually be utilized and where the particular needs and desires of the user can be given consideration, and the essential
servicing provided in a reliable and economical manner. In effect
what is now being demonstrated is that the long-run cost of transferring ideas, skills, and organizational patterns from one place to
another is far lower than the cost of continuously transporting
merchandise.

People not in international business rarely understand the extent
to which international direct investment today involves such a

transfer rather than the mere migration of surplus capital. Much of
the capital from U.S. direct investment in recent years has come
from local and other non-U.S. sources: local investors and suppliers, banks, governments, and international agencies. The American investor's most valuable contribution hasn't been cash but know-
how and management skill. Moreover, as restrictions on capital
exports diminish, European, Japanese and other non-U.S. investors
are beginning to emulate U.S. companies, with parallel benefits to
the economies in which their investments are made. The U.S. has,
of course, no monopoly on advanced technology and management,
and will itself benefit from direct investments made by European
and other foreign companies in this country.

Abstract but Compelling

It is thus not amiss to argue that the increasingly abstract character of competitive advantage is the chief reason that international
investment tends to displace exports in importance. While such investment also creates further opportunities for the export of components, raw materials, supplementary models, etc., the relative
importance of overseas production steadily increases.

What benefits have foreign countries gotten out of the supple-
mentation of management, skill and technology represented by the
over $40 billion (by 1963) of U.S. investment in foreign enterprises?
First, an enormous increase in production—as indicated, perhaps
$60-$70 billion per year, including wages and salaries paid almost
entirely to workers and employees of the host countries. Secondly,
substantial interest and profit payments to local lenders and equity
investors participating in the projects. Third, $1.5 billion of rein-
vested U.S. profits in 1963, representing new savings and investment. Fourth, a large volume of profits taxes collected, which could
easily have totaled around $1.5 billion, or even more, in that year.
Fifth, and crucially important, an enormous contribution to foreign
exchange earnings: these came to $4.7 billion from exports of manu-
factures alone generated by these investments. Adding the exports
generated by mining and petroleum would easily double this figure.
Furthermore, that part of overseas production which was not sent
out of the country may be regarded as in some sense a substitute for

imports that the host country would otherwise have had to purchase. The cost to the host country for all this was $4.5 billion of U.S. profits, of which, as we have noted, only $3 billion was withdrawn. Moreover, nearly $2 billion of this $3 billion was offset by new U.S. direct investment.

Private Investment in Public Enterprise

Demonstrably, international investment is a fruitful source of cooperation for economic progress among western nations. But of what relevance is this to countries where the means of production are not privately owned? Certainly, communist society would appear to provide little place for foreign private investment. However, if we remember that the essential aspect of such investment may be viewed as a transfer of skills, ideas, and techniques—to be paid for with fees or royalties—rather than primarily as a migration of capital —to be remunerated by a dividend or an interest payment—it is possible to discern a basis for East-West collaboration. Such a basis already underlies many joint-venture situations. Here, the foreign investment process is looked upon as an export of equipment paid for in installments over an extended period, plus royalty payments for the licensing of new technology, know-how or trademarks, and management fees for the costs of advising and administering the new operation, transferring the new technology, etc. Comparable arrangements can also be made between East and West. Alternatively, one can avoid the need for an agreement in financial terms altogether by simply deciding to divide the physical output of the joint venture in agreed proportions, with the private-enterprise partner free to retain the foreign-exchange proceeds from the foreign marketing of his share of the output. There are a number of other formulas that will serve equally well.

This mechanism has come to be called "co-production." Such an arrangement usually involves the use of advanced Western technology, equipment and management by a productive enterprise in an East European country in a partnership arrangement with a capitalist production unit. The East European partner normally contributes the labor, the raw materials, and the plant—and often some of the components. The Western partner supplies advanced equipment and know-how, product design, often at least part of the management, and—what is extremely important—international marketing channels.

This concept is certainly rather a startling one. Not only is it hard to see how a communist society could accept private foreign investment, it is equally difficult to understand how Western managers could participate in running a unit of a centrally planned economy which would presumably issue directives to the enterprise inconsistent with the profit-maximization objectives of Western entrepreneurs. Yet surprising or unbelievable as the idea of co-production may seem, the fact is that such ventures actually exist, that they are increasing in number, and that many more are currently being explored as possibilities, or are in the stage of active negotiation. Let me mention a few examples.

The West German firm of Rheinstahl has entered into a joint venture with the Hungarian Ministry of Machine Building for the construction in Hungary of quarrying equipment, machine tools, and other steel products, utilizing Hungarian as well as German semifinished components. The Austrian firm of Simmering-Graz-Pauker has a joint venture with the Hungarian group called Komplex to build power plants in India, financed through Hungarian-Indian bilateral clearing arrangements. IKEA, a Swedish furniture company, supplies machinery and designs for the semimanufacture of furniture in Poland under its own technical control. The semimanufactures are shipped to Sweden for finishing and marketing. The British firm of Walmsley (Bury) Group Ltd. has agreed with Poland's Metalexport to supply paper-making machinery to Poland (and thereafter to sell it to other Soviet bloc countries) which will after a time contain components made in Poland with Walmsley technical assistance. The British firm of Callaghan & Son, Ltd., and the Czech firm of Kdynske Strojirny have an agreement to manufacture jointly a line of automatic textile machinery, and to market and service the machinery throughout the world on a pre-arranged basis. A great many other examples could be cited.

It is important to be clear about the economic bases of such ventures. What is in it for each side? For the East the answer is obvious. The Eastern partner is enabled to produce the sort of items for which there already exists a large demand in Western markets, to reach and maintain the necessary quality standards, and to make and service the goods as they must be manufactured and serviced to win and hold Western customers. But what offsetting special advantages can be offered by the Eastern countries to the Western partners? Why bother to produce in Eastern Europe items to be sold in the West?

Surprisingly, the most important advantage offered is the eastern labor force. Overfull employment in Germany, Switzerland, and other countries of Western Europe has generated severe manpower shortages, relieved only by expensive importation and on-the-job training of foreign workers, with considerable social dislocation and expensive new requirements for housing, schools, etc. The Eastern European countries, on the other hand, still have considerable labor surpluses in agriculture, or even inefficiently employed in industry, owing to the requirement that enterprise directors find employment for a given work force whether they really need them or not. (Of late, the growing freedom granted to managers to disregard such considerations has begun to create overt unemployment, especially in Poland.)

What is more, the East European labor force has some especially valuable properties from the point of view of Western management. First, it is relatively cheap. Living standards are still considerably lower in Eastern than in Western Europe, and workers in communist countries are not free to have independent unions or strike. Thus the cost of labor is not only low, but is relatively stable over the production planning period. Finally, the East European work force contains a high ratio of relatively skilled people; it is particularly strong in middle-grade technicians, engineers, and scientists, who have been trained in large numbers as part of the communist ideological commitment to education and science.

Boon to Trader

A second advantage that co-production ventures can offer Western firms is markets. While the Eastern partner will ordinarily reserve for itself the marketing of the joint venture's finished products in the countries of COMECON (Council for Mutual Economic Cooperation), the Western firms may gain important Eastern outlets for components and materials. Moreover, through its growing familiarity with trade and other officials of the communist country, it may ob-

tain orders (directly or as an intermediary) to supply other finished
goods that the communist country needs to import. In the case of
the joint venture between Simmons Machine Tools in Albany, N.Y.,
and the Czech industrial complex, Skoda, Simmons found an advantageous and inexpensive source of supply in Skoda for certain
machine tools which Skoda could deliver in three to five weeks
(compared to over a year for comparable items from western firms),
while Skoda is to provide an East European market for some Simmons tools that are superior to eastern models.

A third, and potentially quite important, benefit to the Western
partner is specialized technology. In a growing number of cases,
the Eastern partner has made certain technological improvements
from which the Western partner could benefit, and this return flow
of technology becomes a significant *quid pro quo.*

The partners in these co-production arrangements can increase
their returns in the same manner as returns are normally augmented
(whether in international or domestic investment)—by raising productivity sufficiently to repay the costs of financing the productivity
increase, including the costs of the machinery, inventions, stocks of
goods, and other forms of capital invested. The role of profits—both
as an indicator of and as a stimulus to success—is equally important
whether the process is carried on by private or by public enterprises,
or by a partnership arrangement using both types, as suggested
above. Nor is there any reason to doubt that the full modernization
of the Soviet bloc economies could be a highly profitable operation
for all participants. In some respects the Soviet bloc is technologi-
cally and economically at about the stage of Western Europe of the
early postwar period. Modernization is an enormous, but by no
means impossible task, and assistance from the advanced private
enterprise economies could greatly shorten the time and sacrifice
required to achieve the goal. A very large amount of private business
would be involved.

Ideology's Irrelevant

The beauty of these co-production arrangements from the point
of view of one who welcomes more interdependence is that they
require a great deal of communication and mutual understanding
on matters which are taken seriously, because they are of obvious
importance to both sides. In such ventures, practical results count,

and ideological differences are pushed into the background. According to a former student of mine who has planned and carried out a number of such operations in Yugoslavia, ideological differences have proved remarkably irrelevant and easy to ignore in this context. Thus, such ventures *can* do much to stimulate interdependence and cooperation.

If co-production succeeds in reducing interbloc tensions and increasing the prosperity of the East, then both East and West can settle down to solving what is perhaps a more fundamental problem than their mutual hostility: closing the gap in living standards between North and South (the developed and the less-developed). The poorer countries of Asia, Africa and Latin America have begun to view their historic poverty as by no means inevitable, but subject to improvement by their own efforts, and with the help of the developed countries. The resulting "demand for development" is a relatively new but already vastly powerful political force in the world, one that contributes enormously to the world's progress, but which may also lead to catastrophic conflict if not accommodated.

As for the traditional economic aid programs, they have been basically undermined by having been so largely planned and administered in the spirit of the cold war. Most of the resources made available for foreign aid have been actually used to obtain or support foreign "client states," ideological converts, military bases, U.N. votes, revolutionary or counterrevolutionary movements, etc. The resulting scandalous confusion of objectives has been extremely prejudicial to a serious attack on the problem of economic development, which is, in any case, a vastly more difficult enterprise than was thought until a few years ago.

The communists can make political gains, no doubt, by cultivating the harvest of hatred arising from past colonialism and neglect. But political gains of this sort are obtainable only at the risk of escalating minor conflicts into major military confrontations; and victories—even if attained—are likely to be evanescent and burdensome. When it comes right down to it, communism has no more of a solution to the demand for a simple and quick route to economic development than capitalism. (Indeed, as even Marx perceived, a rather high degree of economic development is probably a prerequisite for the effective running of a centrally planned economy.) A long-term and responsible view by the Soviet bloc leaders could therefore lead them to pass up such easy but illusory "victories," and to turn, in partnership with the West, if indeed the latter is willing, to coping with the real and vast problems of world economic growth.

If this partnership were to be effected, the problems of world economic development would begin to look manageable. Even if disarmament remained elusive, one could count in such a case on tens of billions of dollars in savings from an arms freeze, and from the phasing out of obsolescent weapons systems. Moreover, much of the released resources in research and development, systems analysis, and large-scale program administration capability could usefully be diverted to the basic analytic, innovational and creative programs required to achieve the needed breakthroughs in the field of economic development. Examples of such potential breakthroughs are the inexpensive desalination of water, the effective tapping of unconventional energy sources, sharply reduced building costs via prefabricated modules, the speedy achievement of universal literacy and advanced skills through the use of teaching machines and satellite-transmitted TV programs, etc. Dramatic progress will probably be required in a number of such fields to enable the tasks of development to be accomplished within a politically tolerable time span.

For many, therefore, everything depends in the end on the capability of both West and East to make the enormous intellectual adjustments to the technological imperatives of the new interdependent world in which we live. Such mental changes, it is clear, are made only with difficulty. The most menacing aspect of the problem is the fantastic speed with which our environment has been changing and the fact that if we fail to meet a single test we may not have a second chance. There is little room for learning by trial and error. Whether the human race possesses the flexibility to adapt to such a rapidly changing environment no one can foretell. Our job is to try.

This article is a revised version of an original paper prepared within the Program of Research on the International Economics of Disarmament and Arms Control (RIEDAC) in the Columbia University Graduate School of Business. It was first presented as the introductory paper at the International Conference on the Economics of World Disarmament and Interdependence, held in Oslo, August 29th—September 1st, 1965, under the auspices of RIEDAC and the Peace Research Institute (Oslo). The article has since appeared in *Disarmament and World Economic Interdependence,* edited by Emile Benoit with the assistance of N. P. Gleditsch, Oslo: Universitetsforlaget and New York: Columbia University Press, 1967.

CHAPTER 3

GILBERT H. CLEE

*The alert world enterprise combines
constancy of corporate purpose with flexibility of
response to local conditions via a three-level
hierarchy of interrelated plans.*

Guidelines for

Global Business

IN TODAY'S ERA OF RAPID TECHNOLOGICAL CHANGE and increasing international competition, the world enterprise occupies a uniquely sensitive position. Operating in a diversity of national environments, allocating resources and making decisions in the light of global alternatives, it must cope not only with a more elaborate set of organizational variables but with a far more complex and sensitive array of external factors than a domestically oriented business. Its sheer size relative to some of the national economies in which it functions often magnifies the economic consequences of its decisions.

Particularly where the tides of nationalism are running strong, the political impact of these decisions—and the burden of responsibility on the decision maker—may be heavy indeed. To assure the long-term profitability of the organization, top management must be sensitive to the complex interrelationships between the world enterprise and each of its national environments. Without this awareness, it cannot hope to plan the future strategy of the enterprise so as to maximize growth and profitability.

Since the end of World War II the multinational company has truly come into its own. The lure of overseas markets has brought about an upsurge of international activity among producers of chemicals and pharmaceuticals, automobiles, synethetic fibers, electronic equipment, and a long list of other products. It has been estimated[1] that thirty of the top fifty American companies, and twenty-six of the fifty largest enterprises elsewhere in the world, could be ranked as truly international companies—an estimate that is probably conservative if we define, as some experts do, an "international company" as any enterprise with 20% or more of its assets invested abroad. And an informed American observer has speculated that two decades hence 600 or 700 of the largest multinational companies may be doing the major part of the world's business.[2]

Impact of World Enterprise

Such figures, however, hardly begin to suggest the manifold ways in which the plans and actions of multinational companies, large and small, affect the host economies in which their subsidiaries operate. Most concretely, there is the injection of capital into the host country, initially from direct foreign investment and later from the reinvestment of local earnings, which tends to mobilize domestic capital for investment in related enterprises and stimulate business activity generally. There is the further benefit of foreign exchange earned by the subsidiary in exporting some or all of its production and, conversely, the unfavorable balance-of-payments effects of repatriation of profits and of raw-materials imports by the foreign-owned enterprise. Beyond its immediate financial impact, the effects of foreign investment are felt throughout the host economy in the form of additions to local resources of knowledge and know-how, competitive pressures, and higher employment.

Initially, at least, the multinational enterprise brings into the host country a cadre of managers and technicians whose knowledge and skills are transferred, in the course of time, to the domestic nationals whom they train. These nationals will, in many cases, ultimately take over responsibilities for local operations, training a new generation of managers and technical workers in their turn. If there is mobility of employment in these occupations, these effects may soon spread to other sectors of the host nation's economy.

The importance of such an injection of managerial and technical knowledge in a developing nation is well illustrated by the case of Africa's only alumina refinery, a $150-million plant operated in Guinea by FRIA, an international consortium of European and American aluminum producers. FRIA's manpower training program, begun nearly two years before its plant went into full operation in 1960, has trained hundreds of African technicians and managers, many of whom were illiterate when hired. By 1962, the company was employing, along with 400-odd European expatriates, more than 900 Africans. The number of its African professional workers had risen from ninety-seven to 476, and its African foremen from two to thirteen. More than twenty Africans, by completing a two-year vocational training course, had become eligible for journeyman and craftsman positions, and some 200 workers had learned to read and write in the company's literacy classes. By 1963 almost the entire initial work force had been upgraded.

Again, the production techniques employed by a foreign subsidiary may benefit local industries in developing nations. Latin America is replete with examples: the improved cotton-ginning techniques and the advances in vegetable-oil refining, handling and transport introduced by Anderson, Clayton & Company into Brazil; the advances in Peruvian fishing methods traceable to the influence of Wilbur-Ellis, the American fish-packing company; and the pre-shrinking of textiles that is now commonplace in the Peruvian textile industry, thanks to the use of the process by a local subsidiary of W. R. Grace and Company. Comparable effects can sometimes be traced to the marketing activities of a world enterprise. Thus, improved paperwork and office procedures have been brought about by the efforts of International Business Machines Corporation to market its computers to the managements of large banks and insurance companies around the world.

No less important than the immediate infusion of knowledge and skills by a world-enterprise subsidiary are its competitive effects.

When a highly efficient foreign producer enters into direct competition with local industry, some inefficient producers may be forced out of business. At the same time, the foreign operation may tend to bid up the price of local capital and labor, adding to the cost pressures on indigenous producers in other industries as well. Though painful, such effects frequently benefit the economies of the host nations in the long run by forcing local producers to improve their efficiency.

A further important impact of multinational enterprise on the host country is, of course, added employment. The dimensions of this contribution are suggested by a U.S. Commerce Department study that put wage and salary payments by foreign subsidiaries of U.S.-based companies at $6.9 billion in 1957, roughly the equivalent of the total private consumption of Belgium and Luxembourg. Overseas payrolls of U.S.-based companies in that year totaled an estimated 3.2 million persons, better than nine-tenths of them local nationals. Roughly 930,000 foreign nationals in that year were employed by U.S. subsidiaries in Latin America, over 1 million in Europe, more than 230,000 in Asia, and nearly 100,000 in Africa. Considering the growth of overseas investments by U.S. companies since then, it is safe to assume that the current employment figures are a great deal higher.

Bowater in Appalachia

An interesting example of the contribution of a multinational company to the solution of a local unemployment problem can be found in Calhoun, Tennessee, near the southern tip of the economically depressed Appalachian region of the United States. There Bowater Southern, a subsidiary of the giant British paper company, employs some 1,300 local workers. In addition to its payroll of about $10 million per year, Bowater Southern pumps approximately $11 million annually into the region's economy by purchases of wood from private landholders.

Besides the local nationals it employs directly, of course, the world-enterprise subsidiary tends to create more jobs in supplier companies and related businesses. In turn, this added employment enhances consumer purchasing power, stimulates demand, and creates further support for future economic expansion. An example of this can be seen in Volkswagen's Brazilian operation, which employs over 10,000 people directly and stimulates the employment of thousands more through the myriad industries that supply Volkswagen with automotive components and accessories. A further illustration is that of Royal Dutch Shell, whose Venezuelan subsidiary, Compania Shell de Venezuela, besides giving work directly to over 9,000 local nationals, helps create countless other jobs by local purchases of goods and services. These totaled nearly $37 million in 1964 alone.

Long-run Compatability Vital

In outlining some of the major effects of multinational enterprise on national economies, I have not meant to imply that the managers of such enterprises should, or indeed could, invariably plan their corporate strategy in such a way as to maximize the immediate economic benefits to the host nations. The basic purpose of a multinational company, like that of any other private business, is the utilization of resources to maximize profit. Its health and survival depend, ultimately, on the vigor, constancy, and intelligence with which it pursues this purpose. But though it cannot invariably act in harmony with the short-run needs of the host economy, the interests of the world enterprise must at least be compatible with those of the host nation over the long run.

Nothing is more basic to the maintenance of a favorable international investment climate than a convincing and continuing demonstration by world enterprise that it can, over some considerable period of time, contribute important and continuing benefits to the economies of the host nations. Indeed, in negotiating with the host government for the protective incentives that are so often a *sine qua non* of profitable investment in a developing economy, the company must generally be able to demonstrate in great detail the nature and dimensions of the long-range benefits its investment may be expected to bring. Thus, in an era of growing nationalism in many areas of the world, the very self-interest of the multinational corporation obliges it to operate with increasing sensitivity to the self-interest of its hosts and to the effects of its activities upon them.

The acute need to harmonize potentially divergent interests has focused attention on the value of detailed, realistic company planning based on adequate information. Effective planning by the multinational corporation inherently acts as a stabilizing force. By shifting the focus of corporate energies from the pursuit of short-term profits to the building of long-term profitability, it reinforces the mutuality of interest between the local subsidiary and the nation in which it operates. This in turn tends to dissipate the specter of a powerful foreign enterprise, unpredictable in its behavior and unresponsive to local control.

Above all, the complexity of the risks, requirements and opportunities in the international field lends real urgency to the need for institutionalization of planning in the multinational corporation. Nowhere is it more difficult to develop a planning system that will integrate the separate contributions of many corporate executives into a single set of formal plans for the corporation and its individual units. Yet the special requirements of planning in the multinational enterprise have until quite recently received little attention.[3]

The Three Faces of Planning

Planning in the multinational company may be viewed as the process of developing a program for future action through rational assessment of company potentials, evaluation of market opportunities in the light of the relevant economic, social and political variables, and selection of alternatives on the basis of expected risk and return. The results of this process are a hierarchy of interrelated plans that define the business or businesses in which the company will engage, identify specific goals to be achieved, and set forth the means of achieving them. These plans may be classified as strategic plans, interim plans, and operating plans.

The *strategic plan* envisions the kinds of business in which the company will engage in its various national environments, defines the role its expects to play in the countries where it operates, and sets forth its long-range objectives. A manufacturer of consumer durables, for example, might have as its goal the production and sale of a full line of home appliances throughout the world. Its strategic plan might stipulate:

¶ That the company will maintain control of its markets and will create a marketing organization wherever a profitable potential exists
¶ That as overseas market volume develops, production will be shifted from the company's domestic plants to foreign manufacturing facilities, to be strategically located with respect to production and distribution economies, long-term competitive strategy, and relevant political considerations
¶ That the company will expand its operations by reinvestment of earnings where feasible, but may speed its growth by acquiring existing overseas marketing and manufacturing facilities if it can do so economically
¶ That the company will seek to build a long-term position in each of its national environments by pursuing policies that will tend to identify its subsidiaries with local interests: employment of local nationals in supervisory and managerial positions wherever possible, establishment of technical training programs in less-developed areas, and responsiveness to local economic considerations and balance-of-payments considerations when making decisions on repatriation vs. reinvestment of earnings—even where no specific commitments have been made.

The function of strategic plans is to show how the basic corporate objective is to be achieved. Thus, their defining characteristic is content, not timing. Although almost all long-range plans are strategic in nature, the converse is not necessarily true. For example, an opportunity may develop to modify corporate strategy by an acquisition that moves the corporation into an unrelated business, or a new national environment, but is nonetheless consistent with corporate philosophy and objectives. Such a short-term move, being strategic in nature, naturally becomes a part of the strategic plan.

Within the framework of the strategic plan, which may extend from ten to twenty years ahead, an *interim plan* specifies more detailed targets and goals for the years immediately ahead. Depending on the nature of the business and the practical reliability of the forecasts for the various host economies, the interim plan may extend from three to ten years ahead; five years is probably close to the mean.

For example, within the context of the strategic plan just hypothesized, an interim plan might commit the company:

To expand its sales in its existing markets by 50% during the next five years

To enter and develop six new major markets, selected on the basis of size, probability that the company will be able to compete in them successfully, available labor and capital resources, and likelihood that the operation would make a needed economic contribution to the host economy

With respect to each of these new national markets, the interim plan would specify, in the form of detailed objectives and action programs:

The market-share target
The products to be used to enter the market
The methods of market entry and development

Finally, within the context of the interim plan, an annual *operating plan* sets forth precise, detailed objectives for the year ahead, designed to bring the company the first part of the way toward its interim and long-range goals. Translated into financial terms, this operating plan often becomes a budget for the ensuing year.

These three plans—the strategic, the interim, and the operating—comprise the total corporate planning effort, which is reviewed and revised annually. As new opportunities for growth or diversification emerge, appropriate modifications can be made in the strategic plan. The interim plan, governed by the strategic plan, can be adjusted to take account of opportunities or problems that are foreseeable during its shorter time span. Within this context, a new annual operating plan will, of course, be established each year. Thus, each year's operating plan will automatically reflect any changes that may have been made in the interim plan.

The integrated planning system comprising these three types of plan should go beyond the effective management and growth of the businesses in which the company is currently engaged throughout the world. It should also provide for the constant exploration and development of new products to round out the company's line of new businesses and diversify its interests. To strengthen the enterprise and maximize its profitability, strategic planning and interim planning are necessarily concerned with global diversification goals as well as with new goals for the present business. Inside the framework of the interim plan, moreover, the operating units will be concerned with product diversification in their own areas of responsibility.

Five Additional Planning Precepts

The relationships I have outlined among strategic, interim, and operating plans are more than familiar and convenient abstractions; they are the practical foundations of the planning structure in a wide variety of large, outstandingly successful companies. But though domestic and multinational business planning rest on the same broad conceptual foundations, unique problems and complexities confront the planners of world enterprise. In consequence, five precepts of corporate planning take on special meaning for the multinational company:

1. The overall corporate plan should be total and comprehensive. It should cover every aspect of the business over the long, medium and short term, including the economic roles of the subsidiaries in their respective national environments, and it should give due weight to political factors at work in various host countries. Particularly in developing nations, these hard-to-quantify political factors, which most domestic U.S. companies can afford to ignore, can and do crucially affect the fortunes of foreign-owned business operations. Finally, the plan should properly relate each element of the business to the others, domestically as well as internationally.

2. The components of the overall corporate plan should be functionally integrated. Especially for a maker of consumer goods, this can be an exceptionally intricate task. In such companies, the basic marketing planning effort must normally be done at the country level so as to take into account varying local conditions and requirements which headquarters planners cannot know at first hand —e.g., different preferences of Danes and Brazilians as to the sugar content of soft drinks. Decisions on sources of supply may also be best made at the local level. Yet these plans, as they are reviewed and coordinated by headquarters planners, will often require modification in the light of overall corporate strategies.

Broadly speaking, the overall marketing plan will serve as a base for the production plan, which in turn will affect the financial plan dealing with capital requirements and capital expenditures. The research and development plan will take into account the long-term objectives of the company as specified in the strategic plan, as well as the immediate short-term marketing goals of the various subsidiaries. The personnel plan, designed to provide for the manpower needs of all parts of the enterprise, may range from such questions as technical training at the local level to the rationalization of management compensation throughout the enterprise so as to permit international transfer and reassignment of key personnel. It in turn will be affected by the production and marketing plans. And the financial plan, developed with due consideration of the company's net economic contribution to the countries in which it operates, will specify how cash flow and profits will be apportioned to provide for the needs of current operations and for possible future diversification.

3. The plans should pinpoint responsibility. Each organizational unit that can be expected to accomplish a goal should be responsible for its own plan. This plan will later be combined with the plans of other units in a total divisional plan, and the divisional plans in turn will be combined in a corporate plan. Any manager can be expected to discharge his cost, service or financial responsibilities most effectively when he is made to do his own planning. For this reason, it is essential to push the responsibility for planning as far down as possible in the organization. To be sure, local managers may at first need to be educated in the techniques of formal planning. Yet without their participation (and without the sensitive understanding of local conditions that they can provide), the chief executive will find it difficult to locate the real problems within the organization, determine how vigorously its opportunities are being pursued, or measure the performance of individual subsidiaries against the plan.

4. The plan should be dynamic. Beside providing for the effective and efficient operation of the current business in all its national environments, it should set forth programs for new or improved products, new or expanded markets, production improvements through better economy or cost reduction, more effective use of cash flow, and improved personnel standards through new techniques of recruitment or personnel development. Moreover, it may well establish diversification targets. To supplement and protect its

existing business, to shift financial resources into faster growing business areas, to add new glamor to corporate stock in the hope of raising its price-earnings ratio, to use corporate strengths more efficiently, or merely to hedge against economic and political uncertainties, the company may find it desirable to move into entirely new businesses. It may wish to diversify its investments so that some of its businesses will be growing when others may be in difficulty. Again, it may wish to spread its investment risk among a number of countries to minimize the effect of political difficulties in any one nation upon the fortunes of the corporation. This kind of planning is especially demanding in the multinational enterprise because of the extraordinary vulnerability of any multinational diversification program to policy shifts as minor as a tariff adjustment by any one of many national governments.

5. The plan should incorporate both qualitative and quantitative standards. Goals and operating programs should be stated as vividly and concretely as possible, e.g., "establish a dominant position in freeze-dried foods by 1975"; "cut our customer-service time to lowest in the industry by 1972"; "become the top company in a foreign market by 1978." These goals and programs should then be quantified, in a budget and financial forecast, in terms of volume and return-on-investment objectives reflecting the varying costs and risks of the respective countries of operation. These financial objectives, in turn, become the yardstick against which to measure the achievement of the unit operating plans.[4] Financial results will gauge the success of the units in meeting their operating plans; it will be immediately apparent from the variances in volume and profit when a unit is exceeding or falling short of its operating goals.

Information Is Vital

Clearly, planning in a successful multinational enterprise is a way of life. It cannot be confined to top management alone or to a small specialized group. Rather, it involves everyone who bears leadership or executive responsibility for the effective operation of any unit of the enterprise. To ensure that all elements of the organization carry out their planning responsibilities in a consistent and coordinated manner, that all plans are properly geared into the corporate planning cycle, and that all are compatible in content and properly supported with data demands not only an effective planning structure but an adequate, current, and meaningful input of planning information. The optimum planning structure for a given company is almost always so intimately related to the nature and organization of the business that generalizations are likely to prove treacherous. Such generalizations are, in any case, beyond the scope of this chapter. The information requirements, however, may be usefully summed up under two heads: accurate assessment of the corporation itself, and alertness to the forces at work in the national environments where it operates. Effective assessment of the company's internal strengths and weaknesses calls, in turn, for three categories of data:

Economic: A continuous record of existing product lines; their current, past and projected growth; their competitive market position; and their contribution to profits. Areas of potential vulnerability and potential growth in existing product lines must be identified. Related product opportunities, especially for vertical and horizontal integration, should be evaluated.

Operational: An inventory of operating strengths and limitations. This requires a continuous critical examination and assessment of all operating activities to identify the areas in which the company is performing well and those in which its capabilities are inadequate. Such an inventory might, for example, reveal a deficiency of marketing skills in a corporation with outstanding research and development resources and a superb capability for low-cost production, but—thanks to a unique product line—without any real experience in competitive marketing. An operational inventory of this kind helps a company build on its strengths while correcting its weaknesses or limitations. It also serves as a valuable guide in a corporate diversification program, by indicating how the parent corporation can effectively supplement the strengths and weaknesses of the company being acquired, or strengthen its capacity to absorb additional product lines or businesses.

Financial: A detailed current portrait of the corporation's financial position and capacity in each of its national environments. This is always important, but never more so than when management is preparing to embark on a program of expansion and diversification. Many aspects of the company's financial position might constitute significant advantages or real drawbacks to such a venture. A large cash surplus and no debt, providing a great reservoir of capital, might encourage ambitious expansion. A high debt ratio, restrictive covenants in borrowing agreements, and a declining cash flow might argue for postponing the program until the company had succeeded in reaching a stronger financial position. There may be reasons for or against the issue of additional common stock. Financial conditions always bear importantly, and often decisively, on the nature and timing of the steps the company should take in carrying out its strategic plans.

The internal information needs I have outlined are, of course, by no means peculiar to multinational business. They are common to all corporate planning; their increased complexity in the multi-national enterprise is a function of the special communications problems that are involved in operating a multinational enterprise, as well as of its characteristically more complex structure.

Likewise, every corporate planning effort requires accurate knowledge of the corporate environment. In the multinational company this requirement is singularly difficult to meet because of the dearth of accurate, readily available market intelligence in many countries. Yet knowledge of the national environments in which it operates is indispensable to the sound and profitable development of world enterprise. It constitutes, in fact, an unprecedented challenge to the skill and vision of corporate leaders and planners in the next few decades.

By the year 2000, most of the world's 6 billion people will be pressing toward the common goal of economic development. When to take economic advantage of the great potential opportunities in these markets, and how to operate in them, are problems of great magnitude and complexity. The changing nature of competition, worldwide, must be understood. New technological developments that may threaten a part of the corporation's product line or provide an opportunity to strengthen its market position anywhere in the world must be identified and analyzed. An understanding of demographic change, of changing consumer tastes, and of changes in consumer purchasing power in all the company's diverse national markets must be developed. The potential effects on the business of government policy and the probable impact of economic blocs need to be analyzed. Potential business opportunities everywhere in the world must be analyzed with skill and discernment if the company is to take the best and most profitable long-term position in all its world markets.

But it is not only in the interest of multinational enterprise itself that the challenge be met effectively. The issue is not one of private commercial advantage, nor even one of national self-interest. For only if its managers plan with vision can multinational enterprise prosper. And only if it prospers can it effectively promote the growth of the developing nations and contribute its full share to the collective economic strength of the free world.

N O T E S

1. *The Economist,* October 17, 1964, p. 271.

2. George A. Steiner in *Economie Appliquée.*

3. A significant publication in this area is *Multinational Corporate Planning,* New York: Macmillan, 1966, the proceedings of a 1964 seminar on multinational planning held at Fontainebleau under the joint auspices of the Institut Européen d'Administration des Affaires and the Graduate School of Business of the University of California at Los Angeles, with the cooperation of the McKinsey Foundation for Management Research.

4. See Millard Pryor, "Planning in a Worldwide Business," *Harvard Business Review,* January-February 1965, for an interesting discussion of the considerations involved.

CHAPTER 4

KENNETH SIMMONDS

When the body's worldwide but the brain is not,
there's trouble ahead, as many firms that neither have, nor
appear to want, foreign nationals in top
corporate posts are bound to discover.

Multinational?
Well, Not Quite

THE MULTINATIONAL CORPORATION is widely described as an entity capable of transcending national interests to operate for the benefit of a worldwide group of investors, employees and customers. Its internationalist character is reinforced by a top management team composed of unusually adaptable and peripatetic executives who are chosen with a praiseworthy indifference to national origins. These managers, it is even suggested, will eventually decide all conflicts of allegiance between corporation and country of origin in favor of the former.

Such is the idyll. The reality is something else. There are a number of reasons to suspect that, particularly in large U.S. corporations with extensive international operations, internationalization of top managements is not expanding in step with worldwide employment but follows only gradually as individual foreign subsidiaries and affiliates approach the size of their U.S. parents.

A tendency for a self-perpetuating management to fill vacancies with men of a similar cultural background would be one reason to expect a lag in movement of foreigners into top management. Altogether apart from any prejudice, such a tendency may be a simple necessity if management does not feel capable of evaluating the potential of someone from a different background. When selecting a top replacement in a billion dollar corporation, it's no time to gamble.

Another advantage of the domestic national is that he has been closer to the head office for a longer time than his foreign counterpart. Unless it seeks replacements among men in their forties or fifties, top management would change so frequently that there would be little opportunity to observe, design, implement, and adjust the corporate course. A foreign national in his mid-forties, regardless of his outstanding record in subsidiary management, is unlikely to have had much exposure to the operation of top corporate management. This lack of exposure is compounded in those worldwide corporations that follow the suggestions of the "how-to-do-it" school of international business and centralize strategic planning and decision making. International Telephone & Telegraph is an example of such a company. As reported recently:

"Geneen eliminated much of the autonomy of ITT's operating managers, and replaced it with a control system tautly run from New York headquarters. From what was once described as a kind of holding company in which, at one point, managers were literally instructed to ignore New York directives and 'just send earnings back home,' ITT became a tightly centralized organization."[1]

The domestic national, on the other hand, is more likely to have been recruited as a management trainee directly from a business school, and to have spent time in corporate headquarters. He will probably have been involved in the details of strategic planning at the corporate level, perhaps helping to establish new plants, integrate new acquisitions and the like. In short he will have a better opportunity to prepare for top management posts than the foreigner.

The more rigid management structure that seems endemic to some foreign countries also makes it difficult for the young foreign executive to climb as rapidly as his American colleague. While he may come into a firm from an educated elite marked for top posts, much as the American comes in as a management trainee from a graduate business school, he is likely to be regarded as young and inexperienced for ten years longer than the American, and he is more accustomed to wait his turn for promotion rather than grab it as and where he can, or sidestep rungs in the ladder by transferring to other firms.

Furthermore, although he generally has a quality university education, the lack of a business education hampers the foreigner in competing with an American for the same top post. The foreigner is not made as vividly aware as are the 7,000 U.S. MBA students graduating each year that it doesn't take forty years of apprenticeship at lower levels of the hierarchy to handle a top-level decision in a competent fashion.

U.S. Management Policies Hurt

The policies of many American corporations toward their foreign subsidiaries tend to reinforce the relative disadvantage of the foreign executive in several ways. True, the American firm makes a determined effort to get the brightest and best foreign management material, if anything because the cost of keeping U.S. nationals overseas is extremely high. ("Hardship" benefits may bring their salaries in uncomfortable cities such as London and Paris up to the level of the top 1% of local executives.) Moreover, the firm needs someone who knows how the foreign culture operates and can find his way around the centers of power and influence. And once it gets this talent the American firm spares no effort in grooming it. But adequate grooming for management of a subsidiary is a different thing from preparation for headquarters management. Subsidiary top management is normally a castrated top management with the truly entrepreneurial function removed.[2] It is usually too costly to create a second or third research establishment at the subsidiary level and more profitable to copy the success of the parent than to mold the subsidiary into a completely different shape. Elementary economic reasoning points to international expansion of activities for which the domestic corporation is well along on the learning curve and has a lead on the competition. Backed by the experience of the parent, the subsidiary stands to do better if it remains in these fields than if it pursues untrodden ways. This is reinforced by the overbearing size and purchasing power of the U.S. market and the keen competition for it, which usually mean that new ideas are exploited there first.[3]

In many cases internationalization of top management may be hindered by the reluctance of the foreign manager himself to move from his subsidiary status. Why leave the top position in a large subsidiary in one's own cultural environment where the headaches of operating at the top are lessened by the load assumed by parent leadership? Furthermore, in seeking educated men, the American firm will in many countries have obtained men from the social and cultural elites for its subsidiary managers. While these men may feel some underlying rancor at continual subjugation to an absent corporate deity, they may find it equally unpalatable to seek a "place in the sun" that involves relocation to what seems to them a cultural vacuum—say, the American Midwest.

Finally, the foreigner who has not spent a considerable time in the United States may be at a considerable disadvantage in a top management post in a company that is responsible to American shareholders, still has a large percentage of its sales in the United States, and therefore requires that the incumbent possess an intimate knowledge of American institutions. This would be particularly true on the government relations side. What foreigner would feel at home with the pantomime performance required at congressional investigating committees before banks of television cameras? Less than a polished grasp of English would also hinder many of the executives who have spent their working life using principally other languages.

The Matter of Proof

Proof that these difficulties currently face foreign executives in moving to the top of the U.S. international corporation would require a careful study of statistics of employment and promotions for different executive levels. As a first step, a study was made of the national origins of the top management of the 150 largest U.S.

industrial corporations in terms of sales. These were taken from the
1965 Fortune Directory.[4] All top *corporate* officers and directors
listed for these firms in Moody's under the management heading
were included in the survey.[5] With double-counting eliminated, this
covered 3,847 executives, an average of 25 per corporation. Table 1
summarizes these results.

TABLE 1: *Foreign Participation in Top Corporate Management*
(150 largest U.S. industrial corporations)

Classification	Number of Managers
U.S. citizens by birth	3,593
Born outside U.S., not identified as U.S. by birth:	
Entered U.S. permanently before age 26[a]	81
Entered U.S. permanently at age 26 or above	34
Resident outside U.S.[b]	25
Insufficient data for classification	114
Total	3,847

[a] Includes roughly 50% identified as non-U.S. citizens at birth.
[b] Excludes corporate officers of Shell and Unilever; also board members
of their U.S. subsidiaries.

Biographical particulars were taken from a range of standard
references and for the large number of executives for whom insufficient data was available from these sources (over 20%), particulars were requested directly. Sufficient information was collected
to classify all but 3% of the total. In this manner most of the foreign
participation in top corporate management in the sample corporations has been traced. Any allowance for errors in published biographies or for executives with "shrinking violet" tendencies should
thus not affect the conclusions materially.

Executives who transferred to the U.S. up to age 25 have been
shown separately. Many of these came to this country in their early
years, perhaps born of American parents outside the U.S. Only a
minority had any business experience outside the U.S. before they
arrived. Every future top executive who was in the United States
permanently by age 26 climbed the ladder essentially on the basis
of American performance. Only those who came here after 25 can be

classified as representative of a corporation's foreign employment. Subsequent reference in this chapter to "foreign participation" will exclude those who emigrated to the United States before age 26.

Before examining the results in detail, a few comments are needed in defense of the most common objections to any conclusions from these figures. First, it is true that top corporate posts in firms of this size both omit many important executive positions and include some relatively unimportant posts in terms of day-to-day operation. But they do take in the presidents, chairmen, vice presidents and internal directors who make up the top echelon. Second, it may be argued that the top-management picture in 1965 does not take into account that many non-U.S. employees are now rapidly climbing the ladder, that most of these large firms had little international activity at the time the foundations for promotion of current top management were being laid, or that, even in those that had, internationalization was impeded by the war. These points may be valid and suggest that the findings of this survey should not be projected into the future without more testing. Even so, many of those in the survey reached top corporate management in the 1960's, and foreign activity of a number of these corporations has for many years been quite substantial.

About one-fifth of the total employment in these firms is foreign, yet only 1.6% of their top corporate management entered as foreigners after age 25 or remain outside the United States (see Table 2). If we had data on companies that do not disclose their foreign employment, those that do not include subsidiary employment in their employment figures, and those that do not classify Canadian employment as foreign, the comparison would become even more dramatic. For 71 corporations with heavy foreign activity, foreign employment jumps to 33% while foreign participation in top management remains at 1.6%. The fairly even dispersion of foreign executives among the three groups of corporations listed suggests that promotion of foreigners to top posts is less dependent on the size of the company's foreign employment than it is on the availability of foreigners in the general pool of competent executives.

No attempt was made to collect figures for foreign sales or sales of foreign production. A *Business International* study of 117 U.S. corporations operating abroad, however, recorded foreign earnings of these firms for 1964 as 26% of total earnings and foreign net

TABLE 2: *Comparison of Foreign Participation in Employment and Corporate Management (150 largest U.S. industrial corporations)*

	Significant Foreign Employment	Little or No Foreign Employment[a]	Data Not Obtained	Total
Number of corporations	71	55	24	150
All employees (millions):[b]				
Total	4.66	1.79	1.10	7.54
Foreign	1.54	.03	—	1.56
% foreign	33.0	1.7	—	20.7
Top corporate management:				
Total classified[c]	1,851	1,263	655	3,733
Foreign				
Employees	21	10	8	39
Outside directors	9	7	4	20
Total foreign	30	17	12	59
% foreign	1.6	1.3	1.8	1.6

[a] These include firms in steel, airframe, petroleum, tobacco, packaging, and food industries
[b] Subject to differences in treatment of employees of subsidiaries and probably undercounting.
[c] Foreign is defined as non-U.S. at birth and not entering U.S. permanently before age 26.

assets as 25% of total net assets.[6] This selection of firms included many of those in the top 150, so the foreign employment figure of 20% shown in the table seems a reasonably representative indicator of "foreign activity," however measured.

The major discrepancy between the percentage of total employment which is foreign and the percentage of foreign participation in top corporate management lends strong support to the contention that the path to the top is more difficult for the foreigner. Even if we allow that many of these firms have penetrated overseas markets only recently, this conclusion still appears valid.

Table 3 contains a further breakdown of the figure of 34 foreigners in top management who transferred to the United States after age 25. Of these only 13 were shifted from a foreign subsidiary activity by American firms with whom they were then employed—not a very large number out of 3,847 executives surveyed. Five of these were transferred in the crucial age period 36-45, three at a younger

TABLE 3: *Management Who Transferred to U.S. after Age 25—*
Type of Transfer and Country of Origin

Country of Origin	Changed Employment at Time of Transfer	Transferred While with U.S. Corporation	Transferred While with Foreign Corporation	Transferred When Foreign Corporation Merged into U.S. Corporation	Total
Canada	2	5	—	4	11
U.K.	4	5	2	—	11
Germany	5	—	—	—	5
France	—	1	1	—	2
Holland	1	—	1	—	2
Austria	1	—	—	—	1
Mexico	—	1	—	—	1
Australia	—	1	—	—	1
Total	13	13	4	4	34

age, and five later in their career. Of those who were not transferred from a foreign subsidiary, 13 seem to have transferred at their own volition, four were initially moved to United States subsidiaries of foreign firms, and four became directors when Canadian firms merged with U.S. corporations. It is noteworthy that of the 13 transferring of their own accord none came after age 41, suggesting a nontransferability of top foreign management skills and experience.

The nationality distribution is far from a representative collection of American subsidiary activity even as it existed fifteen years ago. The only South American had an MIT degree, and the Europeans came mainly on their own. As might be expected, Canadians and Englishmen make up a large proportion of the total, and if these were excluded there would be only three executives promoted from overseas. While promotion from subsidiary to top management is more common for Canadians than others, few Canadians have come to the United States on their own later in their careers and made it to the top of the corporations included in the survey. Both Canadians shown in this category were under age thirty at the time they transferred.

A further 25 members of top corporate management who have not transferred to the United States were shown in Table 1. These

TABLE 4: *Foreign Management Who Have Not Transferred to U.S.*

Country of Origin	Officers of Subsidiaries on Parent Board	Foreign Outside Directors	Total
Canada	5	14	19
U. K.	1	2	3
France	1	—	1
Switzerland	1	—	1
Argentina	1	—	1
Total	9	16	25

are analyzed more fully in Table 4. Here again Canadians predominate and there is a surprising lack of any attempt to add nationals of other countries to the top corporate group even where they hold top posts in subsidiaries or affiliates.

It might be thought that some firms would have quite advanced foreign representation in top corporate management, even though the top 150 corporations as a group show such a small participation. But there are no outstanding exceptions. Only one or two corporations had more than three members of their top team who were either nonresident foreigners or had transferred after age 25.[7] Moreover, a study of the biographies of the foreign executives concerned ruled out any possibility that these firms were beginning a concerted effort to internationalize at the top. Of the 13 foreigners actually transferred from a subsidiary or an affiliate of a U.S. corporation, no firm had more than two. These are surprising results from a group of companies that contains ITT, which has a foreign employment of around 165,000 out of 200,000; Ford, with 160,000 foreign employees; and Singer, with 63,000, to mention but three examples. Of none of these three corporations could it be argued that their international activities have just taken root. Each has had significant foreign employment for thirty years.

This picture suggests that a determined effort will have to be made to promote foreign personnel into top management ranks if, within the near future, there is to be anything approaching an international team in the 150 top corporations investigated. Even if all foreseeable vacancies were to be filled with foreigners, the snowballing of American foreign investment, coupled with existing managerial turnover patterns, may mean that the proportion of overseas employment for some firms will continue to increase faster than their foreign participation in top management.

But it is unlikely that many firms will switch rapidly to favor foreigners in promotions to top management. Besides those arguments mentioned earlier, two further reasons may be advanced. A number of executives interviewed in the course of this study expressed a firm conviction that it was right and necessary to retain what is American for Americans. Another group pointed out that American business is not run for charity and that the firm should always look for the "best" man regardless of nationality, but be quite contented if this usually means an American.[8] The argument that an international top management should be internationally planned seems to carry little weight with these respondents.

Also emerging from discussions with executives of international corporations was a feeling that there were few, if any, ways in which subsidiary management could bring pressure to bear on corporate management without taking actions that were not in the best interests of the firm as a whole. And to take such actions invites dismissal, not promotion. As long as corporate management retains a firm grip on strategic planning and decision making, the power seems to lie all on its side.

Pulling these ideas together, sketchy though the evidence may be, leads to the conclusion that only as individual subsidiaries become large and complex, generating new products and large income, will the subsidiary executive gain the status and experience that will lead to promotion into top corporate management. As decentralization of top decisions grows, internationalization of top management will follow. With the business literature pointing toward centralized strategy formulation, however, this seems likely to come about more as a result of very gradual evolution than as a consequence of planned internationalization.

The alternative to internationalization is an American "master race" of top executives ultimately controlling a large segment of business activity outside the United States. Any reasonable projection of foreign direct investments of U.S. corporations shows astronomical figures even ten years hence. With this the case, candid advice to the bright young foreigner starting his career may increasingly take the following lines: "If you are thinking of working up the ladder in an American-owned subsidiary, don't. Buy a one-way ticket to New York and get on the right escalator."

It's Just Bad Business

Another consequence of the noninternational top corporate team is that it is likely to be less effective than if it were to be internationalized. Whatever the top American manager may wish to believe, he is a creature of his American culture and no amount of overseas experience can simulate the depth of understanding of the foreign environment that the foreign national himself possesses.

But the major problem will be an increasing strain between corporate and subsidiary management that affects corporate performance. Even though the subsidiary executive may not have the power to engineer his promotion, he may adopt a more nationalistic stance than would otherwise be necessary, fail to tell corporate headquarters the full story, or vent his dissatisfaction with permanent subsidiary status in many other ways. An example of the sort of problems that can arise is illustrated in a *Sunday Times* article on Ford's operations in Britain. Whether these claims are just or not, the significant point is that they were made and have reflected on the firm's reputation and performance:

"Four directors have quit Ford U.K. in a year: those of finance, sales, industrial relations, and the head of the Basildon tractor operations. All but the last resigned largely because of the tightening American control.

"In two years, more than 20 key men in Ford U.K.'s finance department have left. They include the investment analysis manager, the purchase analysis manager and within a few months, three successive administrative managers under the American director of engineering.

"From Ford U.K.'s product-planning section, the manager has left. So have the market research chief and the product-planner of the Cortina. With the labour relations director went one of his top executives. Ford U.K.'s controller of metal stamping has left, so has his right-hand man. So has the manager of operations in Ford U.K.'s new foundry, technically ahead of any other in Europe.

" 'This is not wastage; this is a haemorrhage,' said one of the most senior men who have left. All these, with other less significant executives who have also left, have gone to excellent, even superlative jobs—Ford executives have a usually justified and always expensive mystique. But virtually all had one motive in common. One ex-manager said: 'I know of no British senior Ford executive who any longer believes that there is a real future for a Briton in Ford.'

"To all this, Ford has an adamant answer: 'We have been since 1960 wholly an American company,' said one director, 'But we are run in Britain by Britons. We are world-wide; our attitudes and needs are not therefore those of Little Englanders. There is not dictation from Detroit.'

"But the total American domination of Dagenham—and the evidence of former executives is too strong to deny—is not a Detroit conspiracy; it is the logical result of Ford U.K.'s own history, Ford Detroit's world plans, the American lead in techniques of management and mass production, and a certain British bloody mindedness. Detroit's 1960 guarantee to the British Government when it sought 100 per cent of Ford U.K.—the promise that 'the majority' of Ford U.K.'s management would remain British—has not been broken. It was irrelevant.

"Ford U.K. now has Americans as managing director, financial director, engineering director, and production planning and styling director. Only four Americans are on the ruling Policy Board of 15, but they are the men with power.

" 'You control a company if you control its capital expenditure, its products, and in great detail its operating budgets,' said one senior ex-finance man. 'All these are controlled by Americans over here, and ultimately by Detroit. The amount of paper flowing to Detroit and back is unbelievable.'

"The other Americans at Dagenham control strategic functions—chief stylist, body construction, paint, data processing, the foundry, a welding and manufacturing engineer, three plant layout men, and a bevy in the truck group. 'The technical men are mostly first-class,' said one departed. 'Ford management is correct when it says Detroit has much technically to teach us. What causes the friction is that the Britons the Americans work with know that it is the American who has the ear of Detroit.' "[9]

Ensuring that top corporate management in the international

corporation does become truly international requires planned action. There are many ways to start. Noteworthy steps include: international executive development programs that concentrate on top management problems, rotation of younger foreign executives through corporate headquarters, decentralization of staff functions to foreign sites, or adoption of policies that treat all executives as internationalists regardless of origin.

The first physical transfer to a foreign site of the corporate head office of any major U.S. international corporation is still a thing of the future. There are plenty of regional offices but these are not the same. Although the foreign executives in regional offices will be better prepared to step into corporate management for having had more experience in policy formulation, the imposition of another executive layer can compound the inaccessibility of the American "gods" at corporate headquarters.

Of course, there are costs attached to passing over more advanced U.S. nationals in order to train foreigners for entry into top posts. But in the longer run there may be greater costs from failure to ensure not only equality of opportunity, but equality of preparation. The far-sighted worldwide firm will be the one that makes sure that its top management is both the best *and* the most international it can get.

NOTES

1. Stanley H. Brown, "How One Man Can Move a Corporate Mountain," *Fortune*, July 1, 1966, p. 82.

2. Allen W. Johnstone presents carefully collected evidence of this in *United States Direct Investment in France: An Investigation of the French Charges*, Cambridge, Mass., The MIT Press, 1965.

3. See Raymond Vernon, "International Investment and International Trade in the Product Cycle," *The Quarterly Journal of Economics*, May, 1966, pp. 190-207.

4. *Fortune*, July, 1965, pp. 149-168.

5. *Moody's Industrial Manual*, June, 1965, Moody's Investors Service Inc., New York, 1965. Group and divisional managers not also holding corporate posts, and some lesser corporate offices such as assistant treasurers and assistant secretaries were not classed as top corporate management and hence omitted from the study.

6. *Business International*, June 11, 1965, p. 186.

7. Excluding Shell and Unilever for which foreign corporate officers sit on the boards of the U.S. subsidiaries.

8. These men were quick to claim that foreign international firms were even more parochial, although the example of Royal Dutch Shell, which recently appointed an American to join a Dutchman and an Englishman as managing directors, would seem to belie this.

9. Extracted from John Barry, "Ford's Top Britons Quit as U.S. Grip Tightens," *The Sunday Times,* November 21, 1965.

CHAPTER 5

DAVID B. ZENOFF

Some companies are "financially kind" to their overseas subsidiaries; others exact pronto dividend remission. But, kind or unkind, the foreign business is only occasionally treated as an integral financial part of total operations.

Slicing the Financial Pie

THE HEAT IS ON treasurers and comptrollers of multinational firms to rethink the matter of slicing up the foreign-subsidiary earnings pie. What portion should be retained overseas and what part ought to be sent home? The foreign component of many companies is now too large, and the implications of the investment guidelines too serious, to permit drift or personal approaches to this question. Effectively run companies are busy inventorying the various factors bearing on the problem and hammering out policies and guides to action. Many are discovering that standby solutions no longer fit very well.

Thirty of the U.S.'s leading multinational firms, accounting for one-sixth of the overseas sales of U.S. foreign subsidiaries, discussed their problems and emerging attitudes with the author.

All agreed that the decision on the amount of earnings to be sent home belongs to the parent rather than the subsidiary. Headquarters staffs understandably believe that the interests of the company as a whole, or those of the parent corporation, will not necessarily be served if a foreign subsidiary decides what its own earnings payout should be. This is particularly so as some respondents note incipient tendencies on the part of subsidiary personnel to "forget" that the capital with which they are working is the original capital of the parent company. As one vice president advises his foreign-based colleagues: "Don't lose sight of for whom you are running the operation; the parent company deserves a return on its investment in your subsidiary."

When the companies speak of income from abroad, they primarily mean six items. Dividends are the most obtrusive of these; but management fees, royalties, repayment of parent loans, trademark licenses, and commissions on exports made by the subsidiary to third countries also figure in the accounting. The amount of funds transferred in each of these "other" forms is based on four main factors: (1) the value of the services and benefits provided to the foreign subsidiary, (2) the amount allowed by foreign taxing authorities as deductible business expenses, (3) the desired contribution of the overseas operations to the overhead expenses of the parent's international division (prorated to each subsidiary), and (4) the overall tax situation, including the availability of foreign tax credits and the possibilities of remitting funds in the form of dividends.

Surprisingly, more than half of the companies determine the size of these "other" remittances independently from the dividend return. Among the firms that don't, two distinctive approaches are taken. According to one, the dividend question is tentatively settled before the desired inflow of funds in other forms is arrived at. After attention has been given to these alternatives, a review is made to determine if the size of the dividend remittance should be altered.

In the second approach the size of the foreign dividend is determined by analysis of the most advantageous ways to remit funds from among dividends, fees, royalties, etc. The firms that follow this approach either agree upon the *total* amount (or percentage) of foreign earnings that should be pulled home and then decide upon the best method to obtain this figure from a tax point of view; or they avoid setting a blanket amount and make individual decisions for each subsidiary, based upon whatever criteria they use, including the tax effects of the various forms of remittance.

Normally, the cash requirements of the subsidiary are one of the weightiest considerations in the foreign earnings remittance process. Most firms allow their subsidiaries to hold on to what they need for working capital purposes and for planned capital expansion within the forthcoming six to twelve months and direct them to remit the "excess." Most of these companies are nervous about the dangers of the foreign environment and greatly prefer the affiliate to operate on foreign borrowings rather than on reinvested earnings, but they will usually compare the costs of borrowing abroad versus reinvestment of earnings.

Another group of companies is less malleable and decidedly more nervous. The firms in this group have a standard operating procedure calling for a 90% to 100% earnings remittance. "Minimizing the possibilities of exchange loss and any uncertainty about how much control we have over these funds" is usually offered as an explanation for such a draconian edict. Subsidiaries of these firms are expected to scratch for foreign capital and are allowed to cut the size of their payout ratios only if they can demonstrate to headquarters *urgent* unsupplied requirements for funds.

A third group of firms may be called "permissive." These companies emphasize the financial self-reliance of the subsidiaries over the desire for earnings reflows. To this end, they tell their subsidiaries to reinvest earnings and "strengthen their balance sheets and enhance their position with foreign bankers." A representative of one of these companies said that its English subsidiary hadn't been paying dividends during the recent years when devaluation was rumored and widely feared, and it wasn't going to pay a dividend in advance of the change of the British tax law because the subsidiary's current position was not "sufficiently solid."

No set of companies, however, is totally blind to the environmental risks. About one-quarter of the respondents, cutting across all three groups, make it mandatory that each of their subsidiaries develops "a pattern of continuity and consistency in its dividend payout." In essence it is believed that the imposition of exchange controls is not a far-fetched possibility, even in Europe or Canada, and if restrictions are placed on capital outflows, their subsidiaries will have a much better chance for approval to remit their dividends than will subsidiaries with an irregular payout record. The key is to point to a history of such outflows, identifiable in terms of regularity in timing and relationship to earnings.

Wanted: Environmental Stability

How do the companies react when faced with an immediate rather than a generalized environmental threat? In most firms the possibility of a currency devaluation within the next six to eight months will provoke "serious consideration" of using a subsidiary's dividend as a method of minimizing overseas exposure. But the majority of these firms doubt that they would actually do much about a rumored devaluation because, as several executives indicated, "it is kind of difficult to outguess the devaluation when even the experts don't agree, and we would just be guessing."

The companies that *do* (or would) use the dividend as an important means to offset exchange losses from expected devaluations all pointed to England as a "developed" host country in which such action has been taken in recent years. As an example, Company R, which owns subsidiaries in Canada, England, Germany and France, received an average of 75% of its affiliates' net earnings between 1960 and 1965; but, whereas it took only 50% of the earnings of its English subsidiary in 1960-1964, it hiked the payout ratio to 138% of current profits in 1965 because it feared devaluation of the pound.

Company Q pursued altogether different policies with its subsidiaries in Canada and England. In Canada, where there haven't been devaluation worries for about five years, the primary determinants of the dividend payout were taxation and the subsidiary's needs for funds. In England, however, the objective was "to make the largest distribution that we can . . . don't worry about the tax effects . . . just try to avoid exchange losses." The payout record of the Canadian subsidiary had been about 25% during the past three years whereas the English affiliate paid an average of 110% of its net earnings during the same period.

The subsidiary's requirement for funds and the exchange-rate risks of leaving cash abroad are two factors (operating on different sides of the ledger) that alter the division between parent and affiliate. A third element, to which we have already alluded, is taxes. Almost no multinational company is indifferent to taxes, but only slightly more than one-half of the respondents make a serious effort to minimize the potential burden to the company as a whole. The ultras among them normally give this consideration higher priority than any other in the dividend decision. However, this attitude is unusual. The more typical company is pluralistic, as is illustrated in the reaction of this manager, who says:

"There are two bases for our dividend decision: the cash position of the subsidiary . . . and taxation . . . we try to 'juggle' to get the best overall tax credit. We calculate the tax effects of various levels of dividends from subsidiaries: in fact, we just hired a new tax man to calculate 'optimum' dividends from a tax point of view . . ."

For a small number of companies, paying taxes to the home government on dividends received from overseas is considered a "fact of doing business," and no special effort is made to delay or avoid this obligation. Their sole purpose is to avoid what they term "penalty" taxes—those which are designed to induce or retard income distribution in particular countries. States one such manager:

"There are two angles of this tax rate which we should not confuse. One is tax penalties—for paying too high or too low a dividend. That we try to avoid at all costs. But that we have to pay a tax on income—which is about the same whether we pay it this year or next year—doesn't bother us. There is no substantial loss [in paying U.S. taxes on foreign dividends] unless one considers the loss from the use of the tax money that may have been paid . . . but for a company like ours that has a substantial amount of ready cash, there is no real loss involved. . . . What I referred to earlier [i.e., penalties] was failure to pay a required dividend and incurring a tax that would not otherwise be paid, such as in Germany. . . ."

Again there are the permissive souls, more oriented to the needs of the subsidiaries than the requirements of the parent in the tax area. Notes this executive:

"Our goal for each subsidiary is financial independence . . . it should build up and maintain a solid current position . . . a dividend will be paid only if the subsidiary has met this objective and has no foreseeable capital requirements . . . taxes are *not* very important relative to other criteria."

Generally speaking, the more tax conscious the company is, the more complex and time consuming its tax analysis will be. Where taxes are considered important, the comptroller usually has the responsibility for advising the decision makers on tax "effects" of various payout decisions which they are considering. Depending upon the composition of the overseas operation (i.e., number of affiliates and their legal forms) and the tax objectives of the firm, the design of the analysis might include the *total* tax burden to the corporation (foreign plus domestic taxes minus any domestic tax credits for foreign taxes paid) which would result from different payout possibilities for each of the foreign subsidiaries. Companies that extend calculations to this level usually also compute the "optimum" foreign dividend—the payout ratio for each of the overseas operations which would minimize the overall corporate tax liability.

Still another factor affecting the dividend split between parent and subsidiary is the company's domestic dividend payout ratio. Three related reasons are marshalled to support the relevance of this element: (1) cash is required by the parent company to meet its own obligations to stockholders, and the subsidiaries must meet their portion of this obligation by providing "their share" of the cash; (2) by paying the parent company the same percentage as the latter pays to its owners, the subsidiary is in some intuitive sense demonstrating its value to the ultimate shareholder; (3) for the many companies that have difficulties in getting dividend payouts from a portion of their subsidiaries in less-developed countries, establishment of a uniform dividend payout rate throughout the corporate system—justified by the "obligation to the stockholders"—will, it is hoped, persuade laggards of the justice of the claim. This is explained by one executive in the following terms:

"Since the company insists on a 55% return from its subsidiaries as a worldwide policy (though, conceivably, some affiliates may provide less than that amount and some more), it would not be unrealistic in the minds of any local national organization—the ministries, the government, or whatever organization there might be—to expect at least a 55% distribution by the subsidiary in that year . . ."

Such are the major influences determining the slicing of the foreign-earnings pie. As might be expected, the impact of each of these elements varies with the type of multinational enterprise. Two broad classes of global company can be discerned. In one are those firms that have years of experience in international business, large numbers of foreign subsidiaries, and the habit of consolidating the results of overseas operations, which constitute a relatively large percentage of the total corporate earnings. In the other grouping are the companies with relatively small foreign earnings, few foreign subsidiaries and a fairly limited experience in international business.

The more internationally oriented of these groups are most influenced on foreign dividends by the payout ratio of the parent companies and by the need to produce patterns of regularity in subsidiary dividend remittances. The importance given to these factors suggests that the decision-making process in these firms is in effect a problem-solving "program" where historically developed rules of thumb and standards of satisfactory performance are used.

The other group of companies appears to take a more "exploratory," cautious, and flexible approach to the foreign dividend decision. Each of the variables considered important by companies in this class—taxation, the threat of devaluation, and the possibility of other forms of remittance—require current analysis by management, and decisions on how to proceed can differ from one year to the next and from one subsidiary to another. The importance of these "mercurial" variables reflects the absence of guidelines and standards which have been tested over the years. And since they have few overseas subsidiaries it is economically feasible for these firms to conduct detailed, time-consuming analyses of these complex matters.

Patterns of Financial Management

For the interested observer of the world of international business, and the practitioner himself, these findings provide a basis for examining an important aspect of the patterns of financial management in the large multinational firms. They highlight a variety of current business practices which may warrant a new look by top management and very possibly revision. Consider, for example, the following areas:

Taxation—Under the existing tax laws of the industrialized countries there is ample opportunity for the multinational company to reduce the size of the total corporate tax liabilities by the proper tax analysis and planning for various movements of funds across national jurisdictions. The tax aspects of the dividend decision should involve the firm in an analysis of the incremental tax payable to foreign countries or the home government on some remittances, the overall tax credit position of the company, the possibilities of making remittances in a number of forms other than the dividend, the existence of a split tax rate in a foreign country which may encourage or discourage a certain level of earnings distribution in that jurisdiction, and the advantages of coordinating the distributions and remittances from sister subsidiaries and overseas branches. Given this approach, many more companies than now devote serious efforts to minimizing the corporation's total tax burden (just over 50%) might be induced to occupy their time profitably in this area.

Tying the Foreign Dividend to the Payout Ratio of the Parent Company—Although companies urge this policy to "meet their obligations to stockholders," it was evident during interviews with the international division treasurers—and it has been reported in studies of corporate debt capacity—that a majority of these firms did not have to ration their financial resources (except during the period of mandatory balance-of-payments restraints), and had not extended their borrowing capabilities to the limit. With this in mind, companies could consider borrowing money for dividend distribution rather than foregoing profitable overseas opportunities to remit funds (often at a tax cost) in order to satisfy stockholder requirements. A decision-rule based wholly on the payout ratio of the parent company is unlikely to be the approach that will maximize the valuation of the firm to its shareholders.

The Approach to Capital Budgeting for Overseas Operations— The method used by many multinational companies to decide on overseas investment proposals has been found to differ in certain important ways from the capital budgeting approach used in domestic situations by the parent company. Foreign investment proposals are *not* normally compared to other possible uses for company funds; few firms think in terms of a *worldwide pool* of company-controlled funds. When a rate-of-return projection is made for overseas proposals, it is calculated in terms of foreign currency and not in terms of the currency of the parent company or on an after-home-country-tax basis. Frequently the analysis of overseas investment opportunities is made *without* any attempt at quantitative measurements of their value.

Presumably the differences in technique can be explained by one of the following reasons: (1) the methods used for domestic operations are not entirely suitable for foreign business operations, (2) managers responsible for foreign business have been slow to adopt the tools of analysis utilized by their counterparts in domestic operations, or (3) it is erroneously concluded that the techniques used for domestic business are not appropriate for international activity.

It has been pointed out elsewhere that important complicating factors do exist in the financial management of an operation which transcends national borders.[1] However it is this writer's opinion that many techniques suitable for domestic operations are also appropriate, with modifications, to the foreign part of the business. That they have not been applied in this area is primarily the result of two "historical" factors: (1) in many companies the overseas operations until recently were managed by men who lacked an integrated view of the firm and its procedures, having had experience only in exporting or in a particular subsidiary and (2) foreign operations were for a long time considered a "marginal" or "special" kind of business, which may have relegated it and the interest with which it was managed to a second-rate status. It is altogether possible that, given the recent buildup of business assets in foreign countries, companies will be moved to challenge traditional practices and undertake remedial action.

NOTE

1. For a discussion of some of the distinctive considerations of international financial management, see Dan Throop Smith, "Financial Variables in International Business," *Harvard Business Review,* January-February, 1966, pp. 93-104; and David Zenoff and Jack Zwick, *International Financial Management,* New York: Prentice-Hall, 1969.

CHAPTER 6

HOWARD V. PERLMUTTER

A drama in three acts . . .

The Tortuous Evolution of the Multinational Corporation

FOUR SENIOR EXECUTIVES of the world's largest firms with extensive holdings outside the home country speak:

Company A: "We are a multinational firm. We distribute our products in about 100 countries. We manufacture in over 17 countries and do research and development in three countries. We look at all new investment projects—both domestic and overseas—using exactly the same criteria."

Company B: "We are a multinational firm. Only 1% of the personnel in our affiliate companies are non-nationals. Most of these are U.S. executives on temporary assignments. In all major markets, the affiliate's managing director is of the local nationality."

Company C: "We are a multinational firm. Our product division executives have worldwide profit responsibility. As our organizational chart shows, the United States is just one region on a par with Europe, Latin America, Africa, etc., in each product division."

Company D (non-American): "We are a multinational firm. We have at least 18 nationalities represented at our headquarters. Most senior executives speak at least two languages. About 30% of our staff at headquarters are foreigners."

While a claim to multinationality, based on their years of experience and the significant proportion of sales generated overseas, is justified in each of these four companies, a more penetrating analysis changes the image.

The executive from Company A tells us that most of the key posts in Company A's subsidiaries are held by home-country nationals. Whenever replacements for these men are sought, it is the practice, if not the policy, to "look next to you at the head office" and "pick someone (usually a home-country national) you know and trust."

The executive from Company B does not hide the fact that there are very few non-Americans in the key posts at headquarters. The few who are there are "so Americanized" that their foreign nationality literally has no meaning. His explanation for this paucity of non-Americans seems reasonable enough: "You can't find good foreigners who are willing to live in the United States, where our headquarters is located. American executives are more mobile. In addition, Americans have the drive and initiative we like. In fact, the European nationals would prefer to report to an American rather than to some other European."

The executive from Company C goes on to explain that the worldwide product division concept is rather difficult to implement. The senior executives in charge of these divisions have little overseas experience. They have been promoted from domestic posts and tend to view foreign consumer needs "as really basically the same as ours." Also, product division executives tend to focus on the domestic market because the domestic market is larger and generates more revenue than the fragmented European markets. The rewards are for global performance, but the strategy is to focus on domestic. His colleagues say "one pays attention to what one understands—and our senior executives simply do not understand what happens overseas and really do not trust foreign executives in key positions here or overseas."

The executive from the European Company D begins by explaining that since the voting shareholders must by law come from the home country, the home country's interest must be given careful consideration. In the final analysis he insists: "We are proud of our nationality; we shouldn't be ashamed of it." He cites examples of the previous reluctance of headquarters to use home-country ideas overseas, to their detriment, especially in their U.S. subsidiary. "Our country produces good executives, who tend to stay with us a long time. It is harder to keep executives from the United States."

Why quibble about how multinational a firm is? To these executives, apparently being multinational is prestigious. They know that multinational firms tend to be regarded as more progressive, dynamic, geared to the future than provincial companies which avoid foreign frontiers and their attendant risks and opportunities.

It is natural that these senior executives would want to justify the multinationality of their enterprise, even if they use different yardsticks: ownership criteria, organizational structure, nationality of senior executives, percent of investment overseas, etc.

Two hypotheses seem to be forming in the minds of executives from international firms that make the extent of their firm's multinationality of real interest. The first hypothesis is that the degree of multinationality of an enterprise is positively related to the firm's long-term viability. The "multinational" category makes sense for executives if it means a quality of decision making which leads to survival, growth and profitability in our evolving world economy.

The second hypothesis stems from the proposition that the multinational corporation is a new kind of institution—a new type of industrial social architecture particularly suitable for the latter third of the twentieth century. This type of institution could make a valuable contribution to world order and conceivably exercise a constructive impact on the nation-state. Some executives want to understand how to create an institution whose presence is considered legitimate and valuable in each nation-state. They want to prove that the greater the degree of multinationality of a firm, the greater its total constructive impact will be on host and home nation-states as well as other institutions. Since multinational firms may produce a significant proportion of the world's GNP, both hypotheses justify a more precise analysis of the varieties and degrees of multi-nationality.[1] However, the confirming evidence is limited.

State of Mind

Part of the difficulty in defining the degree of multinationality comes from the variety of parameters along which a firm doing business overseas can be described. The examples from the four companies argue that (1) no single criterion of multinationality such as ownership or the number of nationals overseas is sufficient, and that (2) external and quantifiable measures such as the per-centage of investment overseas or the distribution of equity by nationality are useful but not enough. The more one penetrates into the living reality of an international firm, the more one finds it is necessary to give serious weight to the way executives think about doing business around the world. The orientation toward "foreign people, ideas, resources," in headquarters and subsidiaries, and in host and home environments, becomes crucial in estimating the multi-nationality of a firm. To be sure, such external indices as the proportion of nationals in different countries holding equity and the number of foreign nationals who have reached top positions, in-cluding president, are good indices of multinationality. But one can still behave with a home-country orientation despite foreign shareholders, and one can have a few home-country nationals over-seas but still pick those local executives who are home-country oriented or who are provincial and chauvinistic. The attitudes men hold are clearly more relevant than their passports.

Three primary attitudes among international executives toward building a multinational enterprise are identifiable. These attitudes can be inferred from the assumptions upon which key product, func-tional and geographical decisions were made.

These states of mind or attitudes may be described as ethno-centric (or home-country oriented), polycentric (or host-country oriented) and geocentric (or world-oriented).[2] While they never appear in pure form, they are clearly distinguishable. There is some degree of ethnocentricity, polycentricity or geocentricity in all firms, but management's analysis does not usually correlate with public pronouncements about the firm's multinationality.

TABLE 1: *Three Types of Headquarters Orientation Toward Subsidiaries in an International Enterprise*

Organization Design	Ethnocentric	Polycentric	Geocentric
Complexity of organization	Complex in home country, simple in subsidiaries	Varied and independent	Increasingly complex and interdependent
Authority; decision making	High in headquarters	Relatively low in headquarters	Aim for a collaborative approach between headquarters and subsidiaries
Evaluation and control	Home standards applied for persons and performance	Determined locally	Find standards which are universal and local
Rewards and punishments; incentives	High in headquarters; low in subsidiaries	Wide variation; can be high or low rewards for subsidiary performance	International and local executives rewarded for reaching local and worldwide objectives
Communication; information flow	High volume to subsidiaries; orders, commands, advice	Little to and from headquarters. Little between subsidiaries	Both ways and between subsidiaries. Heads of subsidiaries part of management team
Identification	Nationality of owner	Nationality of host country	Truly international company but identifying with national interests
Perpetuation (recruiting, staffing, development)	Recruit and develop people of home country for key positions everywhere in the world	Develop people of local nationality for key positions in their own country	Develop best men everywhere in the world for key positions everywhere in the world

Home-country Attitudes

The ethnocentric attitude can be found in companies of any nationality with extensive overseas holdings. The attitude, revealed in executive actions and experienced by foreign subsidiary managers, is: "We, the home nationals of X company, are superior to, more trustworthy and more reliable than any foreigners in headquarters or subsidiaries. We will be willing to build facilities in your country if you acknowledge our inherent superiority and accept our methods and conditions for doing the job."

Of course, such attitudes are never so crudely expressed, but they often determine how a certain type of "multinational" firm is designed. Table 1 illustrates how ethnocentric attitudes are expressed in determining the managerial process at home and overseas. For example, the ethnocentric executive is more apt to say: "Let us manufacture the simple products overseas. Those foreign nationals are not yet ready or reliable. We should manufacture the complex products in our country and keep the secrets among our trusted home-country nationals."

In a firm where ethnocentric attitudes prevailed, the performance criteria for men and products are "home-made." "We have found that a salesman should make 12 calls per day in Hoboken, New Jersey (the headquarters location) and therefore we apply these criteria everywhere in the world. The salesman in Brazzaville is naturally lazy, unmotivated. He shows little drive because he makes only two calls per day" (despite the Congolese salesman's explanation that it takes time to reach custimers by boat).

Ethnocentric attitudes are revealed in the communication process where "advice," "counsel," and directives flow from headquarters to the subsidiary in a steady stream, bearing this message: "This works at home; therefore, it must work in your country."

Executives in both headquarters and affiliates express the national identity of the firm by associating the company with the nationality of the headquarters: this is "a Swedish company," "a Swiss company," "an American company," depending on the location of headquarters. "You have to accept the fact that the only way to reach a senior post in our firm," an English executive in a U.S. firm said, "is to take out an American passport."

Crucial to the ethnocentric concept is the current policy that men of the home nationality are recruited and trained for key positions everywhere in the world. Foreigners feel like "second-class" citizens.

There is no international firm today whose executives will say that ethnocentrism is absent in their company. In the firms whose multinational investment began a decade ago, one is more likely to hear, "We are still in a transitional stage from our ethnocentric era. The traces are still around! But we are making progress."

Host-country Orientation

Polycentric firms are those which, by experience or by the inclination of a top executive (usually one of the founders), begin with the assumption that host-country cultures are different and that foreigners are difficult to understand. Local people know what is best for them, and the part of the firm which is located in the host country should be as "local in identity" as possible. The senior executives at headquarters believe that their multinational enterprise can be held together by good financial controls. A polycentric firm, literally, is a loosely connected group with quasi-independent subsidiaries as centers—more akin to a confederation.

European multinational firms tend to follow this pattern, using a top local executive who is strong and trustworthy, of the "right" family and who has an intimate understanding of the workings of the host government. This policy seems to have worked until the advent of the Common Market.

Executives in the headquarters of such a company are apt to say: "Let the Romans do it their way. We really don't understand what is going on there, but we have to have confidence in them. As long as they earn a profit, we want to remain in the background." They assume that since people are different in each country, standards for performance, incentives and training methods must be different. Local environmental factors are given greater weight (See Table 1).

Many executives mistakenly equate polycentrism with multinationalism. This is evidenced in the legalistic definition of a multinational enterprise as a cluster of corporations of diverse nationality joined together by ties of common ownership. It is no accident that many senior executives in headquarters take pride in the absence of non-nationals in their subsidiaries, especially people from the head office. The implication is clearly that each subsidiary is a distinct national entity, since it is incorporated in a different sovereign state. Lonely senior executives in the subsidiaries of polycentric companies complain that: "The home office never tells us anything."

Polycentrism is not the ultimate form of multinationalism. It is a landmark on a highway. Polycentrism is encouraged by local marketing managers who contend that: "Headquarters will never understand us, our people, our consumer needs, our laws, our distribution, etc. . . ."

Headquarters takes pride in the fact that few outsiders know that the firm is foreign-owned. "We want to be a good local company. How many Americans know that Shell and Lever Brothers are foreign-owned?"

But the polycentric personnel policy is also revealed in the fact that no local manager can seriously aspire to a senior position at headquarters. "You know the French are so provincial; it is better to keep them in France. Uproot them and you are in trouble," a senior executive says to justify the paucity of non-Americans at headquarters.

One consequence (and perhaps cause) of polycentrism is a virulent ethnocentrism among the country managers.

A World-oriented Concept

The third attitude which is beginning to emerge at an accelerating rate is geocentrism. Senior executives with this orientation do not equate superiority with nationality. Within legal and political limits, they seek the best men, regardless of nationality, to solve the company's problems anywhere in the world. The senior executives attempt to build an organization in which the subsidiary is not only a good citizen of the host nation but is a leading exporter from this nation in the international community and contributes such benefits as (1) an increasing supply of hard currency, (2) new skills and (3) a knowledge of advanced technology. Geocentrism is summed up in a Unilever board chairman's statement of objectives: "We want to Unileverize our Indians and Indianize our Unileverans."

The ultimate goal of geocentrism is a worldwide approach in both headquarters and subsidiaries. The firm's subsidiaries are thus neither satellites nor independent city states, but parts of a whole whose focus is on worldwide objectives as well as local objectives, each part making its unique contribution with its unique competence. Geocentrism is expressed by function, product and geography. The question asked in headquarters and the subsidiaries is: "Where in the world shall we raise money, build our plant, conduct R&D, get and launch new ideas to serve our present and future customers?"

This conception of geocentrism involves a collaborative effort between subsidiaries and headquarters to establish universal standards and permissible local variations, to make key allocational decisions on new products, new plants, new laboratories. The international management team includes the affiliate heads.

Subsidiary managers must ask: "Where in the world can I get the help to serve my customers best in this country?" "Where in the world can I export products developed in this country—products which meet worldwide standards as opposed to purely local standards?"

Geocentrism, furthermore, requires a reward system for subsidiary managers which motivates them to work for worldwide objectives, not just to defend country objectives. In firms where geocentrism prevails, it is not uncommon to hear a subsidiary manager say, "While I am paid to defend our interests in this country and to get the best resources for this affiliate, I must still ask myself the question 'Where in the world (instead of where in my country) should we build this plant?' " This approach is still rare today.

In contrast to the ethnocentric and polycentric patterns, communication is encouraged among subsidiaries in geocentric-oriented firms. "It is your duty to help us solve problems anywhere in the world," one chief executive continually reminds the heads of his company's affiliates. (See Table 1.)

The geocentric firm identifies with local company needs. "We aim to be not just a good local company but the best local company in terms of the quality of management and the worldwide (not local) standards we establish in domestic and export production." "If we were only as good as local companies, we would deserve to be nationalized."

The geocentric personnel policy is based on the belief that we should bring in the best man in the world regardless of his nationality. His passport should not be the criterion for promotion.

The EPG Profile

Executives can draw their firm's profile in ethnocentric (E), polycentric (P) and geocentric (G) dimensions. They are called EPG profiles. The degree of ethnocentrism, polycentrism and geocentrism by product, function and geography can be established. Typically R&D often turns out to be more geocentric (truth is universal, perhaps) and less ethnocentric than finance. Financial managers are likely to see their decisions as ethnocentric. The marketing function is more polycentric, particularly in the advanced economies and in the larger affiliate markets.

The tendency toward ethnocentrism in relations with subsidiaries in the developing countries is marked. Polycentric attitudes develop in consumer goods divisions, and ethnocentrism appears to be greater in industrial product divisions. The agreement is almost unanimous in both U.S.- and European-based international firms that their companies are at various stages on a route toward geocentrism but none has reached this state of affairs. Their executives would agree, however, that:

1. a description of their firms as multinational obscures more than it illuminates the state of affairs;

2. the EPG mix, once defined, is a more precise way to describe the point they have reached;

3. the present profile is not static but a landmark along a difficult road to genuine geocentrism;

4. there are forces both to change and to maintain the present attitudinal "mix," some of which are under their control.

What are the forces that determine the EPG mix of a firm? "You must think of the struggle toward functioning as a worldwide firm as just a beginning—a few steps forward and a step backward," a chief executive put it. "It is a painful process, and every firm is different."

Executives of some of the world's largest multinational firms have been able to identify a series of external and internal factors

TABLE 2: *International Executives' Views of Forces and Obstacles Toward Geocentrism in Their Firms*

| Forces Toward Geocentrism | | Obstacles to Geocentrism | |
Environmental	Intra-organizational	Environmental	Intra-organizational
1. Technological and managerial know-how increasing in availability in different countries	1. Desire to use human vs. material resources optimally	1. Economic nationalism in host and home countries	1. Management inexperience in overseas markets
2. International customers	2. Observed lowering of morale in affiliates of an ethnocentric company	2. Political nationalism in host & home countries	2. Nation-centered reward and punishment structure
3. Local customers' demand for best product at fair price	3. Evidence of waste and duplication in poly-centrism	3. Military secrecy associated with research in home country	3. Mutual distrust between home country people and foreign executives
4. Host country's desire to increase balance of payments	4. Increasing awareness of and respect for good men of other than home nationality	4. Distrust of big international firms by host-country political leaders	4. Resistance to letting foreigners into the power structure

5. Growing world markets

6. Global competition among international firms for scarce human and material resources

7. Major advances in integration of international transport & telecommunications

8. Regional supranational economic & political communities

---

5. Risk diversification by having a world-wide production & distribution system

6. Need for recruitment of good men on a world-wide basis

7. Need for worldwide information system

8. Worldwide appeal of products

9. Senior management's long-term commitment to geocentrism as related to survival and growth

---

5. Lack of international monetary system

6. Growing differences between the rich and poor countries

7. Host country belief that home countries get disproportionate benefits of international firms profits

8. Home country political leaders' attempts to control firm's policy

---

5. Anticipated costs and risks of geocentrism

6. Nationalistic tendencies in staff

7. Increasing immobility of staff

8. Linguistic problems & different cultural backgrounds

9. Centralization tendencies in headquarters

that contribute to or hinder the growth of geocentric attitudes and decisions. Table 2 summarizes the factors most frequently mentioned by over 500 executives from at least 17 countries and 20 firms.

From the external environmental side, the growing world markets, the increase in availability of managerial and technological know-how in different countries, global competition and international customers, advances in telecommunications, regional political and economic communities are positive factors, as is the host country's desire to increase its balance-of-payments surplus through the location of export-oriented subsidiaries of international firms within its borders.

In different firms, senior executives see in various degrees these positive factors toward geocentrism: top management's increasing desire to use human and material resources optimally, the observed lowering of morale after decades of ethnocentric practices, the evidence of waste and duplication under polycentric thinking, the increased awareness and respect for good men of other than the home nationality, and, most importantly, top management's own commitment to building a geocentric firm as evidenced in policies, practices and procedures.

The obstacles toward geocentrism from the environment stem largely from the rising political and economic nationalism in the world today, the suspicions of political leaders of the aims and increasing power of the multinational firm. On the internal side, the obstacles cited most frequently in U.S.-based multinational firms were management's inexperience in overseas markets, mutual distrust between home-country people and foreign executives, the resistance to participation by foreigners in the power structure at headquarters, the increasing difficulty of getting good men overseas to move, nationalistic tendencies in staff, and the linguistic and other communication difficulties of a cultural nature.

Any given firm is seen as moving toward geocentrism at a rate determined by its capacities to build on the positive internal factors over which it has control and to change the negative internal factors which are controllable. In some firms the geocentric goal is openly discussed among executives of different nationalities and from different subsidiaries as well as headquarters. There is a consequent improvement in the climate of trust and acceptance of each other's views.

Programs are instituted to assure greater experience in foreign markets, task forces of executives are upgraded, international careers for executives of all nationalities are being designed.

But the seriousness of the obstacles cannot be underestimated. A world of rising nationalism is hardly a pre-condition for geocentrism; and overcoming distrust of foreigners even within one's own firm is not accomplished in a short span of time. The route to pervasive geocentric thinking is long and tortuous.

Costs, Risks, Payoffs

What conclusions will executives from multinational firms draw from the balance sheet of advantages and disadvantages of maintaining one's present state of ethnocentrism, polycentrism or geocentrism? Not too surprisingly, the costs and risks of ethnocentrism are seen to out-balance the payoffs in the long run. The costs of ethnocentrism are ineffective planning because of a lack of good feed-back, the departure of the best men in the subsidiaries, fewer innovations, and an inability to build a high-calibre local organization. The risks are political and social repercussions and a less flexible response to local changes.

The payoffs of ethnocentrism are real enough in a short term, they say. Organization is simpler. There is a higher rate of communication of know-how from headquarters to new markets. There is more control over appointments to senior posts in subsidiaries.

Polycentrism's costs are waste due to duplication, to decisions to make products for local use but which could be universal, and to inefficient use of home-country experience. The risks include an excessive regard for local traditions and local growth at the expense of global growth. The main advantages are an intensive exploitation of local markets, better sales since local management is often better informed, more local initiative for new products, more host-government support, and good local managers with high morale.

Geocentrism's costs are largely relegated to communication and travel expenses, educational costs at all levels, time spent in decision making because consensus seeking among more people is required, and an international headquarters bureaucracy. Risks include those due to too wide a distribution of power, personnel problems and those of re-entry of international executives. The payoffs are a more powerful total company throughout, a better quality of products and service, worldwide utilization of best resources, improvement of local company management, a greater sense of commitment to worldwide objectives, and last, but not least, more profit.

Jacques Maisonrouge, the French-born president of IBM World Trade, understands the geocentric concept and its benefits. He wrote recently:

"The first step to a geocentric organization is when a corporation, faced with the choice of whether to grow and expand or decline, realizes the need to mobilize its resources on a world scale. It will sooner or later have to face the issue that the home country does not have a monopoly of either men or ideas. . . .

"I strongly believe that the future belongs to geocentric companies. . . . What is of fundamental importance is the attitude of the company's top management. If it is dedicated to 'geocentrism,' good international management will be possible. If not, the best men of different nations will soon understand that they do not belong to the 'race des seigneurs' and will leave the business."[3]

Geocentrism is not inevitable in any given firm. Some companies have experienced a "regression" to ethnocentrism after trying a long period of polycentrism, of letting subsidiaries do it "their way." The local directors built little empires and did not train successors from their own country. Headquarters had to send home-country nationals to take over. A period of home-country thinking took over.

There appears to be evidence of a need for evolutionary movement from ethnocentrism to polycentrism to geocentrism. The polycentric stage is likened to an adolescent protest period during which subsidiary managers gain their confidence as equals by fighting headquarters and proving "their manhood," after a long period of being under headquarters' ethnocentric thumb.

"It is hard to move from a period of headquarters domination to a worldwide management team quickly. A period of letting affiliates make mistakes may be necessary," said one executive.

Window Dressing

In the rush toward appearing geocentric, many U.S. firms have found it necessary to emphasize progress by appointing one or two non-nationals to senior posts—even on occasion to headquarters.

The foreigner is often effectively counteracted by the number of nationals around him, and his influence is really small. Tokenism does have some positive effects, but it does not mean geocentrism has arrived.

Window dressing is also a temptation. Here an attempt is made to demonstrate influence by appointing a number of incompetent "foreigners" to key positions. The results are not impressive for either the individuals or the company.

Too often what is called "the multinational view" is really a screen for ethnocentrism. Foreign affiliate managers must, in order to succeed, take on the traits and behavior of the ruling nationality. In short, in a U.S.-owned firm the foreigner must "Americanize"—not only in attitude but in dress and speech—in order to be accepted.

Tokenism and window dressing are transitional episodes where aspirations toward multinationalism outstrip present attitudes and resources. The fault does not lie only with the enterprise. The human demands of ethnocentrism are great.

A Geocentric Man—?

The geocentric enterprise depends on having an adequate supply of men who are geocentrically oriented. It would be a mistake to underestimate the human stresses which a geocentric career creates. Moving where the company needs an executive involves major adjustments for families, wives and children. The sacrifices are often great and, for some families, outweigh the rewards forthcoming—at least in personal terms. Many executives find it difficult to learn new languages and overcome their cultural superiority complexes, national pride and discomfort with foreigners. Furthermore, international careers can be hazardous when ethnocentrism prevails at headquarters. "It is easy to get lost in the world of the subsidiaries and to be 'out of sight, out of mind' when promotions come up at headquarters," as one executive expressed it following a visit to headquarters after five years overseas. To his disappointment, he knew few senior executives. And fewer knew him!

The economic rewards, the challenge of new countries, the personal and professional development that comes from working in a variety of countries and cultures are surely incentives, but companies have not solved by any means the human costs of international mobility to executives and their families.

A firm's multinationality may be judged by the pervasiveness with which executives think geocentrically—by function, marketing, finance, production, R&D, etc., by product division and by country. The takeoff to geocentrism may begin with executives in one function, say marketing, seeking to find a truly worldwide product line. Only when this worldwide attitude extends throughout the firm, in headquarters and subsidiaries, can executives feel that it is becoming genuinely geocentric.

But no single yardstick, such as the number of foreign nationals in key positions, is sufficient to establish a firm's multinationality. The multinational firm's route to geocentrism is still long because political and economic nationalism is on the rise, and, more importantly, since within the firm ethnocentrism and polycentrism are not easy to overcome. Building trust between persons of different nationality is a central obstacle. Indeed, if we are to judge men, as Paul Weiss put it, "by the kind of world they are trying to build," the senior executives engaged in building the geocentric enterprise could well be the most important social architects of the last third of the twentieth century. For the institution they are trying to erect promises a greater universal sharing of wealth and a consequent control of the explosive centrifugal tendencies of our evolving world community.

The geocentric enterprise offers an institutional and supranational framework which could conceivably make war less likely, on the assumption that bombing customers, suppliers and employees is in nobody's interest. The difficulty of the task is thus matched by its worthwhileness. A clearer image of the features of genuine geocentricity is thus indispensable both as a guideline and as an inviting prospect.

N O T E S

1. H. V. Perlmutter, "Super-Giant Firms in the Future," *Wharton Quarterly*, Winter, 1968.

2. H. V. Perlmutter, "Three Conceptions of a World Enterprise," *Revue Economique et Sociale*, May 1965.

3. Jacques Maisonrouge, "The Education of International Managers," *The Quarterly Journal of AIESEC International*, February, 1967.

MULTINATIONAL
BUSINESS
CONFRONTS
NATIONALISM

CHAPTER 7

JOHN FAYERWEATHER

*Hope of softening the animosity between
nationalism and the multinational corporation
rests on the strong presumption that the latter is
a potent catalyst of economic advance.*

19th-Century Ideology and 20th-Century Reality

ONE OF THE MORE DISTRESSING FEATURES of our day is the continuing conflict between two of the strongest and potentially most constructive forces in modern society: nationalism and the multinational corporation. From time to time the conflict erupts in spectacular form in expropriations of property—electric utilities in Brazil and Castro's sweeping takeover of U.S. investments in Cuba. But more common and actually of greater overall importance are a multitude of lesser points of conflict—over the share of capital and control a foreign company may hold in a local venture, the degree of regulation foreign governments exercise over foreign operations and many other facets of overseas business.

While each of the points of conflict has some specific logic in itself, underlying them all is the massive sentiment of nationalism limiting the ability of sincere men on both sides to act dispassionately. For example, the question of how much profit a foreign company should be permitted to repatriate is debatable in rational economic terms. On the one hand, there are the rights of the contributor of capital to a payment for the use of his money. On the other, there are pressing demands in the host country for importation of capital equipment and the materials needed for economic development. But to anyone who observes negotiations on this issue it is readily apparent that emotional value judgments are often controlling. The foreign investor is not just receiving "a payment for the use of his money," a cold, economic-legal concept. Rather he "is draining the host nation of its wealth," a phrase emanating from a politically sensitive mentality attuned to the feelings of the general populace. As often as not, in developing nations with colonial pasts, there are further undertones of "the obligation" of the West to finance development regardless of reward, in order to compensate for excessive profiteering and failure to support development in earlier periods.

Thus, no matter how effectively we may deal with the cold logic of the problems confronting the multinational corporation, we cannot hope for a major breakthrough on many of the critical issues unless the nationalistic component of the conflict is resolved. This is no simple problem, and there is little indication that we are yet even close to solving it. I propose to look carefully at the nature of both nationalism and the multinational corporation, defining the elements in each which are pertinent to the problem and considering the direction in which each might evolve to reach some greater accommodation with the other.

What lies at the heart of the conflict between nationalism and multinational business? To answer that question we had best look at the essential characteristics of each.

Nationalism as we know it is of quite recent origin. While it had assorted early forebears, it was not firmly established until the beginning of the 19th century. Prior to that time patriotism, i.e., loyalty to one's country and its monarch, existed. But nationalism goes a good deal beyond patriotism and did not emerge until the majority of the populace achieved a real identification with the state through the middle-class revolutions. A citizen might admire, respect, and love his king and feel emotional ties to his country, but feelings of a quite different order were tapped when the people felt that the nation and its government were truly theirs.

Although nationalism is relatively new, its psychological roots are not. Nationalism is a new manifestation of a fundamental human trait. The key motivation at work is the quest for security, reinforced by other social satisfactions which come from participation in a group. From earliest times these feelings have brought people together into groups with a high degree of internal cohesion and sharp separation from external elements. Social scientists use the term "we-group," which aptly describes the attitudes of the participants. They feel a strong identification with the group, thinking of it and acting in it on a "we" basis and treating those who are not in the group as a distinctly different category: "they," "outsiders," "foreigners." The individual is raised in the traditions, culture, and values of the we-group. He is expected to and generally does willingly accept them and give them strong emotional loyalty and support. Doing so contributes greatly to his own security, for he gains both emotional and physical security from the sense that his group is good and right and strong.

Basis of New Nationalism

For centuries these feelings found their main expression in groups which lived in relatively close physical proximity—the family, the clan, the tribe, the village, and even the city-state. These were units in which the individuals could effectively share in a common life and have a sense of participation in the group. There were larger government units to be sure, but the mass of people were too poorly educated to have much knowledge of or sense of unity with "countrymen" beyond their immediate community, and they had too little participation in the government to feel full identification with it. But there was nothing in the psychological forces involved which inherently limited we-group attitudes to small units, and two important changes, reinforced by other developments, brought forth the new nationalism: mass education and popular government.

As literacy became more common, facilitated by the printing press, people became better acquainted with the world around them and found in this knowledge an identification with the language, traditions, literature, culture, and often religion of their national group as distinguished from the foreignness of other peoples. Concurrently the rise of the middle class was being fostered by economic growth and by the new social structure associated with the industrial revolution and large-scale manufacturing. The middle class soon developed a strong interest in the functioning of the national government and a capacity to participate in it which superseded that of the feudal-landowning aristocracy.

These limited observations, of course, gloss over a quite long and difficult transition. But in broad outline we can see how and why the we-group psychology was elevated to the national level. From its middle-class base in Europe and North America, nationalism has now spread, in this century of popular government, mass communications and independence movements, to every part of the globe and deep into the ranks of the lower classes, leaving only the more primitive tribal groups outside its influence.

This historical review has two implications for the future. First, since the underlying psychology of nationalism is basic, it will not disappear. Second, changes in the way in which this psychology is manifested may occur. We must look therefore at the developments under way in the world today to see where they may be leading.

Following this train of thought, one's instinct is to look for signs that we are moving toward a yet broader span of we-group structure —the family, the tribe, the city, the nation, now an international cohesion. And, indeed, there are numerous things we can point to which seem to fit the requirements for such a transition. Mass communications media are making people all around the world aware of each other and familiar with their ways of life. There has been a steady growth of what might be called international subcultures. Teenagers, for example, in virtually all countries share tastes in hair styles, music, and the like. To at least a limited degree they show a mutual identification rising above national affiliation. We have similar trends among international businessmen, scientists, chess players, radio hams, and assorted others.

The increasing integration of the world economy is also an encouraging sign. Just as the emergence of nationalism coincided with, and apparently was related to, the economic suitability of the nation-state as the industrial revolution got under way, our modern economy seems to require a cohesion and cooperation among nations. The International Monetary Fund (IMF), the General Agreement on Tariffs and Trade (GATT), the European Economic Community (EEC), the Latin American Free Trade Association (LAFTA), and similar mechanisms rising above national sovereignties are critical to world trade and thus to the welfare of people in all nations.

The Threat that Binds

But despite these favorable elements, there are some reasons for doubting that we are on the threshold of a true international we-groupism. First, if we look at the past, we find that no we-group has ever existed without a "they." The need for security is generally accepted as a critical motivation in the individual's commitment to the we-group. While a person may need security in relation to the unknown or in isolation, his concern about tangible external threats is strong and its absence removes a significant support of any we-group affiliation. The communist threat has created a degree of cohesion in the free world, but these ties are limited by the affiliation of large portions of the populations of many countries to communism. It is hard therefore to visualize the peoples of the world being drawn together tightly in the absence of a threat from outer space.

Likewise, for all the development of international subcultures, the differences among the nations are still very great and in important respects show little sign of diminishing appreciably. In such vital respects as language, religion and cultural values the Indian, the Japanese, the German and the American are still a very long way apart. One cannot therefore readily conceive of the rise of an international we-groupism strong enough to rival the national variety.

Nationalism is especially strong in the area of business, chiefly because of the heavy influence external business has exerted on the internal social and political affairs of many nations, especially the less-developed ones. This is the dominant theme in Richard Robinson's searching historical analysis of the effect of Western investment.[1] Animosity toward foreign investment is therefore part of the nationalistic tradition which binds these peoples together. Thus we start at a tremendous handicap in proposing that multinational business affairs become disassociated from nationalism.

Hope from History

On the other hand, it is hard to ignore the historical indications that government policies have always tended to synchronize with the basic economic and business system which was desirable for the effective use of the technology of the day. Throughout history, business institutions and political structures have evolved in constructive directions both independently and in their mutual relations. New forms of business units have appeared which were effective in utilizing the technology of the times, and political systems have developed which were appropriate to prevailing economic conditions.

In the Middle Ages, for example, the simple manufacturing technology which for the most part functioned effectively within quite limited geographic areas was satisfactorily utilized by the artisan system. The city, supplemented by the guild, provided adequate social services and control for the artisan economy. As wealth and regional interchange grew, the great trading companies appeared, and at the same time national governments capable of such complementary roles as protection of shipping emerged. The industrial revolution brought with it the large, publicly owned corporation, with its capacities for bringing together large amounts of capital and operating huge production facilities serving major marketing areas, and the parallel evolution of stronger national governments which built the essential infrastructure and maintained broad controls over business.

If the multinational corporation is in fact beneficial economically, there is a supposition here that government policies and the national sentiments behind them will in some way be adjusted to accommodate it. In speculating about ways in which this might happen another feature of past history is worth observing. Throughout the prenationalistic eras, various forms of internationalism have existed. There have been administrative unifications like the Roman and Ottoman empires in which bureaucracies recruited locally served what were for those times truly international systems, despite the gulf between their masters and the local we-groups to whom they had an initial loyalty. Likewise, in the Renaissance period in Europe the elite, the intelligentsia, were in a sense a distinctive we-group unto themselves, separate from the masses. They spurned localism in favor of a common mission in a unified Catholic society. Can international business and the government officialdom that must work with it around the world achieve such a sense of unity and disassociation from nationalistic patterns? At the moment we can only speculate. But the prospects will certainly be influenced greatly by the extent to which the multinational corporation proves of benefit to the world community.

In examining the benefits conferred by the multinational corporation, we are of course focusing on the social utility of the organization, not on its business efficiency. This distinction is important, for what is profitable for the company, even in a sound long-term view, is not necessarily beneficial to society as a whole. We hope it may be, but we have to prove it.

Is the multinational corporation socially useful, and if so, in what form? Some people have suggested that the hope for the future of international business lies in the creation of a "supranational" corporation chartered by the United Nations, with its headquarters in some center with minimal national character (like Luxembourg), owned by stockholders of a broad range of nationalities and managed as a true world enterprise without partiality to any country. While this is an appealing ideal conceived in conjunction with a transition from nationalism to internationalism, its inadequacy as a means of minimizing the conflict with nationalism is readily apparent. It is effective in removing the impact of the nationalism of the home country of the multinational corporation, but it really does nothing to alter relations with other countries. The supranational corporation is still an outsider, still a "they," whether it be of United States origin or United Nations origin. If and when the peoples of the world start to transfer their we-group emotions to the United Nations in substantial measure, then the device may be really meaningful. But we have seen that this is not a promising outlook, and in its absence I would suggest that the idea has to be viewed with considerable skepticism. Moreover, the change may amount in large part to a fiction, if as seems likely, the capital and management of the corporation still come from a limited number of major industrial countries. Furthermore, for all their negative comments about foreign capital, many nations may have considerably more confidence in the beneficence and responsibility of highly developed business communities than in the qualities of a floating corporation chartered by a very weak government institution and presumably virtually free of overall government control. This is not to say that the concept may not in fact prove sound, but only to emphasize that at the moment it is unduly favored by the age-old advantages of "the grass in the next pasture."

I think therefore that we should more logically look in the other direction; namely, whether, to minimize the conflict with nationalism, the multinational corporation could evolve into a system of national units whose external ties are nonexistent. This is a contradiction in terms and is an unlikely, if not definitionally impossible, outcome. External ties are basic to the concept of the multinational corporation. They are the channels along which benefits flow. One can legitimately ask whether these ties can be reduced or severed without at the same time diluting the benefits. Yet since any progress along these lines would cut down on nationalistic antagonisms, it seems worthwhile to consider the extent to which we may move in this direction.

The multinational corporation's external ties may for convenience's sake be subsumed under four main headings, representing the basic flows within a business organization: product, finance, technology and management.

Product Flow: The social utility of the flow of products from one country to another scarcely needs defense. A host of scholars since Adam Smith and Ricardo have so established the concept of comparative advantage that the fact of the flow of goods into a country is thoroughly accepted.

The identification of products with the external multinational corporation by trade names and brands is another matter. In the less-developed countries and to a degree in more advanced industrialized areas like Europe, U.S. companies have found that their brand names are profitable assets because United States industry in general and they in particular have a reputation that attracts consumers. This is seemingly inconsistent with the "anti-they" attitude of nationalism. Suffice it to say that foreign nationals tend to be ambivalent: as practical consumers they want the specific brands, but as nationalists they feel constrained to attack their entry. Polish hams in the U.S. may be a reverse example.

Do multinational brands serve a socially useful purpose? This is a difficult question that cannot be answered clearly. On the surface the value is not apparent. But digging deeper one may suggest that the consumer acceptance the brands achieve is an important vehicle for market expansion and economic development. We enter here into the question of whether a number of aspects of aggressive commercial marketing make significant contributions to the expansion of a national economy. Theory in this regard is still crude and inconclusive, so all we can do is leave it as an open question.

A final question is whether control of the marketing process must remain in the hands of the home office. It should be noted that the marketing function is one which traditionally has been most readily transferred to independent local businesses. That is, multinational companies both at home and abroad have turned over a large part of their distribution to local wholesalers, import merchants, dealers, and the like. However, we also observe that corporate efficiency motives have led many firms to withhold the marketing of at least the first level of distribution in foreign markets from local firms. Their objectives have been to sell more aggressively, to provide better direction of dealer organizations and other ends which add up to "better" distribution. Thus, in judging whether these penetrations into foreign nations have social value, we are back again to the unanswered question of the contribution of marketing to economic development.

Finance Flow: The input of capital and the return of earnings are fundamental to private business interest in foreign operations. In Europe and other highly industrialized areas, it is doubtful whether the imported capital is of significant value to the host nation, but in less-developed areas it has an acknowledged beneficial role. Indeed, both the U.S. government and the receiving nations have made major efforts to increase the flow of capital. There is the theoretical possibility that capital needs might be supplied by indirect investment; for example, by purchase of stock of local companies by U.S. investors. The practical prospects in this regard are not good, however, as portfolio investments in the less-developed areas are still living down the adverse experience in the interwar period.

The chief vehicle for inducing a capital inflow but moderating the nationalistic reaction against it is the joint venture—a partnership of foreign and national capital. This may be a partial answer but it appears to dodge the issues, especially when, as most new nations prefer, the foreign company interest is limited to less than 50%. First, any arrangement which uses local capital to substitute for part of the investment a foreign company might make reduces the net inflow of needed external capital. Second, in the opinion of the majority of multinational companies a joint venture is managerially less effective than one with single control and may thus weaken the contribution to industrial growth. This is another complex subject which we can only leave as an open question.

It seems reasonable to conclude that the industrialized nations can manage without large capital infusions from abroad. The policies of Japan in the post-war era have followed this general line with success. But in the less-developed countries the social value of inputs of capital tied to managerial control to assure their effective use seems beyond question.

Technology Flow: The flow of research-derived technology for use in products and production processes would seem to provide the strongest basis for the multinational corporation, both in business terms and in terms of social value. Certainly it is in the fields where technology counts most that international firms have been strongest—chemicals rather than textiles, office machines rather than bread, etc.

The economic efficiency of doing research in a limited number of centers rather than duplicating it in every country of the world appeals to simple logic. We may have a cross flow of technology between developed areas, as we do between Europe and the United

States. But since it seems almost certain that the less-developed nations will lag behind in technology for many years, the technological flow between the developed and developing will be predominantly in one direction.

Can this flow be severed from ownership through licensing agreements? The existence of a vast number of such arrangements is ample proof that it can be done. But we are again confronted with a practical block and a theoretical question. Most large companies would prefer to control the operations rather than turn their technology over to others. They feel that they can do a better job, especially in the developing countries where many of the potential licensees are at a generally lower level of managerial competence than their own organizations. This leads to the same type of question we encountered in the marketing area. If the multinational corporation can do a better job of implementing the technology, is it not the more desirable vehicle for development of the national economy?

Managerial Flow: The substance of this part of the multinational business is hard to describe in concrete terms, especially to the antagonistic nationalist. Yet it has a real meaning. The ability to blend a group of people together into an efficient business organization and to formulate and execute effective policies is recognized as one of the main strengths of the industrialized economies. The application of this competence in foreign countries has given many multinational corporations a basis for superiority well beyond what their products, capital or technology could provide. The social value of inflows of this managerial skill is certainly attested to by the way all countries have sought to draw on the management skill of the more developed. Consider, for example, the multitude of invitations to U.S. management professors and consultants to work in other countries, as well as the activities of the International Executive Service Corps. And while there is the possibility that the inflow might be provided by individual contributions rather than through the organizations of multinational corporations, there are so many proponents in government and academic circles, as well as business, of the thesis that an integrated, going organization is the best transmission device for managerial know-how that one must accept this as a strong presumption.

After we have looked at each of the components of the multi-national corporation's activities, there is still something more to be considered in appraising the value of a unified business organization. Just as there is a historical evolution toward large we-groups, there is steady progression toward larger business organizations in which capital, technology and management are integrated with varying degrees of vertical control in the acquisition and distribution of products. We know that this progression has not excluded the existence of smaller enterprises and that a number of enterprises can coexist. It is not impossible therefore to conceive a world in which all corporations would be confined to their own national borders, but would engage in exchanges of products, capital, technology and management skills by arm's length bargaining. But this conception runs counter to the trend of history. It is far easier to accept what we see today as the natural evolution—great corporations efficiently accomplishing these flows through their own integrated operations spreading across national borders.

Accommodation Not Easy

These views of the component flows and integrated character of the multinational corporation give us a basic perspective on its capacity to accommodate to nationalism. The outlook does not appear highly promising. This is not to say that the corporation cannot act in ways which minimize the effects of nationalism. Much has already been written by this author and others about the practical actions which companies may take to meet nationalistically motivated desires, including the use of local nationals in management, employment of local capital and sympathetic relations with foreign governments.[2] While the details of these actions involve numerous questions, I am here accepting them as obvious and sound basic policies. The present analysis has been pitched to a different level. My concern is that even after we have implemented these basic policies to the point which is typically sound from a business efficiency point of view, we find that the external ties remain so significant that the conflict with nationalism retains a solid core of substance.

My purpose has been to examine the fundamentals of the structure of the multinational corporation to see whether a quite different concept could be conceived which would achieve both business efficiency and social utility. The picture as I have drawn it does not suggest this to be the case. But it should be cautioned that we do not have the type of well-documented, thoroughly analyzed research we need to reach considered conclusions on many aspects of this subject. My primary aim has not been to reach conclusions but to outline the character of the issues and the ways in which we may usefully think about them. As a conclusion it is adequate therefore to observe that there is a very hard core of conflict between nationalism and the character of the multinational corporation and that it is difficult to see how this conflict can be ultimately eliminated.

Where does this leave us? Will the conflict be a permanent one or will a pattern of mutual accommodation evolve? No one really knows. Taking a final look backward, however, we can find encouragement in the way other conflicts within society have found resolution, at least to a fair degree. For example, there is an apparent conflict between the acquisitive, materialistic character of modern industry and the tenets of Christianity. Yet, the two have been effectively married in Western Europe and Anglo-Saxon countries by the Protestant Ethic, which in giving religious sanction to hard work encouraged industrial productivity and justified the rewards of industry on this earth. John D. Rockefeller could thus feel no basic conflict in being a good Baptist and making millions of dollars. Likewise, the conflict between job security and the advance toward higher productivity has been always with us, whether in the English Luddites, who smashed textile machinery in the 1810's, or the railroad featherbedding issues of the 1960's. Yet labor has increasingly recognized the social utility and ultimate benefit to itself in more productive industrial methods. In a few notable cases it has even provided leadership in introducing labor-saving devices, e.g., John L. Lewis in the coal industry.

The proposition that the activities of the multinational corporation within various nations have social value has not been proved here, but it does appear to have strong support. If it is valid, then our historical perspective gives encouragement that a resolution of the conflict with nationalism will evolve. Although the change may come through some broad movement from nationalism toward political internationalism, it is more likely to occur through a mutual recognition of self-interest on the part of businessmen and business-oriented government officials around the world, a decline in the nationalistic preoccupation with business affairs, and a reduction of the external ties of the multinational corporation in each nation to the minimum that is clearly socially useful.

N O T E S

1. Richard D. Robinson, *International Business Policy*, New York, Holt, Rinehart & Winston, 1964, pp. 1-44.

2. For example, see my article, "LRP for International Operations," *California Management Review*, Fall, 1960, pp. 23-29.

CHAPTER 8

C. P. KINDLEBERGER

*So long as European companies eschew mergers
while their governments rebuff the
U.S.-based world corporation, integration will remain
a shining but largely unrealized goal.*

European Integration and the International Corporation

MY THESIS IS that economic integration cannot be achieved by customs unions alone, but requires factor movements, and that factor movements on an adequate scale to achieve or closely approach integration require institutions beyond those normal to factor markets.

In particular, to make substantial progress toward economic integration probably necessitates the development of corporations that are equally at home in the various political entities party to the integration attempt. Ideally, in the European integration contemplated by the Rome Treaty, it would be a European corporation, reconstituted under European charter or resulting from mergers that transcended national lines to create a truly European, not a national, decision-making entity. Or the effective institution might be an international corporation with a home base outside the Common Market and therefore indifferent in its dealings with one or another country of the Six. At the moment, when provision for European incorporation in the European Economic Community has been tabled, it looks as though the international corporation, typically that with headquarters in the United States, is the leading prospect for the effective instrument of European integration. If the Common Market repulses the American giant corporation and fails to establish European incorporation, the European movement may fall short of real integration.

But it is necessary to proceed more systematically. Permit me to discuss the two substantives in the title of this chapter separately before I develop the connection. Economic integration I define as factor-price equalization, that is, the equalization of wages, interest and profits. This definition is more far-reaching than those which emphasize merely the elimination of restrictions on the movement of goods. It makes integration a standard, like absolute zero in temperature, which can be approached or moved away from, but is seldom if ever reached.

Factor Movements Essential

Of course, freedom-of-goods movement is an important ingredient of integration, as the factor-price-equalization theorem suggests. If two countries produce goods in the same way, equalization of goods-prices will result in equalization of the prices of factor inputs—land, labor and capital—provided certain rather restrictive assumptions are met about the unimportance of transport costs, the identification of certain goods with certain factors, the production of every good in all the countries, perfect competition, constant returns to scale, etc. So restrictive are the assumptions, however, that few economists believe that goods-movements alone can produce economic integration as here defined. It probably requires as well the movement of factors, which the classic economists thought did not occur in international, as contrasted with domestic, trade.

The Rome Treaty establishing the European Economic Community provided for freedom of factor movements. Yet large-scale movements of capital have not taken place within the Common Market. To the extent that the capital markets of Europe are joined, it was, before the announcement that the President would seek passage of an Interest Equalization Tax in July, 1963, principally by means of New York. European borrowers would sell bonds in New York, and European lenders would buy bonds. Some of the bonds were identical, i.e., bought by Europeans from Europeans in New York.

Another institution for moving capital from one national money or capital market in the EEC to another is the large American bank with branches in the separate countries. This device is not available for integration in the United States, since branch banking is forbidden in most states. Nor has it gone far elsewhere. But it is interesting to observe that there are no European-wide commercial banks except the Chase Manhattan, the First National City, the Bank of America, and the Morgan Guaranty. French, German, Italian, Dutch and Belgian commercial banks cooperate, and regularly participate in consortia for successive loans; but the identity of interest is limited. A new decision is made each time for each operation; there is no mechanism for borrowing in one market and lending in another automatically, such as occurs in the single bank which receives deposits here and makes loans there.

Integration through factor movements also takes place by means of movements of labor, and these, too, operate in Europe largely by outside mechanisms. It is true that Italy has provided the largest number of foreign workers for Germany, France and Belgium (leaving out Switzerland which has half a million Italians but is not a member of the Common Market). But the numbers of border workers who cross from Belgium into France or the Netherlands and France into Germany, are trivial compared to the large inflow from Eastern Germany to the West, from North Africa to France, and from Portugal, Spain, Greece and Turkey into Germany, France and Belgium.

Moreover, the outsiders with no roots are more mobile than Bretons are in France or East Bavarians in Germany and far more mobile than nationals between the separate countries. It has been noted that wage equalization is taking place between Southern and Northern Italy by means of Switzerland and Germany. Southern Italians go to Switzerland and Germany at the same time that Italian employers are recruiting Italian workers in those countries to bring them to Northern Italy. Similarly, 12,000 Moroccans leaving Northern France for the Ruhr when their contracts in the French coal mines are up raise wages in France and lower them in Germany, a step in the direction of wage equalization.

But the tendency toward equalization of factor prices does not always occur through organized markets—for goods or for labor and capital. In the United States an important contribution to integration has been the national corporation. This borrows in New York and invests where it can assemble materials and labor in least-cost combinations relative to market outlets. The economic historian, Alfred Chandler, dates the rise of the national corporation in the United States at the 1890's, and observes, interestingly, that with the change of scale and horizon, there was also a change in behavior, as the national corporation took marketing back from wholesalers and discharged the function itself. A national corporation that shuts down production in a high-cost and expands in a low-cost location provides a mechanism of integration connected with, but significantly differentiated from, the markets for goods and factors.

Jet-age Flowering

The rise of the international corporation is more difficult to date. Some American companies "went international" shortly after becoming national, at the turn of the century. By 1929 there was a sizable list. But it was not until the development of the aircraft, and especially the jet aircraft, that the international corporation came into its own. As Stephen Hymer has pointed out,[1] international operations are expensive. They require face-to-face contact, expensive communication by telegram and telephone. They involve misunderstandings and loss. They can be undertaken, therefore, only when they offer a particularly high return. Hymer's point is that direct investment is not simple capital movement. That could take place more cheaply through capital markets. Direct investment implies coordination of company operations to take advantage of super-profits. The basis of the higher-than-noraml profits may be a monopoly in technology, or access to extra-large amounts of capital, or capacity to coordinate operations in several parts of the world in ways which cannot be managed through the free play of market forces.

A few further remarks about the international corporation before coming to grips with the connections between it and European integration. There is a theorem set out by Irving Brecher and S. S. Reisman that since people in the same position trying to maximize profits will necessarily behave in identical fashion, it makes no difference whether a given company in Canada is Canadian or American: the economic result will be the same. I doubt this. Two decision-making units trying to maximize profits within the same horizon, spatially and through time, will behave in the same fashion —assuming equal intelligence and managerial capacity—but if one is a national corporation and the other an international one, their horizons will differ and so may their behavior. The international corporation will be keeping an eye on profit opportunities, governmental intervention, political pressures, and so on all over the world. To meet a local demand, the local company will expand in the local area. The international corporation might well supply the demand from abroad. Moreover, if demand contracts in the market, the local corporation is likely to cut production and dig in. The international corporation may close down altogether.

The differences between the national and the international corporations explain why joint ventures are such failures as an answer to the problem of direct investment—one partner wants income and the other wants capital gains, or one partner wants profits from refining and distribution and the other wants profits from selling the basic material. They also explain why the international corporation's answer to the demand for local participation—why don't you buy shares in the parent corporation?—usually falls on deaf ears. (Note the exception of the Libby-McNeil-Libby case in France, however.) Local capital is limited to a local horizon. It sees a local profitable enterprise owned abroad, and it wants a piece of it, including the wealth that comes from capitalizing the super-profits from the particular operation. On Hymer's principle of the need to overcome costs of foreign operations, direct investment must earn not only a higher return than the company could earn at home, but also a higher return—owing to the monopoly—than a local company can make in the host country. Since they operate with different horizons, the international corporation and the local investor or government have a hard time agreeing on what constitutes optimal behavior.

Dim Outlook for Continental Corporation

Now to join up European integration and the international corporation. As previously noted, my hypothesis is that if European integration is really to be achieved, there must develop European corporations, maximizing profits over some appropriate time profile, within the geographical limits of the Common Market. I do not see such corporations coming into being. To the extent that international corporations operate in the Common Market, the bulk of them will be American, with most of their interests outside. But I doubt that there will be enough American corporations operating in the Common Market to achieve much of the indicated integration by this mechanism.

There are some European corporations, to be sure. The 1964 merger of Agfa and Gevaert in the photographic-film field, a German corporation and a Belgian, was viewed by some as the beginning. But the two firms maintain separate identities for their products, separate boards of directors, separate bodies for decision-making. It is said that they will start by merging their distribution facilities, and move on after that to research. The test of a merger, however, is whether there is finally one decision-making unit, and whether the decision can be taken to close out an activity in one location (read country) when it is found less efficient than in another location where operations can be expanded. Cooperation between two locations that are both maintained stops short of integration in the sense I mean it. The forms of integration may be adopted without the substance.

To illustrate, let me cite the story of a Sloan Fellow at MIT—a junior executive studying for a year—who wrote a master's thesis on oil imports. Like most Sloan Fellows, he liked to interview—it gives one a chance of looking over the rest of the industry with a good cover. In New York he asked the assistant to the chairman of a large oil company what its views on oil imports were, and was told that the company had none. Expressing incredulity, he was told more candidly that the company had two views which the board of directors was unable to reconcile, one of the domestic and one of the foreign-operating subsidiary. The fact that the foreign subsidiary earned a higher return on its investment than the domestic subsidiary might have been expected to push the board of directors in favor of its position. But the domestic subsidiary was not without its strengths. For one thing, it had support in the Congress of the United States which neither the foreign subsidiary nor the main company could muster. This was not a merger into a single company, but an alliance of sovereigns.

United Steel in Britain, which maintained inefficient production at Cumberland and hesitated to expand efficient capacity in the East Midlands between the wars, may provide another example.[2] While it is too soon to estimate how the Agfa-Gevaert merger will develop, the initial arrangement, which perpetuates both companies under the direction of a joint board, suggests that decisions will not be taken solely on the basis of profitability, regardless of where that standard leads.

There have been many international corporations of European origin. Some of the most impressive of these, where integration is complete, have been Anglo-Dutch in character, especially the Shell and Unilever companies. These breach the lines of division between the Common Market and the European Free Trade Area under British aegis. Others have had a purely national base, like Philips, Siemens, Solvay or Dunlop. Still others—ARBED of Luxembourg in iron, or Alsthom in electrical products—are most clearly international in character.

For a while in 1963 and 1964, it looked as if the Agfa-Gevaert merger would be followed by many others. Citroën bought into the German firm NSU, which owns the patents to the Wankel gas-turbine engine, and plans were laid in 1965 to construct an engine plant in Germany and a chassis factory in France. Henschel in Kassel and Berliet in Lyon cooperate in trucks. Alfa Romeo and Renault and a number of other pairs of automobile companies have marketing agreements. Philips has talked to Siemens, and joint actions have been taken by Société Carbochimique of Belgium and Société Chimique d'Auby of France, Royal Dutch Shell and Montecatini. But agreements, talks, and cooperation are not mergers in which the identity of the parent company is mingled with that of another nationality; nor is this true when new joint subsidiaries are created. Rheinische-Westphalische Oel is a new subsidiary, owned jointly by Shell and I. G. Leverkusen, and Shell and Badische Anilin, another I. G. Farben descendant, cooperate in plastics. But these efforts are not only limited, as compared with complete mergers; they are confined for the most part to pairs of national companies. When Shell and Badische Anilin tried to form a subsidiary in France to make polyethylene, the Ministry of Finance reminded them icily that authorization was required for foreign firms to operate in France.[3]

Cartels Are the Norm

The fact is that the European tradition calls not for merger but for business agreement, or cartels. The Rome Treaty forbids cartels, but the European Economic Commission, in the course of applying the provisions of the Treaty, has chosen to distinguish between good agreements and bad ones. In the early period of the Common Market a number of agreements between national firms were made in the interests of rationalization. One company would make this product, and the other that. The need to maintain a complete line behind a tariff wall gave way to specialization and exchange within the Common Market, with large economies of scale, according to observers like Herbert Giersch, arising from rationalization cartels. But when Nordhoff of Volkswagen publicly proposed that the various national companies of Europe specialize by model size[4] as a means of meeting American competition, he was indignantly refused. Professor Valetta, of Fiat, who had earlier suggested an agreement of the European producers for pricing, purchasing (especially steel) and selling as a means of heading off American competition, but was turned down because his scheme was obviously in contravention of the Rome Treaty, rejected the Nordhoff proposal. Fiat has a full line of cars, and Volkswagen has specialized. The Volkswagen proposal for specialization patently favors Volkswagen and hurts producers with a more balanced set of models.

The automobile industry furnishes an excellent example of the problem. The United States, with a single market of 194 million consumers, has three or possibly four producers. Europe, with more than 200 million consumers, has had forty altogether and possibly fifteen to twenty substantial producers, but is surely going to find itself reduced to a smaller number. A semimerger took place in France between Citroën and Peugeot, which formed a special company, a fifty-fifty subsidiary to produce parts common to both, including certain transmissions and truck engines.[5] Volkswagen originally bought up DKW but has since sold it to Mercedes-Benz. It is significant that these are national mergers. Italian, French and even German interests are fearful of American "monsters," but the answer to them seems thus far to have been merger at the national level rather than the development of the European corporation. apart from the Citroën interest in Wankel with NSU and Henschel-Berliet in trucks, there have been no international mergers.

Contrast the position of the American Big Three. General Motors has the fast-rising Opel in Germany and Vauxhall in Britain, and has announced a $100 million expansion of its Belgian assembly plant in Antwerp. Ford is well established in Germany and England with local models, with a new plant in Belgium. Chrysler has acquired interests in Simca in France, Rootes in England, and a Spanish subsidiary, and is said to be looking for a suitable company to buy in Germany. These firms are already in position to adjust production internationally.

Europe generally is made unhappy by the size of American corporations. It is pointed out that General Motors alone grosses as much as the thirteen largest German companies (and that is 10% larger than the gross national product of the Netherlands); or that General Motors' profit has been larger than Renault's turnover. This was in 1963, before its record $1.75 billion profit in 1964. Among the world's sixty biggest corporations, forty-nine are American and only eleven European,[6] and of the 100 top firms in turnover in 1962 Germany placed only thirteen, with its largest, Volkswagen, thirty-fifth on the list.[7] Of the giant companies of the world, the Americans listed an average five times larger in size than the leading British or German corporations in their field and ten times larger than the French companies.[8]

But these figures, as economists know, are not only difficult to interpret, depending upon whether one chooses assets, net worth, turnover, profits, or cash flow; they are also of doubtful relevance. The amount of funds which an American company will invest in Europe is limited, and it is this limited portion of assets, profits, sales, cash flow or whatever which should be compared with European companies. Even so, the comparison is frightening for Europe.

Specific Objections

France objects to the American companies on more than mere size. These companies, it is held, can frustrate the French Plan. The plan is implemented to a considerable degree through the control which the Commissariat du Plan exercises over the flow of government funds and public savings. With an underdeveloped capital market, savings move from household to French business largely through government institutions. This is especially true when profits are squeezed by rising costs so that investment depends more on outside and less on internal funds. Foreign corporations with access to outside sources of capital can escape governmental control.

The other concern of the French is that the technological fallout of international corporations will occur outside of France. When General Electric buys Machines Bull and parts of Olivetti, the research will be done in Schenectady rather than in Paris or Ivrea.

A General Unreadiness

Neither of these objections is very compelling. As to the first, the plan has thus far been a success because it pushed for expansion. To worry that investment may occur which is not wanted is to anticipate a shift in the thrust of planning to restraint, higher prices, less growth. There have been symptoms of this attitude in France from time to time, but happily they have been fleeting. If American companies want to invest their own money or money borrowed outside France, they are sensible or foolish. If they are sensible, France benefits, as well as the company; if foolish, it is their money which is lost, not French, unless their expansion leads to intense competition and losses for other manufacturers.

The more fundamental reason, it seems to me, is that the French are unwilling yet to be truly international, nor even, as I shall suggest in more detail shortly, truly European in their economic life. This attitude is not solely French, by any means. Industrial associations in Germany last winter were studying whether European industry should be delivered to United States capital power. The great German banker, Herman Abs, is said to be restive under the threat of United States direct selling of securities by American brokers to Europeans, instead of through German banks, and German banks dislike the international corporation because it weakens their monopoly on capital by providing the firm with access to credit abroad. The Dutch are regarded as international and maintain strong ties to Britain and the United States, but this sometimes appears less as a positive attitude of faith in internationalism than a counterpoise to the domination of Germany and France in the Common Market. There are times, exemplified by their attitude toward Mediterranean labor, to which they have not extended a warm welcome, when they seem slightly nationalistic too. But the French are outstanding in independence of trans-Channel or trans-Atlantic suggestion or leadership, and we can use them to illustrate the vestigial importance of national life in the Common Market.

The French opposition to the international (read American) corporation is partly its freedom from capital control, and partly the fact of technological fallout abroad. But fundamentally the trouble with these corporations is that they are not French. The French want a French and not an international technology, just as they want a French and not an international deterrent. This is true in atomic energy, in supersonic aircraft, in computer technology and everything else. It is widely believed by American officials in Europe that the French opposition to American "monsters" is a smokescreen under which the Conseil du Patronat Français hopes to soften up the Community's antimerger and anticartel actions. But this is too subtle. The point is that the French are not ready for the European corporation, much less for the international corporation.

This can be demonstrated partly by the absence of international mergers in Europe involving French and partner companies. It is also mirrored in the actions of others. Take the attitude of American corporations. When the Common Market was initially organized, it was believed that American firms operating in the separate markets would rationalize their operations. IBM, for example, was said to have maintained plants in separate countries assembling separate machines, the components of which were produced in several other countries. This layout was believed to minimize the danger of nationalization, since no country taking over a plant would acquire an integrated operation. When the Common Market took effect, this rather expensive arrangement could be abandoned for a more efficient organization of production. Or in the case of companies making a single line, scale economies might make it sensible to substitute one plant for five after the internal protective tariffs were eliminated.

The notions of investment creation and investment diversion were evolved to parallel (verbally, though not analytically) trade creation and trade diversion in the economic analysis of customs unions. Investment creation was the response by the outside producer to the stimulus of trade diversion. Unable to lick them, he joined them, establishing a plant inside the Common Market to fill the market from which discrimination cut him off. This was the widespread American response to the Rome Treaty and is completely analogous to a tariff factory—that is, a manufacturing operation called into being by a tariff on finished products. Much of the effect of the Common Market in attracting United States investment was not investment creation in the sense that investments in Europe which were not profitable with internal tariffs separating the four countries and the Belgian-Luxembourg customs union became profitable when these were removed. It came from the attention which the Common Market drew to investment opportunities in Europe which had previously passed unnoticed, having lain beyond the horizon of the American businessman still preoccupied after the war with the American market.

Investment diversion, as contrasted with investment creation, was to stem from the anticipated reorganization of the European investment of outside companies that were already established in Europe to take advantage of newly arisen opportunities for economies of scale and specialization. The creation and the diversion effects could be intermingled. The Common Market could lead to both expansion and reorganization. But investment diversion, so far as is observable from the outside, is negligible. American companies seem to have decided that the anticipated opportunity to rationalize was illusory. It was put to me once in 1964: "To sell in France, build a factory in France." General Motors Frigidaire incurred the displeasure of the French government when it closed down its small plant at Gennevilliers in 1962. This was required by the force of Italian competition in automatic refrigerators. If the cause had been company rationalization, the indignation would doubtless have been greater. It is true that there is considerable interplant exchange between Ford of Limburg in Belgium and Ford of Cologne—enough, it is said, to have increased the ratio of Belgian foreign trade to national income in recent years (without affecting the balance of trade). The General Motors investment in Antwerp may be more than a mere duplication of Opel and Vauxhall facilities in Germany and Britain, respectively. But investment diversion by American plants does not seem to have been significant.

It is not only the international companies of American origin which encounter problems in France. The rebuff to Shell and Badische Anilin has been mentioned. At the time of the General Electric purchase into Machines Bull of France, it is said that a private banker had tried to interest Siemens and Philips, separately, in the venture. These two companies, like General Electric, have need of a ready-made entry into the computer field, where they have fallen behind. Capital problems may have contributed to the decision not to pursue the matter, but it is said that each company lacked the assurance that it would be treated in the long run as a national in France.

Trade discrimination is possible under GATT because the world has made provision within the most-favored-nation clause for customs unions and free-trade areas, to bridge the gap between free trade (in the national market) and tariffs. In the corporate field, no such discrimination has been possible. The standard here is national treatment, in which foreign corporations are treated like national corporations.

No Right in Law

For example, national treatment of each other's corporations is provided by the Franco-American Convention of Commerce, Friendship and Navigation, the latest of which was signed in November, 1959, even though the French have disregarded it in announcing

restrictions on foreign investment in April, 1965. Foreign corporations can be discriminated against as a class by legislation or by
administrative action. But while it is possible *administratively* to
favor corporations from some foreign countries over those of others,
there has been in the past no recognized right *in law* to discriminate
in favor of the corporations of one nation over those of another.
This right is now claimed by Article 52 of the Treaty of Rome which
grants national treatment to the companies of partner countries, but
not to those of outsiders, a claim which has still to be tested in
diplomacy and in international law. If it is successfully defended,
and if the conditions for establishing corporations are made uniform
in the Community, as had been sought but tabled in 1961, there
would be created in effect a European corporation.

Note that the concept of a European corporation presupposes
the development of a corps of European executives who are mobile
from Catania to Friesland. The European bureaucrat has been
developed, ready for quick relocation to Brussels, Paris, Geneva and,
with less grace, Luxembourg and Strasbourg, but the European
executive is less inclined to pull up stakes—and far less inclined than
the business school graduate in the middle rank of executives in the
United States, who is prepared to transplant his family and chattels
from San Diego or Miami to Seattle or even Calais.

Yet despite the readiness of American executives to follow orders
from the vice president in charge of foreign operations, unless the
international corporation is assured of national treatment over a
wide area, it can have no greater mobility than the single domestic
company. If risks attach to the mobility, rather than extra profits,
the international corporation will operate a series of separate foreign
investments rather than a single efficient and factor-price-
equalizing one.

Would the United States object to discrimination in the Common
Market in favor of Common Market corporations? The subject is
evidently complex and involves legal considerations of a sort that a
mere economist hesitates to contemplate. There are those who think
retrospectively that this country made a mistake in encouraging the
Common Market with its trade discrimination against United States
exports. They, and doubtless others, would insist that while the
goal is national treatment for foreign-owned corporations, there
must be at minimum nondiscriminatory treatment of foreign-owned

corporations. This would make the European corporation wait until there was a European sovereignty. The question is academic in view of French hesitation to take a European rather than a French view of economic, social and political life in the Common Market. But it may not remain so.

N O T E S

1. "The International Operations of National Firms: A Study of Direct Investment," unpublished doctoral dissertation, MIT, 1960.

2. See Philip Andrews, *Capital Development in Steel*, Oxford: Blackwell, 1951.

3. Paris edition, *New York Times*, July 24, 1964.

4. *Le Monde*, July 26-27, 1964.

5. *France Actuelle*, November 15, 1964.

6. *New York Times*, July 28, 1964.

7. German Embassy, *The Bulletin*, September 22, 1964.

8. *France Actuelle, op. cit.*

CHAPTER 9

JACK N. BEHRMAN

> *Loyalty is a widely proclaimed virtue.*
> *Multinational corporations necessarily have divided*
> *loyalties. Both companies and governments are*
> *skirting the issue, uncertain how to resolve it.*

Multinational Corporations and National Sovereignty

THERE IS AN UNEASY FEELING among those watching the international business scene that a basic conflict exists between what is called the "multinational enterprise" and national sovereignty. The potential conflict is from the enterprise itself, or through it, from another government. The use of the enterprise by the home government through its control of the parent company permits that government, for example, to interfere in the affairs of another, or host government. As the host government sees it, there is a challenge to its sovereignty by the home government through the multinational enterprise, which is legally under the jurisdiction of both governments. Parts of it are incorporated under different governments. It therefore serves several "sovereigns."

Losses of national sovereignty are not new. National sovereignties have been eroding for some time. The debates on acceptance of the Bretton Woods proposals, creating the International Monetary Fund and the World Bank, included considerable discussion of whether the agreements were an "exercise" or a "loss" of national sovereignty. The conclusion was that they were both. A nation does not lose sovereignty if it retains the privilege of opting out—or if it can exercise the ultimate power of destroying the particular entity which presents the challenge. Yet, an agreement in which members deny themselves the use of certain powers and procedures does reduce the exercise of sovereignty.

There is no doubt that governments have an ability to opt out of a situation resulting from the existence of affiliates of multinational enterprises; they can destroy, alter or control any affiliate within their borders. During World War II, both the Allies and the Axis powers took over foreign-owned entities for their own use. There was no conceivable challenge to the sovereignty of these governments from affiliates of foreign-owned companies. Ultimate power resided in the governments. This power continues to reside there today.

The government may also desire to exercise that sovereignty by ceding some of its authority and responsibility to another entity, which assumes that power under the terms laid down by the government. The terms will reflect essentially what the government wants, if it has given thought to the issues at hand. If it has not, then it may at times cede power by inadvertence. In creating one situation (incorporation of affiliates) and offering the privileges of establishment, it may reap results which it had not anticipated.

The increasing significance of unanticipated results has given rise to concern. The Canadian tariff was erected to protect and stimulate Canadian industry, but the same duties made investment by foreign companies in Canada more attractive. The result was a different kind of invasion—not by goods but by capital. A technique adopted for one purpose brought a different and unanticipated result. The same thing is occurring with the right of establishment, which permits a foreign company to enter, incorporate and do business under local laws just as a domestic company does. The extension of the rights of private property to foreign corporations, coupled with the reduction of barriers, has generated a form of enterprise not anticipated when the rights of incorporation and liberal trade policies were adopted.

Now the question arises as to whether the impact of the multi-national enterprise is desired by host governments and, if not, what should be done about it. Several complexities make it difficult to come to grips with this problem. One is that the factors and relation-ships involved are not quantifiable: how does one measure national sovereignty or determine how much has been relinquished? Another is that there is no theory which can be applied directly to the analy-sis of the costs and benefits of direct investment; there is one for the movement of goods, one for capital and one for the integration of economies. There is no theory of the costs and benefits of integrating economies through direct ownership of industry—of the new struc-ture of international production and distribution which is substi-tuting for trade and investment. It is, therefore, not easy to balance the net gains of the impact of multinational enterprises against a loss of sovereignty.

Certain questions relating to the exercise of power by a govern-ment over the multinational corporation may clarify the problem and provide a better understanding of the conflict.

Right of Intervention

1. What right does a home or parent government have to inter-vene in the activities of a foreign affiliate when the factors employed by it are predominantly domestic and under the jurisdiction of the host government?

Given the lack of clear definition of rights of nation-states, the tentative answer to the question lies essentially in their ability to interfere. If the national government has the ability and willingness, "right" tends to become a legal issue, and there are no courts to deny governments the exercise of rights that they wish to employ. To date, there is no system of "rights" and "non-rights" concerning the multinational enterprise on which one government can rely to determine its appropriate role in commanding company behavior. Policies toward the separate functions and elements of the enterprise tend to be formed out of the total foreign economic and political policies of governments—as to exports, capital flow, taxes—rather than being focused on the enterprise itself.

2. *Should national governments tie their hands because multinational enterprises exist? If so, at what cost in terms of national policy?*

Even if the parent government has the right to exercise authority, it may be willing to limit its own use of that power. Intergovernmental agreements illustrate this willingness to seek accord on the use of power. In what areas should there be agreement among governments to limit their authority over the acts of the multinational enterprise?

We have had suggestions for Codes of International Investment. These would limit the authority of the host governments to impose restraints on the foreign investor and, presumably, require some sort of "appropriate behavior" from the investing company. They do not cover interference from the parent government. The codes have not been accepted, partly because they do not reach the critical problems as seen by host governments. They are a means of expanding multinational enterprises and the power of parent governments—not of circumscribing them.

There are, of course, agreements between Canada and the United States which attempt to limit the exercise of the power of the U.S. government in the areas of export control, antitrust and now balance-of-payments controls. These have taken the form of either "consultation" or "exemption." They have not, however, limited the power of the U.S. government over U.S.-owned affiliates. in Canada.

Is it unreasonable to expect that the government (and Congress) would unilaterally (and voluntarily) accept a limitation on the exercise of its power? Nations do refrain from exercise of power, but usually only when the potential costs are high or the gains uncertain and diffuse. In the three areas mentioned above, gains from the exercise of power seem certain but the costs diffuse. The multinational enterprise is available as a tool of foreign policies, and the U.S. government does not see the particular benefits of intergovernmental agreements covering the activities of the enterprise.

For the enterprise not to be under control of the U.S. government would mean that the government had abdicated a series of important economic decisions to the board rooms of these companies. In this case the basis of the decisions may not be the same as that desired by the government. Control remains because the interests of the government and the parent of the multinational corporation diverge at critical points, or because foreign governments can induce affiliates to act against the wishes of the U.S. government.

3. *Are there any limits to the exercise of authority of the parent government over affairs of the multinational enterprise arising out of conflicts with foreign economic objectives?*

There are situations in which the exercise of power or authority produces results which are contrary to other objectives of the government, raising the question of the costs of interference. For example, the pursuit of antitrust objectives, without modification or amelioration for over-all foreign policy purposes, may well prevent the achievement of other, high-priority foreign economic goals. There are frequent arguments that antitrust problems have given U.S. companies pause in pursuing opportunities in the developing countries, where markets and government attitudes would permit the creation of a monopoly position that would enhance the opportunities for U.S. exports. Companies have avoided opportunities to gain earnings for the United States because of a fear of antitrust implications. Sometimes the reluctance is overcome by the support of a government agency, and the company moves abroad, only to find that in subsequent years the Department of Justice decides it has an interest in the sponsored activity. This potential interference affects decisions of multinational enterprises on foreign operations.

Prevention of exports to communist countries has precluded a contribution to U.S. balance of payments and permitted sales by allies, strengthening their payments position and increasing the drain on U.S. gold. Restrictions on foreign investment have tended to reduce the flow of funds to the developing nations, and reduction of dollar outflows tends to slow the rate of growth in countries such as Canada.

Even though the U.S. government is unwilling, in principle, to deny itself the exercise of power over the multinational corporation, it has modified the use of that authority in specific situations: those that would produce costs greater than the benefits. For example, the exemption of Canada in the payments guidelines and the preferential treatment of developing countries reduce the benefits of controls in favor of other objectives. It is conceivable that the expansion of multinational activities into many items of the balance-of-payments accounts will raise the cost of using restrictions to cure deficits; the complex linkages of payments elements through the enterprise will cause some controls to be counter-productive. If, as some argue, there is a direct relationship between foreign investment and exports by the parent, a reduction of capital outlays abroad reduces the export surplus.

Even the question of whether flexible, fluctuating or free exchange rates are bearable can no longer be determined simply on whether forward markets are functioning properly, on whether short-term capital will move smoothly or even on whether long-term capital flows will be damaged. The accounts of the multinational enterprise permit a variety of means of switching funds so as to mitigate such movements or, alternatively, heighten the fluctuations of exchange rates.

The means of balance-of-payments adjustment are altered by the existence of the multinational enterprise. The cost of interference may simply become too high. However, little analysis is being done by governments or economists on precisely what the existence of the multinational enterprise may mean to the adjustment process or the degrees of freedom left to governments.[1]

Reduction of Interference

4. Even if no government is willing to limit its authority voluntarily, are there ways by which the host government can reduce the level of foreign interference?

This question can be asked another way. Can host governments impose sufficient penalties on the parent government, directly or indirectly, economically or politically? Obviously, host governments have the right to impose counter-restrictions. They have a unit of the multinational enterprise within their boundaries, and they can impose regulations countering the orders of the parent government on repatriation of earnings, inflow of funds, export sales and even competitive relationships. They can also raise the political cost of interference by claiming that it goes beyond some "rule of reason," and by demonstrating to other countries the dangers of permitting political intervention through multinational corporations.

These responses can impose substantial costs on the parent government either through frustration of its original objectives or disruption of relations with other countries. The imposition of these penalties is not without some cost to the host government, however, for the issues are raised immediately to the diplomatic level and are injected into the over-all balancing of interests taking place between the two governments. The host government will tend to feel, whether or not the feeling is justified, that the parent government will penalize it in one area for having fought back against its interference through the multinational enterprise. An illustration is the reported French fear in 1968 that the U.S. government would favor Belgium in the U.S. capital controls if Belgium would buy its fighter planes from the United States instead of France. In this case, the status of international investment would be dependent on a rather complex analysis involving defense strategy, NATO, Belgian fear of a French embargo on planes (as with Israel), fighter capability, delivery and price, capital-import needs, personality conflicts among heads of state, and the French position on British entry into the Common Market.

Though the host government can impose countervailing restrictions of its own, whether it will do so is another question. It is likely to do so only when it considers that it can succeed without endangering other objectives which are equally or more important. Essentially, decisions which by their nature are primarily economic will be made in terms of political realities and political goals.

5. *Is the tactic of attempting to achieve given policy objectives through private corporate relationships an appropriate substitute for the inability to obtain intergovernmental agreements on antitrust and denial controls?*

Host governments have complained that the exercise of controls through the multinational enterprise is, in a sense, "dirty pool." The parent government is attempting to gain through private channels what it cannot gain directly through diplomatic channels—as with denial controls and repatriation of earnings. Foreign governments have been unwilling to accede to the desires of the U.S. government in restricting certain exports to the Soviet Union or China, and they have not been willing to lend sufficient dollars back to ease U.S. payments pressures. Now, the United States achieves some of these same ends through the private sector.

The host government complains because it does not want to prevent the exercise of power by the U.S. government through this medium; it simply prefers that the power not be exercised. Essentially, the United States is doing what it is able and willing to do, while the host government is not willing to do what it is able to do: counter the restraints. The Canadian government, for example, is certainly able to implement the recent proposal by the Canadian Task Force to establish a government agency for trading with the Soviets and China, frustrating U.S. controls over subsidiaries in Canada.[2] But it will probably not be willing to do so because of the additional conflicts which would arise from such a confrontation with the U.S. government.

One of the more interesting questions on the relation of companies to governments—not asked by the U.S. government but of great concern to the enterprises—is: to what extent should any multinational enterprise be penalized when it is forced to comply with U.S. regulations? U.S. export control officials are not empowered to ask how much income is being lost because of a denial; yet the evidence is that exports worth several hundred million dollars might be possible from the United States to the Eastern European countries and China in the absence of the controls. For example, the $800 million Fiat contract with Russia, as well as the Olivetti one for calculating machines, might have come to U.S. companies.

While foreign policy objectives may not have a price tag in this sense, any given restraint does have a dollar impact. One request by the U.S. government that a company refrain from a given business opportunity overseas—when there was no law covering the situation —cost the company about $50 million. The company did not mention this loss in conversations with the government, nor did the government ask the price tag. In fact, U.S. companies are loath to argue the dollar-income question partly because they do not care to be pilloried in Congress for putting profit before patriotism.

Management Responsibility

6. What is the responsibility of the owners or management of a multinational company to the parent government in following the spirit of its laws rather than the strict letter? What of its response to mere requests? Does it have similar responsibilities to host governments?

The responsibility of the multinational company to the parent and host governments is usually spoken of rather loosely by corporate officials—not that they take the matter lightly. They simply find it so complex and difficult that it is easier to speak in generalities. The usual comment is that "we are good citizens and try to do what is good for each government—parent and host."

On the whole, the multinational company will try to decide what is good for the company and then fit its explanation of what it is doing to the expressed objectives of each government. It rationalizes what it is doing as "good for the government and country," not publicizing some of the things it is doing about which public officials might have some doubts. The company may be right that what it is doing is, in fact, better for the country than the practices sought by government officials. Further, it is conceivable that the current government is out of step with what a succeeding government will want. Companies tend to take a longer view of national interests than some governments do, for the latter are in office but a few years, while the company must stand over a long period of time on its behavior record.

There is surprise in some quarters that such a long-term, apolitical view is taken by U.S. business. For example, *Le Monde* reported that "For the American businessman, there are not two categories of Africans—one having a favorable attitude to the United States and the other an unfavorable attitude; but rather, Africans with whom it is possible to do business and others with whom it is impossible."[3]

An analysis of governmental controls over the multinational enterprise reveals that it can hardly accede simultaneously to the desires of all governments. In almost all instances where the squeeze is tight, it is the parent government that wins. In others, there is a neat balancing act for which there are no principles to determine how the situation should be finally resolved. Game theory is probably more appropriate here than any other theory of corporate behavior.

There is another aspect of this question of responsibility that requires airing: what is the allegiance of the company to the over-all foreign economic policy of any government when there is no specific requirement expressed about particular behavior? Should the multinational enterprise reflect a given national policy or are multinational enterprises stamped with the policy of parent governments despite their own wishes in the matter?

In many countries, the company and its affiliates are associated by the public with responsibility for foreign economic and political policies of the parent government, including military policy. Some corporate officials in the United States have felt the burden of the Vietnam war, just as early in 1968 the U.S. consumer rebelled against French goods and *haute couture* because of President de Gaulle's policies.

There is no simple pattern of loyalties among corporate officials. They are primarily loyal to the company, but this primacy can be upset by one's wife, mother, God or taste for expensive trips on company expense accounts. The list is complex enough for each individual to carry multiple loyalties at any given time and to express them in different situations during the same day—loyalty to the parent government on one decision and the host government on another. Neither government has yet determined precisely what issues require what kind of expressions of loyalty, from whom, and when.

Nor do the various host governments expect similar behavior from foreign-owned affiliates within their borders. Governmental powers are unequal. Both a European subsidiary of a U.S. enterprise and a U.S. subsidiary of a European enterprise will follow to the letter U.S. export control requirements, even if the European parent company may be following different directives from his own government. The European-owned affiliate is also subject to the antitrust laws of the U.S. government, as is the U.S.-owned affiliate in Europe, when it affects U.S. trade. According to the testimony of some European multinational enterprises, they have instructed their U.S. affiliates to adhere to the payments guidelines and not repatriate earnings to the parent during the dollar deficit.

But what if a European government concludes that the U.S.

payments constraints are not appropriate and will heavily damage its own position? The constraints do not prevent a U.S. affiliate of a European company from remitting earnings, but such an outflow damages U.S. payments. How is this affiliate to respond? Should it try to help its mother country offset the effects of the U.S. guidelines? Given the present balance of investment between the United States and Europe, such an outflow is probably of less concern to the U.S. government, if it takes place, than a return of foreign earnings from affiliates in Europe. But what of the foreign government's interest in such remissions to the U.S. parent? Only if there are clear and non-contradictory directives from each government can the affiliates and parents of a multinational enterprise feel certain that they are fulfilling their "responsibilities."

The practice of host governments of making "unofficial requests" of the parent company to control the behavior of a subsidiary in a given way places the multinational enterprise in a difficult position. It has no clear mandate to "enforce" action, but it may be "honor bound" to comply or may even be subject to "sanctions." The techniques available to the host government to penalize non-compliance are substantial—even if the government does not employ them.

It may be something of a paradox, but despite its use of controls and interference, the U.S. government does not recognize an equal right on the part of a foreign government to persuade the foreign affiliate of a U.S. company to adopt a certain action inimical to U.S. interests, as in the area of antitrust. The terms of reference are, essentially, that a "requirement" of the host government (not simply a "request") must exist to exempt the parent from liability under the regulations. This requirement must be statutory or regulatory and not merely an oral (and especially not a secret) request.

There also appears to be a lack of similarity in the responsibility of companies within their jurisdictions to comply with different types of governmental directives. The responsibility lessens if the requests come from lower echelons of governments. Some of the lack of parallelism among and within governments is probably a reflection of the different intensity of interests on the part of governments in using foreign companies for purposes of foreign policy. Some of it also arises from a lack of clarity of the principles and impact involved, which in turn stems from the unwillingness of officials of the multinational enterprise to challenge governments strongly or to force the issue to the level of principles. They would, in the main, prefer to temporize, work around, live with or bear up under whatever is imposed upon them rather than face it squarely on the merits or on principle.

Though the tensions and potential conflicts which have been experienced over the use of multinational corporations to implement policies of parent governments are certainly real, there is no evidence that parent governments will act unilaterally to remove their own contributions to these tensions, and host governments will probably not consider the specific conflicts sufficiently critical to raise them to the diplomatic level. The multinational enterprises will prefer not to have the tensions resolved in ways which inhibit their operations. Interference by governments through the multinational enterprise in the affairs of other national sovereignties is therefore likely to continue without a definitive response from host governments, since the results of alternative responses are not clearly discernible. The enterprise will continue to challenge national sovereignty and be a channel through which home governments interfere in host economies.

N O T E S

1. Two studies have been made recently: G. C. Hufbauer and F. M. Adler, "Overseas Manufacturing Investment and the Balance of Payments," U.S. Treasury Dept., Tax Policy Research Study No. 1, 1968; and my critique of this analysis in "Direct Manufacturing Investment, Exports and the Balance of Payments," National Foreign Trade Council, New York, 1968. See also Professor Adler's commentary on the Treasury study in the *Columbia Journal of World Business,* May-June 1968.

2. "Foreign Ownership and the Structure of Canadian Industry," Ottawa: Queen's Printer and Controller of Stationery, 1968.

3. *Le Monde,* January 5, 1967.

CHAPTER 10

I. A. LITVAK and C. J. MAULE

Foreign corporations, when successful, can be a disturbing element to host governments. They create fears of extra-territoriality and loss of sovereignty. This need not be.

Guidelines for the Multinational Corporation

FOREIGN TRADE AND FOREIGN CAPITAL have played, and will continue to play a vital role in Canada's economic well being. The openness of the Canadian economy is exemplified by the fact that exports of goods and services represent about 22.5% of Canada's Gross National Product, while foreign interests have a total stake of $33 billion in Canada's economy. More than 50% of this foreign investment represents ownership of Canadian enterprises, concentrated primarily in the areas of manufacturing and mineral production. Foreign-controlled companies account for three-fifths of Canada's manufacturing and mining and three-quarters of her petroleum and natural gas industries.[1]

To lend further perspective to Canada's openness, approximately two-thirds of Canada's export and import trade respectively is with the United States, and more than three-quarters of the foreign ownership is in the hands of residents of the United States. In fact, the Canadian industrial structure is often viewed as a miniature replica of its neighbor. Most leading U.S. companies have subsidiaries in Canada, and in many cases their competitive position in Canada is similar to that in the United States. For example, the U.S. "Big Three" automobile manufacturers are also the Canadian "Big Three." Another fact worth noting is that U.S. companies, in an attempt to maximize the return on their investment, have successfully concentrated their investment in growth industries.

From the U.S. viewpoint, however, its export and import trade with Canada accounts for about one-fifth of its foreign trade and is a much less significant figure in terms of its Gross National Product. Further, Canada as an investment site accounts for slightly less than one-third of U.S. foreign direct investment. Finally, Canada's persistent deficit on current account, which in one year exceeded one billion dollars, is chiefly due to its trade with the United States. This has been offset, however, by the large inflow of U.S. capital.

This flow of trade and capital have made the two economies interdependent. Nonetheless, it is questionable whether this state of interdependence is one of equal mutual dependence, and it is therefore inevitable that the very nature of such a relationship would give rise to friction between the two countries. Although the recent introduction of the Canadian Guiding Principles of Good Corporate Behavior for Subsidiaries in Canada of Foreign Companies is a result of this friction, it merely deals with the symptoms of the friction.

The Debate

The topic of direct foreign investment, specifically that involving U.S.-owned and -controlled firms, has been a recurring debate in Canada. However, it is only during the past decade that this topic has become a significant political issue. This period in Canada has been characterized by an emerging sense of nationalism, traceable in large measure to the increasing awareness by Canadians of the extent of U.S. influence in their economy and over their lives. To illustrate the intensity of this awareness, every major Canadian political party has incorporated into its party platform a plank dealing with Canadian-U.S. economic relations.

There can be little doubt that the hearings conducted by the Royal Commission on Canada's Economic Prospects some twelve years ago and the studies published by the Commission helped to crystallize dramatically the magnitude of U.S. control and influence on the Canadian economy.[2] There is even less doubt that Walter L. Gordon, the chairman of the commission and Canada's most influential economic nationalist, was primarily responsible for highlighting the question of foreign ownership, especially its economic and political effects on Canada. Mr. Gordon expressed a national concern over the distinct possibility that U.S. subsidiaries, most of which are wholly owned, would, when faced with conflicting loyalties between U.S. and Canadian interests, opt for the U.S. position.

To prevent the erosion of Canadian sovereignty through the vehicle of direct foreign investment, the Commissioners recommended that foreign-owned subsidiaries take action to "Canadianize" themselves. This included appointing Canadians to their boards of directors, staffing key positions with Canadians, issuing a sizable minority of their equity stock to Canadians, publishing financial data about their operations, purchasing from Canadian suppliers where feasible, and aggressively seeking out export markets. These recommendations are similar to the present Canadian guidelines. In fact, they may be viewed as part of what constitutes the Canadian policy toward foreign investment.

Since 1956, Gordon's report and Mr. Gordon have gained increasing prominence as areas of friction between Canada and the United States developed over such issues as trading with the Communists, U.S. antitrust legislation, the interest equalization tax, military alliances, labor relations on the Great Lakes, tariff changes and U.S. balance of payments guidelines. In each case, the consensus in Canada among many politicians and others was that Canada's national sovereignty was being either violated or threatened. Some viewed the subsidiaries as Canada's own fifth column.

To preserve Canada's cultural integrity, and to protect her sovereignty, Canada's two major political parties found it necessary to introduce several pieces of legislation over the last decade for the purpose of defining the rules of the game for foreign investors. These pieces of legislation represent further scraps of Canada's policy towards foreign investment.

Guiding Principles of Good Corporate Behavior for Subsidiaries in Canada of Foreign Companies

1. Pursuit of sound growth and full realization of the company's productive potential, thereby sharing the national objective of full and effective use of the nation's resources.

2. Realization of maximum competitiveness through the most effective use of the company's own resources, recognizing the desirability of progressively achieving appropriate specialization of productive operations within the internationally affiliated group of companies.

3. Maximum development of market opportunities in other countries as well as in Canada.

4. Where applicable, to extend processing of natural resource products to the extent practicable on an economic basis.

5. Pursuit of a pricing policy designed to assure a fair and reasonable return to the company and to Canada for all goods and services sold abroad, including sales to the parent company and other foreign affiliates.

6. In matters of procurement, to search out and develop economic sources of supply in Canada.

7. To develop as an integral part of the Canadian operation wherever practicable, the technological, research and design capability necessary to enable the company to pursue appropriate product development programs so as to take full advantage of market opportunities domestically and abroad.

8. Retention of a sufficient share of earnings to give appropriate financial support to the growth requirements of the Canadian operation, having in mind a fair return to shareholders on capital invested.

9. To work toward a Canadian outlook within management, through purposeful training programs, promotion of qualified Canadian personnel and inclusion of a major proportion of Canadian citizens on its board of directors.

10. To have the objective of a financial structure which provides opportunity for equity participation in the Canadian enterprise by the Canadian public.

11. Periodically to publish information on the financial position and operations of the company.

12. To give appropriate attention and support to recognized national objectives and established Government programs designed to further Canada's economic development and to encourage and support Canadian institutions directed toward the intellectual, social and cultural advancement of the community.

Source: Department of Trade and Commerce, *Foreign-Owned Subsidiaries in Canada,* Queen's Printer, Ottawa, 1967, pp. 40-41.

People shape events. First Mr. Gordon, then former Prime Minister Diefenbaker, and later Eric W. Kierans, an aspirant to the leadership of the Liberal party, have emphasized the interdependence of the United States and Canada and the constraints placed on Canada by the United States.

In 1966 Eric W. Kierans, then Minister of Health for the Province of Quebec, put into focus for Canadians the basic political issues of extra-territoriality and the international or multinational corporation. His concern was not with the business performance of the subsidiaries in Canada, but rather with the extent to which these subsidiaries had to compromise their economic pursuits in the light of legislation enacted by the U.S. government. Unlike Mr. Gordon, he welcomed foreign investment and its accompanying benefits. His quarrel was not with U.S. investors, but rather with foreign government policy or action which would have the effect of compromising the activities of subsidiaries in a host country. He saw the net result as a flagrant violation of the sovereignty of the host country.

When the U.S. government made public its guidelines for direct investment in 1965, it gave rise to a series of reactions on both sides of the 49th parallel which finally resulted in the formulation of the official set of Canadian guidelines. These formally present U.S. subsidiaries, for the first time, with the real difficulties of divided loyalties. To whom do they owe their primary loyalty and allegiance?

On February 1, 1966, in an address to the Toronto Society of Financial Analysts, Mr. Kierans included the following remarks: ". . . But when the United States dictates the investment policy, dividend policy, purchasing policy of the greater part of the Canadian manufacturing, mining and petroleum industries in Canada, it is directly interfering in the operations of Canadian business and controlling the activities of Canadian citizens subject to our laws and economic objectives . . . We are no longer dealing with the large numbers of economic theory but with a single directing voice; not with the disparate and independent decisions of thousands of businessmen but with hard government policy."

Mr. Kierans argued that "the U.S. guidelines will have a disastrous impact on the structure and organization of the Canadian economy." Lower direct investment outflows to Canada, reduced exports (from subsidiaries to parents) and accelerated imports from parents to subsidiaries would result from the application of the U.S. guidelines, and Canada's balance of payments would suffer accordingly. The Canadian government, therefore, had to introduce countermeasures or face the prospect of having Canada's future shaped in Washington. He repeatedly emphasized that he did not oppose private foreign investment, whose "net economic and social advantages . . . outweigh the ill-defined and vague dangers to political independence that some have seen . . . only the most emotional and chauvinistic could imagine a concerted effort by businessmen to undermine political authority."

By 1967, the issue of national sovereignty was receiving considerable publicity in Canada, and *The Task Force Report*,[3] which must be viewed against this backdrop of previous events, chose national sovereignty as its underlying theme. Although the Report contains no terms of reference, certain issues are listed as central to its investigations and recommendations.

Report of the Task Force

The Report makes the point that while the realization of Canada's future economic goals hinges on its ability to continue to attract foreign capital and technology, Canadians are worried that the present level of direct foreign investment may threaten Canada's future national independence. The multinational corporation is viewed as the medium through which this threat may be transmitted. The Report sets forth a series of proposals to ensure that the behavior of the multinational firm is consistent with Canadian national policies. The proposals essentially take the form of countervailing measures designed to obviate actions by foreign governments and companies which would be inconsistent with Canadian aspirations.

Any attempt to evaluate the Report's recommendations for legislative actions must first include a statement of the conclusions derived from the analysis. According to the authors of the Report, "Six major issues face Canada and its policy-makers as a result of foreign ownership and control of Canadian economic activity."

1. To ensure that Canadian subsidiaries of multinational corporations adhere to Canadian law and policy.

2. To require all corporations in Canada to disclose more information about their operations and activities.

3. To stimulate competitive conditions and Canadian entrepreneurship by amending existing anti-combines legislation and tariff policies.

4. To improve the performance and efficiency of Canadian firms, both Canadian-owned and foreign-owned, by the promotion of management education and research and development.

5. To enact new Canadian laws and to establish administrative machinery designed to countervail certain U.S. government laws and policy, such as laws on freedom to export, U.S. anti-trust law and policy, and U.S. balance of payments policy.

6. To guarantee that Canada benefits from direct foreign investment by increasing Canadian participation in the management of multinational corporations. The Canadian tax system should be altered to achieve this objective.

Recommendations

To increase the benefits and reduce the costs of foreign ownership, the Task Force recommends a series of proposals which include:

1. Creating a government agency to handle surveillance of multinational corporations operating in Canada;

2. Making more effective use of certain laws and policies such as the Canadian company law, bankruptcy law, securities legislation, the Corporations and Labour Unions Returns Act and the guiding principles of "good corporate behavior": the information gathered under these laws would enable the government to improve decisions in the area of foreign ownership;

3. Amending tariff policy and reorienting anti-combines legislation simultaneously to promote greater international competition and to encourage rationalization of industry through amalgamation;

4. Improving the quality of Canadian business and entrepreneurship through federal support of management, education and training programs, research and development incentives, relaxation of restrictions on closed-end investment funds, and formation of a Canadian Development Corporation;

5. Countervailing the U.S. law which restricts subsidiaries from exporting to Communist countries by establishing a government trade agency with powers to promote such trade in accordance with Canadian law and foreign policy.

While the tone of the proposals appears to be nationalistic, the Report does give full recognition to the benefits which have accrued to Canada as a result of foreign investment and it is clearly stated that ". . . any wholesale substitution of domestic for foreign capital over any short period of time is neither feasible nor desirable."

The Report is concerned with maximizing the benefits and minimizing the costs of foreign investment. Essentially the view of the Task Force is that the benefits are economic and the costs political. Certainly one can point to economic costs as well, such as the miniature replica effect, which results in Canadian industries having too many firms of suboptimal size, but it is the political costs that receive greater emphasis in the Report.

The Report contains a number of policy recommendations of which the major ones are (1) the State Trading Corporation, (2) countervailing U.S. anti-trust laws, (3) the Canada Development Corporation, and (4) other measures to offset U.S. influence in Canada.

The proposal for a government trading agency stems from the

fact that the U.S. government prohibits U.S. citizens from trading with Communist China, and the prohibition applies to firms owned or controlled by U.S. citizens in Canada. Under the Trading With the Enemy Act, any U.S. citizen found guilty of trading with certain countries such as Communist China may be fined and imprisoned. It is public knowledge that certain U.S.-owned companies in Canada have been forbidden to do business with Communist China and that the U.S. executives who control these companies could be held responsible for their actions by the U.S. government. In fact, this has meant that Canadian companies owned by Americans have been subject to Canadian and U.S. legislation, with the latter overruling the former in the event of any conflict.

To overcome this problem of conflicting national sovereignties, the Report recommends that ". . . a government export trade agency be created with the necessary powers to ensure that export orders are filled when they conform with Canadian law and Canadian foreign policy. State trading organizations of Communist countries could register orders placed with Canadian firms with the agency . . . If the agency judges the sole inhibition to be American foreign-assets-control regulations, the agency would purchase the item on its account for resale to the state trading organization. . ."

On March 6, 1968, the Canadian Export Association, which numbers among its members both U.S.-owned and Canadian-owned firms, took special issue with the above recommendation and termed it one of the "most controversial."

"Whatever the original reasons for setting up an agency, the ultimate results could be embarrassing. Under the present arrangements, whenever a state trading nation such as the Soviet Union has pressed Canada to buy an agreed amount of its goods in return for Soviet purchases in Canada, Ottawa has always been able to reply—honestly—that, under the free-enterprise system, the Canadian government cannot possibly commit itself to buy anything. The only customers, these state traders are told, are companies and individuals, and they buy whatever they like.

"If you want to sell in Canada, the argument continues, you have to deal directly with the customers. The creation of a state trading agency, even though it was intended purely as a selling and not a buying machine, could be the thin end of the wedge. Ottawa, it is feared, might find it difficult to convince its Communist trading partners that it no longer had the power to do state buying as well as selling."[4]

There are other weaknesses associated with the proposal. For example, what will happen to the price of the product ordered? If the proposed federal agency is to act as a wholesaling intermediary, it will incur operating costs. Who will absorb these costs, the Communist customer or the Canadian taxpayer? If it is the former, the product will probably be priced out of the market. Furthermore, who will service the order? Certainly not the U.S.-owned firm. Is it realistic to suppose that the agency will possess the staff and the expertise to service all such orders? What about the precedent which such an agency will establish? Every time the U.S. government position differs with the Canadian on similar issues, will a new government agency be organized or an existing one expanded?

The proposal is simply not operational. Recent developments in Communist countries suggest that more and more of their producing enterprises are dealing directly with Western firms, bypassing Western wholesalers and, in some instances, even Communist foreign trade corporations. Emphasis is now being placed on joint industrial cooperation between producing firms. Furthermore, the need for such an agency can be questioned on other grounds. Existing machinery between the U.S. and Canadian governments in recent years has tended to mitigate the negative effects of this problem. If it can be shown that the U.S.-owned firm in Canada is the only firm capable of servicing a particular "communist" order, exceptions such as these have been allowed. The proposal, in short, would only serve the Communists as a propaganda tool, and, in fact, might embarrass Canada more than the United States.

The probability of this proposal being legislated is minimal. It has yet to be shown that substantial export orders have been lost to Canada, and until this is done, no moves are likely to be taken in Canada.

Ten years ago Kingman Brewster, now president of Yale University, carefully documented instances of U.S. anti-trust laws being applied to resident Canadian companies.[5] The Report provides very little additional information on this problem, except to state that it is a problem. One case mentioned in the Report is the proposed takeover by Schlitz of Labatt's Breweries in Canada, which was blocked by the Federal Trade Commission. This case is a poor example, since it is patently not an infringement of Canadian sovereignty for a U.S. firm to be told by an agency of its own government what firm it may or may not acquire.

In recent years this problem has been dealt with through intergovernmental discussions which appear to have been adequate, since no further cases have recently come to light. The Report suggests the addition of a number of measures such as forbidding compliance with foreign anti-trust laws by firms resident in Canada and forbidding removal from Canada of commercial records resulting from a foreign court order.

If this were a problem of major impact and importance and if existing measures were insufficient to deal with whatever problems existed, additional measures might be required. Since, however, neither of these conditions exist, it is unlikely that these recommendations will be given high priority in the legislative proposals of any Canadian government which may be formed in the near future.

An idea which originated with Mr. Gordon and which, if properly organized, could prove to be beneficial to Canada's development is the Canada Development Corporation. This corporation would be expected to play an entrepreneurial role. As a Crown corporation, it would pool sufficient management skills and capital to undertake new ventures in areas of resource development, expansion of export industries and industry reorganization. Further, it would also compete with foreigners in possible takeovers which might involve key industries in Canada, and would, through share purchase, establish a Canadian interest in some foreign-controlled firms.

The success of such a Corporation will hinge on the kind of financing role it will play: equity versus debt financing. If it is the latter, business will not feel itself threatened by a new dimension of competition—government, and needed foreign capital will not be scared away. On the other hand, if it is the former, business will have to be confident that sufficient private capital is not forthcoming and that foreign capital is not discriminated against. If discrimination does occur and foreigners lose confidence in Canada, so will Canadian investors.

Unlike the State Trading Corporation, the idea of a Canada Development Corporation has been around for five or six years and has already been proposed by Liberal governments. While it is quite possible that such a Corporation may become a reality, its effectiveness will depend on the skill of its managers and the financing which it receives. The latter would seem to be the major potential stumbling block to its achieving the role envisaged for it by the Task Force. However, a Canada Development Corporation in some modified form is likely to emerge.

The Canadian government to date does not possess adequate knowledge about the operations of foreign subsidiaries, since it does not require private companies, many of which are U.S.-owned, to report details of their operations. Consequently, the Canadian government is not in position to determine the extent to which U.S. subsidiaries react to policies such as the U.S. balance-of-payments guidelines.

However, the January 1968 U.S. balance-of-payments executive order, which required American firms to repatriate a portion of their earnings from overseas investments, led to a severe run on Canadian foreign exchange reserves. Special representation had to be made by Canada to claim exemption from the U.S. executive order. This was later obtained. This incident clearly indicates the high degree of interdependence on those industrialized economies which invest in each other. Unless each country appreciates the effects of its actions on others, steps are likely to be taken to insulate countries from such adverse effects. These steps can only be protectionist, which will not be in the long-run interest of the world economy.

Mandatory Guidelines?

To obtain such information and to prevent U.S. guidelines from affecting the behavior of U.S.-controlled subsidiaries in Canada, the Report proposes that the Canadian guiding-principles questionnaire be made mandatory. Further, it recommends that the application of the Canadian guiding principles be strengthened by establishing a government agency to coordinate policies for multinational corporations.

The guiding principles questionnaire recommendation is a realistic one, so long as all companies, Canadian- and foreign-owned, are required to report. Eric Kierans has stated: "A full disclosure of the operations of Canadian companies, foreign and domestic, would reveal the information needed for analysis and sound policy-making. The reporting has been required for decades in the United States . . . Attempts made by the Bank of Canada to carry out simple flow-of-funds analyses of Canadian industries were frustrated by the lack of information on subsidiary operations. No data is available on parent-affiliate transactions except through American sources. Subsidiaries are considered private companies because they have a single shareholder. This ludicrous aspect of our Companies' Act should have been removed years ago."[6]

It is probable that the Canadian government will require greater disclosure on the part of all firms in Canada. However, it is doubtful that a special agency will be created for the purpose of discriminating between Canadian- and foreign-owned companies.

According to the authors of the Report, national independence and a rising standard of living are the overriding objectives of Canadians. Because Canadian savings are insufficient to promote the economic goals of the nation, the Canadian government will continue to promote a climate conducive to attracting foreign capital. It is reasonably certain that future national policies will not be designed to discriminate between domestic and foreign capital. On the contrary, recent actions by the Canadian government suggest that the intent will be to bolster confidence in the economy and to encourage entrepreneurship by all Canadian firms regardless of the nationality of the owners. Nonetheless, such an environment will not be nourished at the expense of Canadian independence.

While the more extreme proposals of the Task Force, such as the State Trading Corporation, are not likely to see the light of day, certain recommendations such as legislating greater disclosure of activities by all Canadian companies, promoting Canadian factors of production, and creating a Canada Development Corporation are likely to be implemented. In the case of the more critical issue of extra-territoriality and conflicting national sovereignties, the Canadian government can be expected to work closely with other governments and international bodies dedicated to the establishment of a set of international laws and standards. These laws and standards will attempt to persuade multinational corporations to behave as good corporate citizens in each country in which they do business.

N O T E S

1. Dominion Bureau of Statistics, *The Canadian Balance of International Payments, 1963, 1964 and 1965,* Ottawa.

2. *Royal Commission on Canada's Economic Prospects,* Final Report, Ottawa: Queen's Printer, 1958.

3. "Foreign Ownership and the Structure of Canadian Industry," *Report of the Task Force on the Structure of Canadian Industry,* Queen's Printer, Ottawa, 1968.

4. *Review and Digest Bulletin,* Canadian Export Association, Montreal, March 6, 1968, pp. 1-2.

5. *Law and United States Business in Canada,* Canadian-American Committee, Montreal, 1960.

6. E. W. Kierans, *Challenge of Confidence,* Toronto: McClelland & Stewart, 1967, pp. 85-86.

CHAPTER 11

RICHARD EELLS

*A new dimension—political in nature—
has been added to the tasks
and talents of multinational managers.*

Multinational Corporations: The Intelligence Function

THE MODERN CORPORATION is one of the major social institutions of our time. It is not simply a device for doing business, nor can its social role be properly assessed in terms of size and business "bigness." More interesting is the fact that the modern corporation represents a new system of cooperative social organization, the bringing together of the intelligence, the labor and the investment of large numbers of men. The old combative individualism, so often idealized in classical economic theory, recedes before the advance of this cooperative effort. Sometimes denounced in outworn nineteenth-century ideological terms as a monster spawned by finance capitalism and "imperialism," the modern corporation in fact has emerged in the twentieth century as a positive social force. It has become a nearly indispensable organizational form in a world of rapid social change.

A necessary link in industrial development and an invaluable source of strength for a modernized nation, the corporation is now being assessed in new philosophical terms. The issue of the role of the modern corporation within a single nation, and its place in the structure and dynamics of that nation, arises not only in the United States but also in every developed and developing nation. It arises, too, in one of the great debates of our age: how to bring into being on our violent planet a civil society that assures a "minimum public order"[1] under a regime of law. It is in the context of this larger global community that we must also ask what the role of the modern corporation is.

With the vast expansion of international business by the great corporations of Europe, the Americas, the Far East and Africa, the modern corporation has become multinational. Its institutional significance, both actual and potential, is often unrecognized. It is capable of active collaboration with states and public international organizations. It can and does undertake cooperative tasks as great as the industrialization of Asia and Africa. It can provide cultural interchange on a worldwide scale through the cumulative effects of its social activities in thousands of localities.

Multinational corporations, simply as business enterprises, have a major part to play in lifting world living standards to a higher level. They scan the world for investment opportunities to maximize the results obtainable from their research facilities, technical skills, patents, equipment, capital and experience. They are perhaps indispensable catalysts in the process of economic development.

Beyond the economic function, the multinational corporation in its most highly developed form offers a type of organization that can be turned to many other tasks, regionally and for the world at large. Minimum public order might possibly be supplied by some form of government at an international or supranational level, sufficiently powerful to effect a reduction in conflict. But in most of the world arena, a public order based upon norms of mutual respect does not seem to be achievable without the collaboration of the ablest private-sector organizations.

The multinational corporation at its best is the servant of no one group or country. Its constituencies include all the interests that must be balanced in a good corporate constitutional government.[2] The essential characteristics of such an organization have only recently begun to be comprehended. One specific aspect is especially interesting: the systems and strategies involved in the use of information for survival and growth and for meeting its social responsibilities in the world arena. Any organization, however large in size or great in purpose, depends upon effective means of knowing what is going on, both within and without its walls, as a prerequisite to wise policy. Workable methods of receiving messages from outside the organization, integrating these messages with already accumulated knowledge, and using the combined intelligence as input for formulating the policy of the organization as a whole; then sending out the necessary messages to external receivers—these methods are standard requirements for survival and growth as well as for meeting responsibilities. In the multinational corporation, however, there are special problems related to the environment in which it functions.

International Systems

There are conflicting theories about the international system as it operates today. There are, in fact, many rival views of "international systems"—in the plural. Nor is this only because the political map of the world arena has changed radically since World Wars I and II. Historically, there have been many kinds of international systems. Even the future of the so-called state system, inherited from the treaties of the early modern period in Europe, is in doubt. No one knows whether the system of 150-odd sovereign states will survive both the rush of new knowledge and revolutionary technology—especially technology affecting the art and science of war, and the ecological crises precipitated by logarithmic population growth and perhaps irreversible pollution of air, land and sea resources. Are we moving toward a new age of regional or supranational government in the world arena; possibly toward an age of "world peace under world law"? Are we headed toward the breakdown of the state system under the weight of numerous ministates that cannot conceivably bear their share of the responsibility for preserving peace and order? Models for "the international system" vary all the way from extreme monism to extreme pluralism. Who knows what units of government will at length prevail in a series of reconstructed international systems—if, indeed, one is justified in using the term "international" when the very survival of nations as major participants in the system remains in question.

There is little doubt about the prevailing theory of the international system. In formal, legalistic and conventional terms it is a system of 126 sovereign states represented in the United Nations together with some thirty or more entities—usually national in one sense or another—that are or claim to be sovereign participants in the system. These are the major "actors" of international law. All other entities on the scene are "minor actors" in the process of making and applying the rules of international jurisprudence. The major actors, the nation-states and other public entities (including public international organizations) are the principals in the use of instruments of national and international policy: diplomacy, economics, the use of force, and communicational or ideological strategy. The international system, so conceived, is pluralistic in a limited sense. It is not a monistic system of supranational authority. On the other hand, it excludes numerous nongovernmental organizations (NGOs) and the innumerable private-sector organizations in the world which engage in significant transnational activities. Recognition of this larger and more complex plural structure of the world arena demands new ways of viewing "the international system" that depart from the traditional and conventional maps.

Both public international organizations and the NGOs pose difficult problems for those who rely on simplistic models of the world arena. Traditionalism has required that the world be divided up into territorially defined nation-states with fixed frontiers that mark jurisdictional boundaries. In addition, there are the open seas, the beds in which they rest and the undivided realm of space. Otherwise, the world arena is patterned as a flat mosaic. Yet public international organizations at a higher level have proliferated since World War II along with an increase in the numbers of sovereign states. At the same time private-sector organizations (often called "international" for want of a better term) have also greatly increased both in numbers and in the scope and importance of their activities in the world arena.

Furthermore, the public international organizations—notably in the common markets—have moved appreciably toward supranational status with consequent undermining of claims to absolute sovereignty on the part of member states. All of these developments may foreshadow the dominance of functionalism[3] over traditional legalism in the structure of the world arena. They also serve to remind us of the shadowy line that separates, or seems to separate, the public from the private character of organizations in this arena. One has to talk of "quasi-public" and "quasi-private" organizations and activities and to abandon the black-and-white distinctions of pure theory.

The pluralistic structure of the world arena reflects the many functions that have to be organized and carried on in response to mankind's expectations. In religion, in education, in the arts, the sciences, in the press and other communications, in transport, in health and hygiene, in sports and recreation, as well as for the economic purposes of industry, agriculture and commerce, the multinational corporation—like the nation-state—finds itself one among many. Some of these entities approach public status. Many of the NGOs, which lie within the penumbra of quasi-public institutions between state and private associations, have consultative status at the United Nations Economic and Social Council. The International Labor Organization is one example. A more recent example is the International Telecommunications Satellite Consortium (INTELSAT), a 71-nation network which relies upon various mixes of public and private ownership in the national user organizations. The interweave and interplay of state and privately owned facilities in INTELSAT is characteristic of many of the new transnational functional devices.

Transnational Trends

This trend, heightened during the past half-century, is a response to many regional and worldwide needs that the conventional international system of sovereign states could not meet effectively. The multiplication of organizations and other devices for meeting these needs is often referred to as the "internationalization" of undertakings. The word is misleading. Some of these efforts are truly international—that is to say, undertaken by the joint action of sovereign states. Others are more properly designated as "transnational," transcending to a degree the political boundaries of states and independent of state action.

Transnational action is required because the forces of life on this planet are increasingly transnational. The reach of world commerce, of all science and art and of the human spirit goes beyond transient political boundary lines. The growing incongruence of parochial political jurisdictions in the face of these more expansive life forces is everywhere evident—in metropolitan government, in a still Balkanized Europe, in a world of nation-states that, like other anachronistic political institutions, may at length be swept into the scrap heap of historic curiosities.

World commerce and industry call for new institutions. One response to this demand is the multinational corporation, which is essentially a cross-boundary operation involving "home" and "host" nations (or "sending" and "receiving" states). Actually, the multinational corporation may take the form of a group of corporate entities acting in unison from numerous home bases, "home" meaning variously the locus of the originating or creating or certifying sovereignty. Eventually we may come to speak of these new institutions of industry and commerce in more appropriately ecological terms, relating them in the usages of language to natural zones or eco-systems of our global biosphere, such as regions, continents and the oceans. Oceanography, in particular, will turn up opportunities for extractive and other industries that will make new demands on our powers of conceptualization. As we turn to agri-business, aquaculture and space-dimensioned corporate efforts, the "multinationality" of these efforts will probably recede in importance as other units of political integration rise to prominence. Think, for example, of corporations organized for the development of the seabed under an ocean regime that may be neither national nor international. The ocean regime of the future may be a new kind of political form not known to the traditional international system.[4]

There is also the darker side of transnational forces. The problem of pollution, like the problem of bacterial and parasitical disease, does not stop at national borders. As Margaret Mead writes, "We are altering man's environment in ways we do not understand and in ways that may be disastrous." Since this planet is hopefully to be the chief habitat of the human race for generations to come, despite the major advances in space exploration, there is a pressing need for a worldwide analysis of all the means by which man is befouling his environment and an equally comprehensive program for halting this menace. Even if international machinery is devised for making this effort, transnational organization must be used to supplement it.

The hard fact is that the modern state stands stubbornly in the way of many vital transnational efforts. It might be said that it stands in its own way. Professor Frank Tannenbaum once declared that the old nationalistic system of sovereign states is ending because it cannot protect the human race from annihilation. Wars and threats of wars traditionally used to protect the state and its citizenry are of little use when war becomes indiscriminatingly destructive. "The peace of the world," Tannenbaum wrote, "must rest on an institutional base indifferent to the idea of national security." He observed that over the centuries political entities rise and fall while trade and commerce go on and on. "If the nation-state goes the way of its feudal predecessor," he believed, "the extra-national corporation may well take over."[5]

Polarities in the World Arena

For the present, however, corporate managers must plan their tasks in a world arena of sovereign states which wield coercive powers based on heavy sanctions. This environment is hardly predictable with certainty. Alternative hypotheses, if only for the purpose of short-range corporate planning, to say nothing of twenty- or thirty-year perspectives, are essential. Some observers suggest that only four political powers will count in the future: the United States, the Soviet Union, a united Europe and Japan. Others say that the age of superstates is nearing its end and we are entering upon an era of functional pluralism in which entities of different kinds can be expected to proliferate in the world arena, some nationalistic, some local, others functional.

Meanwhile, the course of the multinational corporation has to be charted amid the bipolarities and the multipolarities of the world arena, amid the economic overlordships of the countries, large or small, in which it does business, and in that vast realm beyond the "open" frontiers with attendant problems of the public order of the oceans and space.

Charting a course in this complex world arena demands certain specific capabilities: knowledge of the decision-making processes and of the strategies of states and other participants in the world arena, and the ability so to define corporate goals that corporate policies can be stated as preferred outcomes and the strategies to achieve these outcomes can be designed.

Decision Strategies

Decision making, whether by nations, groups or individuals, can be regarded in part as a continuous process of combining the informational streams that come to the decision maker from the outside world and from within the organization. And there is a stream of messages moving from the subliminal to the conscious levels of the mind, made up of memories, experiences apparently forgotten and all the psychological events that shape and condition the human personality.

The world arena, because it is not a regime of law, is a place where all participants at times fall back on four types of strategies: coercion, negotiation, use of economic resources and persuasion. It is not realistic to expect that these strategies will be in fact (although in theory they may be) monopolized by sovereign states so long as nonstate claimants can command large powers. Yet there are important differences which relate to any discussion of the strategies of multinational corporations. This is apparent in an examination of the parallel strategies of corporations and states.

Force can seldom be used by corporations directly, except for local police purposes in industrial plants and communities. With multinational corporations in host or receiving countries, it is always questionable whether corporate policy can or should be pursued by means of supportive strategies—military or other—of the home or sending country. A full spectrum of possibilities has to be considered. At one end the citizen, organization or corporation of any nation can hypothetically be left entirely on its own, with no support whatsoever from the home or host governments. At the other end of the spectrum one would postulate unlimited intervention by sovereign governments on behalf of or hostile to a corporation. Neither extreme is realistic. In practice, all corporations make direct and indirect use of the powers and strategies of public governments.

The strategy of negotiation is an essential tool of both corporate and national policy, not only for economic advantage but more importantly for status in the world arena. Status as a matter of law, of prestige or rank, of preferred position in a given situation is an outcome that depends as much on negotiating capability as it does on economic assets. Corporations, which are not among the major "actors" of international law and diplomacy, are nevertheless frequently represented in national capitals and other power centers. Their representatives may be received with more consideration, if less pomp and circumstance, than ambassadors, and the weight of their words may be far more persuasive if for no other reason than corporate command of valuable informational flow.

Economic power is often regarded as the sole key to the role of multinational corporations in world affairs. But the economic instruments of corporate policy are only part of the story. Economics, in national strategy, involves the effective allocation and use of scarce resources, as it does in corporate strategy. But the assets of nation and corporation include all resources that can be sold or withheld from the market. Insofar as these resources include land (the title to which is controlled by sovereign states), minerals, money and other negotiable instruments (the value of which is subject to legal regulation), it seems that economic strategy is heavily derivative of national policy. The dependence of multinational corporations (operating as they do in an arena without an over-arching regime of world law) upon the laws of many different—and sometimes hostile—regimes makes economic strategy in the world arena something different in kind from that of a corporation operating entirely within the home nation. For the multinational corporation, as for the modern corporation generally, the strategy of economics always has to be aligned with the public interest. The economic goals of the corporation cannot safely be at odds for extended periods with the goals of national communities in home and host countries.

The use of persuasion and ideas also has its special character in the multinational corporation. The use of communicational and informational systems is of paramount importance in this type of strategy, since it involves both input and output. The concern is mainly with input. In national governments this is ordinarily called intelligence. One can also speak of corporate intelligence. However, this is but one aspect of communications strategy in general. Intelligence, narrowly viewed, is the knowledge that highly placed government officers and military men must possess to safeguard the welfare of a nation. Intelligence, broadly viewed, is the knowledge that any person or group must have to safeguard the welfare of that person or group.

Corporate Intelligence

As regards corporations, intelligence[6] deals in certain kinds of knowledge. It is produced by the activity of a special kind of organization. It has three principal aspects. The knowledge essential for intelligence of any sort includes: (1) basic descriptive content, (2) current reportorial content and (3) speculative-evaluative content.

Descriptive knowledge is needed of all of the geographic regions where a multinational corporation operates and where social, political, economic or military developments may affect company operations adversely or favorably. Current reportorial content is needed, of course, to keep the basic content up to date. The speculative-evaluative element in corporate intelligence necessarily includes studies of the strategies of both nations and the private-sector groups. It is noteworthy that strategy in this wider sense is a rapidly growing field of the social sciences, in which there are such new topics as conflict-resolution and such new areas of study as the policy sciences.

A special kind of organization is needed to produce such knowledge. Its nature is suggested by the observations of two students of the art and science of intelligence, one of whom (Sherman Kent) specialized in national intelligence, the other (Harold L. Wilensky) in corporate intelligence. The former has observed the intelligence organization of a national government. National intelligence organizations require certain of the characteristics of good business organizations. Kent finds it natural that the language of intelligence organizations should be weighted with words from business. These organizations are engaged in "the manufacture of a product (knowledge) out of raw materials (all manner of data) and labor (highly skilled, but not practical in the business sense of the word)."

The resultant product has to be packaged in ways to suit the diversities of consumer demand, namely in governmental bureaus that use the intelligence output. Some consumers want this output in semi-finished form, for example, as field notes with accompanying comments. Others want it finished, in bulk and in encyclopedic form. The most demanding want it "in small amounts done up in gift wrapping (the one-page summary of the world situation in words of two syllables or less)." In its packaging, the product must both direct and reflect the fluctuations of consumer requirements, the consumer in this case being the receiving corporation.

If a country threatens to go communist, the intelligence on that country must be stepped up. If another country gets ready to take a stand against the intelligence-gathering nation in the matter of bases, then information on that country will have to be increased. Like many a producer of consumer goods, an intelligence organization will have "its greatest marketing success when its product bears the unmistakable signs of superior research, cautious development, sound design and careful production."[7]

Attention can be profitably given to the proper organization of the intelligence function in industry. Harold L. Wilensky, in his study[8] of the way in which knowledge shapes policy, suggests that while some gains in the quality of intelligence are possible from a reorganization of the intelligence function, two points need to be kept in mind to avoid "information pathologies." First, the attitude of the top executive toward knowledge is crucial. This attitude is "a product of his own education and orientation, his exposure to independent sources, his capacity to break through the wall of conventional wisdom." Secondly, the intelligence specialist himself can affect the general tone of policy discourse. This sound advice bypasses excessively elaborate discussions focussed solely on intelligence organization and gets to the heart of the matter: an appreciation by corporate leaders of the need for new knowledge and their respect for its uses in shaping policy.

This may seem elementary advice at a time when science and technology are recognized as major keys to economic growth and development and to the modernization of societies. Yet there is far less recognition of this fact with respect to social sciences than in those branches of knowledge that produce hardware. Wilensky speaks of "structural and doctrinal distortions of information" that seem less likely to occur in rapidly growing organizations that are in contact with a fluid environment, as against dangers that appear in the more established and slower-growing organizations. The alert executive has to know how, in any case, to reach out into a population of "unofficial intelligence agents" as well as to tap often unused sources within the organization itself. The more imaginative administrative leaders "looking toward the bottom, rely on internal communications specialists such as education directors and auditors; looking outward, they rely on contact men such as press officers, lobbyists, mediators. They talk to reporters and researchers investigating their organizations; they establish study commissions or review boards comprised entirely of outsiders, like the members of British Royal Commissions; they institutionalize complaints procedures and thereby subject themselves to systematic, independent criticism from below, as in the case of the ombudsman; they assemble ad hoc committees, kitchen cabinets, general advisors, personal representatives." The unofficial intelligence agents Wilensky regards as independent enough to provide detached judgment yet sufficiently sensitive to the culture of the executive to communicate. He sees them as bringing to bear "the multiple perspectives of marginal men."

This counsel against undue emphasis upon intelligence organization at the expense of sound top executive attitudes toward knowledge—its sources, its substance, its uses—is undoubtedly a counsel of wisdom, and it may be needed in corporations even more than in government bureaus.

One has to be on guard against what Wilensky calls "the anti-intellectual spirit and crude empiricism" that one may encounter not only in unofficial intelligence agents but in intelligence specialists themselves. There remain, however, hard issues of organization of the intelligence function of multinational corporations, and there is little evidence that these issues are sufficiently visible today. Does the new information technology, with the advent of whole staffs of specialists in linear programming, simulation, operations research, electronic data processing, systems analysis, lead to disruptive developments in the authority structure of a company? The new technology is here to stay, but the new specialists are suspect by the old guard in gold braid or in mufti. The old guard fears a take-over by the "Whiz Kids." In corporations, the parallel may be seen in old-guard resistance to the idea of new knowledge as against the "wisdom of the ages" and rejection of the input of a radically revised intelligence function as against the received dogmas of conventional wisdom about trade and commerce.

The fact is that the multinational corporation of today and tomorrow is not adequately conceptualized in the conventional wisdom of economics and politics for effective use of communicational strategy. The intelligence component in the multinational corporate organization must be fitted for use in a new kind of transnational entity vying for place and meaning in the world arena, an arena that is neither an "international market" (whatever that means) nor an "international system" (again a doubtful term).

The world arena is a condition, as well as a place of contention for power, for wealth, indeed for a wide range of goal values. The range of values is not perceived, typically, either in board rooms or in top executive levels of many multinational corporations. How to introduce a modern intelligence function into these corporations, with attitudes and an organization that meet the onrush of change in the world arena, is one of the most challenging tasks of business management today.

Lest anyone think that organization of the intelligence function in the multinational corporation is merely desirable but not vitally important, it is well to consider some of the substantive issues that now confront many multinational corporate managers.

1. Whose instrument is the multinational corporation? The stockholders'? The home country's? The host country's? Is it perhaps an indispensable instrument of mankind in its search for a viable structure of world economy and, more basically, man's search for a way to preserve our invaluable biosphere?

For several generations managers have not thought of multinational companies as the instrument of any group. They have sought, in theory, to be impartially responsive to stockholders, consumers, workers and suppliers. They claim to be responsive also to the requests of the government of whatever country they are working in. But what would the working policy of the company be if it referred these received doctrines to the hard-nosed analysis of its intelligence staff? Does that staff insist upon balance in the intelligence input? The intelligence files of the company now contain far more intelligence about consumers of its products than about any other group. This preponderance of data may reflect the doctrine that by reason of the economic votes consumers cast when making market choices, they will affect the future of the company immediately and directly, as though all mankind were made up of consumers. Intelligence input might well correct this perilous imbalance.

2. What, if any, are the economic, social and political responsibilities of a multinational corporation to the home country and the host countries? Let us assume that established policies include the following general features: a) good products at fair prices, b) the rights of employees, c) economic and social cooperation with the government when requested, d) initiative in local and transnational community problems, e) conservation of natural resources, f) better international communication and understanding, g) support of cultural traditions and popular aspirations. Is this a complete and timely list?

The intelligence organization of the company should systematically collect data pertinent to all of these but should not stop there. It should ask how these responsibilities are to be exercised, on whose behalf and with what measures of accountability. Most importantly it should ask whether the very concept of corporate responsibility requires complete revision in the light of conditions that prevail in the world arena. Only in the local community does the company take initiative, and even there it strives to keep its role inconspicuous. In several underdeveloped countries, for instance, the local school system developed out of the company's training programs, and company managers are in effect the directors of that system, but they never admit to being anything more than consultants.

3. What sanctions, if any, are available to enforce the economic, social and political responsibilities of the multinational corporation?

Apart from commercial codes and antitrust laws, which the company strictly obeys, there would appear at first to be few formal sanctions. The effective sanctions seem to be informal and popular. The general public is made up of consumers. If only a small percen-

tage of them were to take offense at the company or any of its
corporate colleagues, sales could suffer severely. The company believes it is guided by "public opinion." For more than a generation
it has been gathering intelligence about public opinion in all parts
of the world. Updating its intelligence function, the company now
finds that there is a wide range of formal and severe sanctions that
both home and host governments command and can use to the
disadvantage, as well as the advantage, of the company. The "public," moreover, which had appeared to be essentially a public of
consumers, now turns out to be strongly imbued with nationalistic
drives.

In some sectors public opinion reflects Third-World commitments of nonalignment in the epochal struggle between East and
West. Does this indicate the need for corporate policy that is
explicitly "geocentric," avoiding either the Scylla of "ethnocentrism"
(home-country orientation) or the Charybdis of "polycentrism"
(host-country orientation)? The "ultimate goal of geocentrism" in
multinational corporations "is a worldwide approach in both headquarters and subsidiaries" in the constructs of Howard V. Perlmutter, and this geocentrism is "expressed by function, product
and geography."[9] The intelligence work of a company will necessarily be geared to meet one or the other of these orientations.

One may assume that multinational corporate enterprise in the
world arena is simply enterprise but that, because of the disorder
which now prevails in that marketplace, managers of such enterprises must do all that they reasonably can to work toward a regime
of minimum public order there. This means heavy involvement of
the corporate intelligence function in both public and private efforts toward the organization of world peace. Or one may assume
that the multinational corporation should go much further than this
and contribute actively and systematically toward a world regime
of optimum public order: embracing, that is to say, "the totality of
a community's legally protected goal values and implementing
institutions" and a public order which seeks "beyond an effective
community monopolization of force, the richest production and
widest sharing of all values."[10]

The relevant community, in the latter case, may not be worldwide for a given corporation; it may be regional or confined to a

noncontiguous group of countries. In any case, it is clear that the future of the intelligence function in multinational corporations will vary greatly, depending upon which of these positions is taken by those who govern them.

N O T E S

1. This term derives from Myres S. McDougal and Florentino P. Feliciano, *Law and Minimum World Public Order*, New Haven and London: Yale University Press, 1961.

2. This subject is discussed in: Richard Eells, *The Government of Corporations*, New York: The Free Press of Glencoe, 1962; R. Eells & Clarence Walton, *Conceptual Foundations of Business*, Revised Edition, Homewood, Illinois: Richard D. Irwin, Inc., 1969; and Sanford A. Lakoff, "Private Government in the Managed Society" in Roland J. Pennock & John W. Chapman, *Voluntary Associations*, New York: Atherton Press, 1969.

3. See Ernest B. Haas, *Beyond the Nation-State: Functionalism and International Organization*, Stanford: Stanford University Press, 1964; Charles A. McClelland, *Theory and the International System*, New York: The Macmillan Co., 1964; James P. Sewell, *Functionalism and World Politics*, Princeton: Princeton University Press, 1966.

4. See Myres S. McDougal and William T. Burke, *The Public Order of the Oceans: A Contemporary International Law of the Sea*, New Haven and London: Yale University Press, 1962; and Elizabeth Mann Borgese, "The Ocean Regime: A Suggested Statute for the Peaceful Uses of the High Seas and the Sea-Bed Beyond the Limits of National Jurisdiction," Santa Barbara, California: The Center for the Study of Democratic Institutions, October 1968.

5. Frank Tannenbaum, *The Balance of Power in Society*, New York: The Macmillan Co., 1969.

6. A basic work on this subject is Sherman Kent, *Strategic Intelligence for American World Policy*, Princeton: Princeton University Press, 1951, which I follow here to some extent. See also Roger Hilsman, *Strategic Intelligence and National Decisions*, Glencoe, Illinois: The Free Press, 1956.

7. Kent, *op. cit.*

8. Harold L. Wilensky, *Organizational Intelligence: Knowledge and Policy in Government and Industry*, New York and London: Basic Books, Inc., 1967.

9. Howard V. Perlmutter, "The Tortuous Evolution of the Multinational Corporation," *Columbia Journal of World Business*, January-February 1969.

10. McDougal and Feliciano, *op. cit.*

CHAPTER 12

FRANK TANNENBAUM

*Political entities rise and fall. Trade and
commerce continue. If today's nation-states go the way
of their feudal predecessors, the extra-national
corporation may well take over, illustrating Darwin's law of*

The Survival

of the Fittest

EFFORTS TO ORGANIZE THE WORLD FOR PEACE past and present have always broken down in the end. This is a simple statement of the historical record. One cannot argue lack of good will or honesty of purpose, lack of or a genuine desire to achieve an effective international body that would take on itself the role of peace-keeping. But, as the whole world knows, successive efforts have been frustrated. The League of Nations was the latest great failure. Unhappy though it is to say, the United Nations may be headed in the same direction.

There are many reasons why this has happened. Human affairs are complicated matters. They have been shaped and influenced by a myriad of "causes" which taken together have given us our present dubious heritage—a threat of human annihiliation, and an apparent inability to stem the drift towards converting the threat into an imminent convulsion. A casual evaluation of the daily record suggests that man seems to have no instrumentality at hand to reverse the armaments race or to stop him from the last decision he would probably ever be called upon to make—give the signal that would release thermonuclear warfare.

Such a possibility would only seem consistent with a world gone mad or held in the grip of individuals who lack "reason," conscience, Christian charity or ordinary common sense. In fact, there are good but worried people now in the United States who are prepared to put the 200,000,000 population underground as a security measure against such a war, and there are others who seem to accept the prospects of a loss of 20 to 30 million American lives in an effort to defeat the enemy.

The mere statement of these matters as possibilities, as reasonable things that prudent men are trying to comprehend and plan for, so as to mitigate what seems to them even greater horrors, raises fundamental questions of why this possibility is upon the world. It will not do to blame it on the scientists who learned how to split the atom and manufacture the atomic bomb. The problem is not a scientific one. It is not even primarily military. It is political because it involves the nature and function of the state itself.

The modern nation-state is of relatively recent origin. Some historians place its emergence as a result of the Reformation. Others mark its beginnings at about the time of the French Revolution, or as one of its major consequences. Be that as it may. The primary definition of the modern nation-state is that it can protect its citizens from external attack and maintain internal order. The emphasis upon protection from external aggression has most clearly set the tone and defined the character of the modern state. Nationalism, in fact, and all that goes with it require the ability to keep the state absolutely sovereign, which in essence means the ability to impede any intrusion upon its territory, interests or dignity.

In a world of competitive nation-states, such as Europe represented after the Reformation when France and Spain were expanding and consolidating their future at the expense of their neighbors, and after the French Revolution when France was trying to impose its rule upon the rest of Europe, questions of national security became the prime consideration. The First and the Second World Wars were logical by-products of this system; so is the Cold War; so is the armaments race; so are the struggles in various parts of the world that have followed the Second World War. In each case the attack is against a "sovereign nation" to subjugate it, to impose upon it another loyalty, and even another system. Fear of conquest governs the political attitude of all nation-states toward the rest of its world.

The many alliances, treaties, understandings, mutual defense pacts, disarmament meetings, peace congresses, and international courts undertaken because of security considerations have all failed in the end. The history of the sovereign state is a bloody one and it could not be otherwise. A state absolutely sovereign as Thomas Hobbes saw it, accepting no infringements on its rights, confined in a geographic boundary, beset by enemies equally sovereign, equally ambitious and presumably equally well or better armed could only be at war or preparing for war. The nation-state system is intrinsically unstable and the prospect of war is ever present. The improved weapons placed in its hands by the new technology have merely increased the size and the human and material costs of warfare.

The attempts to form international organizations have not seriously changed the nature of the system or the relations of the states to each other. The League of Nations witnessed Mussolini's attack upon Ethiopia, Japan's invasion of China, the Chaco War in South America and other conflicts as well. The United Nations have seen numerous small wars, the blockade of Berlin, the Korean War, the war in Vietnam, the very real danger of a war between Greece and Turkey and the conflagrations in the Middle East, to mention only a few of the more evident examples. And one should not forget the confrontation over Cuba between the United States and Russia.

An organization of the world made up of sovereign states is not a satisfactory base for maintaining international stability. Each member in any real crisis, or even in lesser matters, behaves as a nation-state; when it takes a position in the United Nations on any subject, it does so in accord with its conception of its own interests. Every debate, every vote, every speech reflects this outstanding fact. Anyone who listened to the debate over the recent war in the Middle East will testify that not a single state put the international order before its own national interest, nor could it do so. The nation-state system by the very nature of its overriding involvement in the question of national security cannot act otherwise. Unfortunate though it may be, there is no evidence that an enduringly effective international order can be built on the political unit we know as the nation-state.

It is not that having described the impasse men and nations find themselves in that I have the answer. I wish I did. The question is of an order to which no answer can be invented. The history, traditions and manner of thought of the last five hundred or more years underlie the present situation. The horror it implies for human destiny is the ossification and obliteration of mankind. Surely not even the vision of the Apocalypse was more convulsive than the horror hidden in the "balance of terror" between the great powers. And all of this is upon us because of the state's search for absolute security—which it is still pursuing and which it must pursue while it exists. How much longer will the national political state survive—(if it is not destroyed by the atomic bomb)—another five hundred years? Probably not. If it can *not* supply protection for its citizens, it has lost its major reason for being. This applies to both the little and the big nation. Nor as we have seen, can the state build a viable international order. Its nationalism stands in the way. It has no possibility of doing so.

If, as some assume, the movement towards European unity suggests a decline of nationalism, then in the present state of affairs it would simply be replaced by a larger nationalism. The appearance of an all-European nationalism would not necessarily advance an international organization; it might even make it more difficult to approve the surrender of a larger sovereignty which would be involved. The point really is that international organization cannot be built on the nation, or a combination of nations with national characteristics; it must have a different genesis.

An Alternative Base

If such a base could be found upon which to build an extranational political institution, then indeed the external role of the nation-state would decline and gradually disappear and the problems of security—national security—would become meaningless. Security for the nation would exist because no one would bother about it just as no one now fusses about religious orders, even those that have an ancient military history. This must sound like the wildest sort of dream, like the emanations of some Utopian prophet with no sense of the real world and therefore irrelevant. I wish it were irrelevant. Then the problem it tries to deal with would no longer exist. But it does exist and it cannot be solved. It can only be bypassed and allowed to wither away. The threat to the security of the nation-state must first become meaningless before the present danger of atomic weapons can come to seem irrelevant to the needs of mankind. The arms cannot be destroyed as long as there is danger to the security of the state. The threat to national security must become meaningless before the sword will be beaten into plowshares.

This seemingly impossible idea, of a disappearing security problem because the nation-state can no longer provide it, is a daily growing phenomenon going unnoticed. If the nation-state can no longer protect its own against annihilation from the outside, it in fact becomes functionless but that in itself would not create the supra-national order. If we are ever going to have an international order, then it will have to rest upon some other base, preferably one that is extra-national by its very nature; one that bypasses the problem of national security. Such a base does exist and is growing stronger and more inclusive with every day that passes. It comes from an existing and expanding body of international organizations which are multiplying daily in function and number. They are supra-national in their very existence, plan and purpose. Their managers, governors, authorities think in extra-national terms; their personnel is indifferent to the nation-state except as an impediment.

This extra-national body is the corporation—the extra-national corporate body as I would prefer to call it. Others have called it the multinational corporation—or even the "cosmocorp." It is natural because it has its origin in performing a needed function. It is as natural as was the slow growth of a trading and commercial community that in the end created the nation-state as a substitute for medieval order.

Other extra-national institutions have long existed. Religious bodies like the Roman Catholic Church, the Greek Orthodox Church, scientific bodies, the International Red Cross and hundreds of other corporate bodies exercise jurisdiction over property, have thousands of employees, have contractual relations in a hundred different countries, have their own internal systems of discipline, their own police force and administrative arrangements. They make rules and regulations that affect the lives, comfort, convenience and fortune of thousands of people in many parts of the earth. These bodies govern the enterprise under their control and in doing so, exercise powers that border on the sovereign.

None of these religious or eleemosynary organizations have demonstrated the vitality and growth of the ubiquitous business corporation. An international telephone company provides a good example of a business penetrating national considerations. It is indifferent to national boundaries and unconcerned about national security. It becomes aware of the state for the most part as an impediment, an obstruction. Its servants are only involved in fulfilling a function wherever it needs to be satisfied: in the Sahara, Switzerland, Vietnam or Paraguay. This is equally true of the international airline company. Its pilots, mechanics, ticket agents, financiers, passengers, may come from any and all places. Its concern is with speed, safety, schedules, costs, landing fields, trained pilots, weather control, absolutely effective communication. The questions that bother the nation-state—security, national interest, customs, tariffs, fear of invasions, danger of violations of the border are in this instance matters of irritation or indifference. Those same considerations apply to international banks, to some of the large manufacturing and distribution companies like Unilever, Philips Lamp, Standard Oil Company (New Jersey), Shell and others.

When an international airline company decides to establish a terminal in a new "nation" for the first time, it has performed an act of greater import to the body politic of that nation than most acts of the government. When an international bank decides to make a loan, it exercises a judgment, the political consequences of which may prove great indeed—it may save the government from being overthrown, or it may stimulate an industry that will provide employment for many, increase the national income and raise the standard of living of all.

When an international oil company opens up an oil field, as has happened in Venezuela or Iran, it may change the face of the nation and lay the foundations of a modern society. In doing so it exercises

authority equal to, or in some instances greater than, the local
government. It makes contracts, acquires land, lays pipelines, brings
in shipping, develops communications, roads, builds schools, brings
in a great variety of skills which are gradually passed on to the
local population, changes the social structure of the body politic,
stimulates a labor movement, a skilled working class, a middle class
of distributors, a wealthy class of lawyers, politicians and local participants; and by the royalties and taxes it pays permits the government for the first time in its history to perform those services
expected of it in a modern society. The government can build schools,
expand its university, develop a national road system, etc., etc. The
powers of the corporate body are very great but its influence upon
the society in which it operates may be greater. The acts of a supra-
national corporate body have in effect the characteristics of a
sovereign state; they may be unavoidable—such as the need for the
right of way for a pipeline which has to be provided or the corporate
body will not be able to function in this place, just as the government cannot build a highway unless its legislature will authorize the
funds and the courts uphold the rights of eminent domain.

The international oil corporation, the international communications corporation, the international bank are natural bodies. They
are called into being by the need in our time for the function which
they and they alone can perform. The modern world is their presence. They are the essence of the extra-national system that has
grown and expanded at a rate faster than the population explosion,
or literary output or whatever. In that sense they perform functions
more essential than that of sovereignty, or better perhaps, functions
that only they can perform and without which the modern state
would be seriously crippled. And these functions have to be performed by an international corporate body and cannot be performed
by any other agency. The nation-state cannot run the international
tele-communication system, or the international airline system, or
the international distributing system.

These are private institutions operating for a profit. The profit is
the wage that keeps the system going. The function is public, essential and indispensable if the people living in the nation are to
share the growing exchange of goods, ideas and people. The picture
is obscured by the presence of a few large nation-state powers like
the United States or Russia. They seemingly could do many things

for themselves, perhaps not as efficiently or effectively, but the smaller political bodies in Latin America, in Europe, in Africa and Asia are completely dependent upon the "sovereign" corporate body —the international banking system, the international oil industry, the international communications system—for their participation in the world. And when an international corporate body decides to build an airfield in a small African or Asian country, it in fact exercises an act of sovereignty—no one can compel it to do so and local government can only stop it from doing so to its own disadvantage and increasing isolation in the modern world. Such an act would be equivalent to a defeat in a war.

An Extra-national Commitment

This corporate body of which we have been speaking is increasing in number, in power, in prestige, in size, in the areas of modern enterprise that it embraces. Its purpose is service—in response to manifest needs—and it has a "life everlasting" as long as the service needs to be performed. Its ownership is irrelevant, for the owner does not either manage or control it except in legal fiction, and it can be owned by people all over the globe. Its management can be drawn from wherever competence is to be found; its profits may be distributed among owners in all nations; its technical personnel and labor force can be, and often are, completely international.

Equally, or more significant, the international corporate body is devoted to the performance of an international function. Its total commitment is extra-national. It has no concern with boundaries, national interest, local cultural pride, regional idiosyncrasies except only as they favor or hinder the performance of the function for which the corporate body has come into existence. This international corporate body is thus autonomous within the state where it operates. It draws its capital, finance, skill, material from wherever it finds it. It is at the service of the nation but is not of it. Its life will go on when the present government has fallen, when the state even has changed its character by merger, annexation, defeat or whatever.

The international communication corporations will go on no matter what the political map will look like fifty years from now. The functional service is more durable than the political form or territorial prescription. The telephone system operates in both East and West Germany, in both North and South Korea. The international corporate body is in fact extra-national and stands indifferent to it. Its personnel thinks, plans, and operates on a supra-national basis. The international corporate body "governs" functionally across all borders wherever it has found a natural role, a service it alone can provide.

We thus really have two systems of "sovereignty" in the world: the state, large and small, and the supra-national corporate body. The first is on the defensive, probably on the decline, troubled by fear, anxious over its security, living by permission of those who could annihilate it on any day. Even the great powers stand in fear that the "balance of terror" will break down or that some fallible human being will miscalculate and blunder to produce a cataclysm which may see the end of all life on the face of the earth.

The nation-state has tried to build an international system for its own salvation but has always failed. Its commitment to absolute sovereignty has impeded its ability to contrive an extra-national body which would submerge and limit the state. If we live by the experience of the past, the modern nation-state cannot build an extra-national body to its own undoing as a nation-state bent on security above all else.

The second "sovereignty" is the extra-national corporate body. It is growing in number, size, influence, power, functions and independence. Excepting for the very great powers, the smaller nations are increasingly dependent upon the extra-national corporate body for the means of economic development, if not for survival. These corporate bodies are service organizations that perform their essential functions for a fee—such as interest on a bank loan, or a profit on oil distribution. They are apolitical but possess great political influence if not political power. Their international character makes them indifferent to local political squabbles. Their supra-national structure places them beyond the need for national security so essential to the state. They have one great vulnerability.

Clearly, if the state manages to blunder into a holocaust which consumes the races of men that people the earth, then the international corporate bodies will go down the stream and be washed away as if they had never existed. But if we assume that life is carried by some creative impulse that will not die, that man has always contrived a new structure when the old one was worn out, when it could no longer provide for, and protect those whom it was meant to serve, then one would expect what has happened in the past to be repeated in the present impasse. The extra-national corporate body would seem the logical basis for the contrivance of a non-military supra-national order.

Precedents

This is a strange destiny for the corporation. But primitive instances of it have been seen in the past: the Knights Templar and the Hanseatic League, for example. These functioned well for a time within the boundaries of the then known world. The reduction of the earth to the size of a large ancient parish with many autonomous governments makes the supra-national corporate body the natural bond between them. The speed of communication, the increased mobility and proliferation of the sciences make corporate organization increasingly evident, necessary and inevitable.

An industrialized world is held together by the large number of corporate bodies and by their widening role. The corporation groups the nationals into a new loyalty—a functional identity across all borders. The day may well come when the majority of people in all nations will have their functional loyalties to one or more supra-national corporate bodies. They may well become conscious of basic commitments, values and interests unrelated to the state or the nation.

This is probably inevitable if the industrial and technological upheaval works its way as it seems bound to do. The international corporate bodies would have differences with other similar organizations. But the differences would have little to do with nationalism or military security. What seems implicit in this development is a new supra-national order based not upon the state obsessed by security needs but resting on the naturally extra-national bodies that are visibly enveloping men and states over a large portion of the globe.

Time is the essence of change and transition. How long will it take for the corporate body to be so evidently the international structure as to make the formal legal organs contrived by the nation-state irrelevant because the state itself will become irrelevant to international dealings? It took many centuries before the commercial revolution gradually evolved a middle class that found the feudal order unacceptable and gradually contrived the nation-state to serve its ends. One cannot assume that so profound a structural change as here envisaged can go on without political implications, and without a shift in political power. It is difficult to see the way this shift of political power will occur—but that it will take place there can be no doubt. It would have been equally difficult to foresee the modern state in the glories of a feudal society.

How long will it take? Will the nation-state hold on long enough to permit this to occur or will it destroy itself and mankind as well? What about Russia and China? The answer here, I think, is clear. If Russia and China are going to become industrialized in the sense that the United States is industrialized, then they will go the same way—the international corporate body will reach over into the closed state as in some measure it already does. The international corporate body is a natural functional institution and it can only be kept from its role if there is no extensive industrial development. In either case the closed communist or the non-communist states will either destroy each other or persevere long enough to allow the unforeseen growth of the international corporate body to take on the requisite political role and bypass the problem of security while leaving to the state the police powers for internal civil needs.

This is the major issue confronting mankind. It is a question of time and no one can say whether man will allow himself the mercy of surviving long enough to find a way of transferring international political powers to the corporate bodies that have come into being unwittingly and whose commitments are primarily functional, to render service where it is needed—indifferent and untroubled by the issues of national security and sovereignty.

III

SOME UNIQUE FEATURES OF WORLD BUSINESS

CHAPTER 13

WARREN J. KEEGAN

*Tax administration requires an appropriate
distribution of multinational corporate income.
Section 482 of the Code provides
the guidelines in the United States.*

Multinational Pricing

Is a Complex Task:

The Case of the U.S.

PRICING IN A SINGLE NATIONAL MARKET is a complex subject that has long baffled student and teacher alike. International pricing, fully in this tradition, has overwhelmed not only students and teachers, but executives and government officials and their legal and accounting advisors. This is not surprising.

In addition to all of the factors which should be considered in pricing for a single national market, the international pricing decision involves multinational accounts demanding equal treatment, transportation costs and product adaptation costs. It also involves problems associated with national tax codes and the authority of tax collectors to review intra-company and inter-corporate transfer pricing (i.e., controlled as opposed to market-determined or "arm's-length" pricing) across national boundaries.

Transfer pricing includes not only the sale of tangible property ranging all the way from raw materials to intermediate and finished goods, but also the pricing of money (loans), services (research and development, consulting, managerial assistance), the use of tangible property (equipment, buildings) and the transfer or use of intangible property (patents, copyrights, trademarks, procedures, forecasts, estimates, customer lists). In addition to the normal internal control problems posed by such transfers in a domestic environment, when a corporation spans national boundaries and tax jurisdictions, such transfers are subject to review and must be accepted by frequently inscrutable national tax authorities whose interests in the transfer and approaches to taxation are potentially in conflict. When the transfer involves tangible property, the customs authorities must also accept the transfer price. Their interest in a high import price to maximize duties is in direct conflict with the income tax authority's interest in a low price, which raises local company income and thereby raises income tax revenues.

For companies headquartered and principally owned in the United States, the U.S. review of transfer pricing is of preeminent importance. It is in the United States that these companies consolidate the earnings of their various foreign activities, and it is there that they have their principal base of manufacturing operations and their major accumulation of know-how. Both the goods and know-how transferred from the United States to foreign affiliates must have a price. The prices and distribution of profits that result from such transfers are reviewed and must be accepted by the tax authorities. Thus the sheer volume of transfers subject to review makes the U.S. enforcement in this area of particular interest because the U.S. government has clearly been a leader among nation-states in the development of policy and rules in this vitally important area. Under the direction of the former Assistant Secretary of the U.S. Treasury, Stanley S. Surrey, extensive and detailed regulations in this area were promulgated last year[1] and now serve as the guidelines against which individual cases will be judged.

The Regulation

SECTION 482

"In any case of two or more organizations, trades or businesses (whether or not incorporated, whether or not organized in the United States, and whether or not affiliated) owned or controlled directly or indirectly by the same interests, the Secretary or his delegate may distribute, apportion, or allocate gross income, deductions, credits, or allowances between or among such organizations, trades, or businesses, if he determines that such distribution, apportionment, or allocation is necessary in order to prevent evasion of taxes or clearly to reflect the income of any of such organizations, trades, or businesses."

Internal Revenue Code, 1954

For the U.S.-based multinational corporation, Section 482, although only one sentence long, is one of the most important single provisions of the U.S. tax law affecting international pricing practice. Interestingly, this section of the code is relevant to international business principally as it has developed during the past two decades. In earlier years, the great bulk of international transactions were in the form of trade between U.S. companies and independent foreign purchasers. Because the parties in this transaction were unrelated, the prices they set were by definition arm's length. In the past two decades U.S. participation in the international economy has been increasingly dominated by direct marketing and direct manufacturing abroad by the subsidiaries of U.S. companies.

There are two basic reasons for the incorporation of Section 482 in the tax code. The first and no doubt the original reason is potential corporate tax evasion. Since no more than $25,000 of income

---

ARM'S LENGTH

In drafting the Section 482 regulations, the U.S. Treasury frequently referred to an "arm's length" price. This is the price which would be charged in an independent transaction between unrelated parties. The application of this standard to transactions between related parties requires the identification of comparable "uncontrolled" transactions.

---

bears the lowest tax rate (now 22%), there is an incentive to multiply the number of corporate entities so that, if possible, no one of them will have income exceeding $25,000.

Internationally, the possibility of deferring U.S. taxes exists wherever there are foreign tax jurisdictions with tax rates lower than the U.S. rate. Under the current tax law, the U.S. shareholder of a controlled foreign corporation is not taxed on his share of that company's income until it is returned to the United States in the form of dividends if more than 70% of the income derives from manufacturing operations within the foreign country as opposed to non-manufacturing income (rents, royalties, licensing fees and dividends) or is income from services performed for related persons outside the foreign country, or income from sales of property to related persons outside the foreign country.

Thus the opportunity for U.S. tax deferral, which is in fact a tax reduction, exists in international operations whenever a company generates manufacturing income in foreign tax jurisdictions and whenever the same company generates income from any source in foreign countries which have tax rates lower than those in the United States.

So long as a tax-haven subsidiary obtains at least 70% of its income from manufacturing operations and sales within the foreign country, it can fully shield non-operating income from U.S. taxes. Since in recent times the philosophy of the U.S. tax system has been income-source neutrality or the application of U.S. taxes to the income of U.S. citizens wherever it is earned, the tax deferral feature of the present tax law is a major deviation from this philosophy and, in the eyes of the Treasury, a tax escape, for which Section 482 is a remedy.

The second basic justification for Section 482 applies even when the tax deferral escape is not a factor, as is the case when a U.S. company has income in foreign jurisdictions which tax income at rates equal to or greater than U.S. rates. From the viewpoint of the U.S. Treasury, Section 482 is still needed to insure that the U.S. government gets its fair share of the taxes on income earned by a multinational corporate system. In order to get its fair share, the U.S. tax authority must insure that multinational corporate systems fully account for all income earned in the United States. In order to do this, U.S. companies in such systems must fully price all transfers to foreign affiliates. When transfers are not fully priced, the income of the company's foreign affiliates will be artificially inflated, and taxes on this income will go to the foreign tax jurisdiction. As long as the United States allows a credit against the U.S. tax liability for foreign taxes paid, any exaggeration of the true income of foreign subsidiaries owned by U.S. companies will increase the tax revenues of foreign tax jurisdictions at the expense of the U.S. Treasury.

Before the Revenue Act of 1962, the U.S. tax on foreign income from all sources was deferred until returned to the United States as a dividend or distribution. Throughout the 1950's, U.S. international expansion continued at a rapid pace. Because of the widespread utilization of tax havens to take advantage of the tax deferral provisions and the growth in volume of transactions between the U.S. parent and foreign affiliates, the Internal Revenue Service (IRS) began to show increasing interest in Section 482 enforcement in order to reduce what was considered to be an escape from U.S. taxes.

Before 1961, the IRS's record of winning cases under this section was not impressive. Treasury representatives, therefore, requested that the section be amended by the Revenue Act of 1962 to expand the authority of the IRS and to provide a formula approach for certain allocations. Congress did not agree to this request, but the Conference Committee report noted that "Section 482 already contains broad authority to the Secretary of the Treasury to allocate income and deductions" and recommended that the Treasury "explore the possibility of promulgating regulations under this authority which would provide additional guidelines and formulae for the allocation of income and deductions in cases involving foreign income."

With this assurance that the existing section of the Internal Revenue Code contained substantial authority, the IRS expanded its International Operations Division and began to exercise authority to a much greater extent. Numerous substantial deficiencies based on new and varied theories were charged. According to one observer, "the IRS apparently took the view that it would determine what authority it did possess under Section 482 and if taxpayers did not wish to accept the deficiencies, the courts would spell out the scope of the Service's authority."[2]

Types of Transactions Regulated

The immediate question facing executives and their tax advisors is what can a company do in the international pricing area in the light of current tax law. The Treasury regulations spell out approaches to international pricing in considerable detail. The IRS is bound to follow these approaches in its enforcement efforts. Very importantly, however, Treasury regulations do not have the weight of law until they are accepted by the courts. Thus, it is important to examine the regulations carefully not because they are the present tax law, but because they will guide the IRS review of transactions between related business organizations during the coming years.[3] They provide rules and procedures for determination of taxable income for five specific kinds of transaction.

Loans and Advances. The regulations provide that an arm's-length rate of interest must be charged for all loans and advances. If the creditor was not regularly involved in making loans to unrelated parties, a mechanical formula is applied which requires that the interest be at least 4% but not more than 6% per annum, unless the taxpayer can establish a more appropriate rate for the specific circumstances involved. These rules apply to all forms of bona fide indebtedness including money or other consideration whether or not evidenced by a written instrument, as well as indebtedness arising in the course of business out of sales, leases or any contribution of capital. The interest period does not commence until six months after the indebtedness arises or a later date if regular trade practices permit comparable balances to remain outstanding without charging interest. The regulations on loans and advances are straightforward and reasonably clear; no problems of interpretation are anticipated.

Performance of Services. The general rule is that when marketing, managerial, administrative, technical or other services are performed by a member of a controlled group on behalf of another member or members, an arm's-length charge must be made to the member or members benefiting from the services. All allocations under this section are subject to a benefits test which provides that allocations made shall be consistent with the benefits intended from the services, not the benefits which actually accrued. The regulations further provide that when the arm's-length charge for services is determined with reference to cost, all costs, both direct and indirect, associated with the groups performing the services must be included.

Fortunately, the regulations conclude by providing that when a company has allocated charges for services "by employing in a consistent manner a method of allocation and apportionment which is reasonable and in keeping with sound accounting practice, such method will not be disturbed." An example in the regulations of an allocation practice which would be acceptable is a reasonable and consistent apportionment of executive officer cost among domestic members of a controlled group. The domestic practice could be the standard for allocations to foreign members.

The regulations also provide that except in the case of services which are an integral part of the business activity of the member rendering the service or the member receiving the benefit of the service, the arm's-length charge shall be deemed to be equal to the costs or deductions incurred in providing the services. Both direct and indirect costs are to be taken into account. An example of a direct cost would be the compensation and expenses of the international division staff. Indirect costs include the overheads of departments incurring direct costs and an appropriate share of the costs of supporting departments and groups. Specific examples in the regulation of indirect costs are compensation of top management and the services of a domestic advertising department which functions for the benefit of a foreign subsidiary.

The problem with these regulations is their dogged adherence to a pristine concept of the arm's-length charge. Unfortunately, for most of the services involved there is no such thing as an arm's-length charge. The headquarters management function is an example. This function is either performed within the organizational framework of a group of controlled companies or it is not performed at all. The same is true of many administrative services. There is no convenient external benchmark to establish the arm's-length price of many corporate services. Moreover, there is frequently no agreement within the controlled system on the value of such services. Headquarters executives may view these services as extremely valuable, while the subsidiary or field executives might view the same services as less than worthless.

Reasonable Allocations of Costs

The possibilities for acrimonious debate about the benefits which are derived from services performed within a system of controlled entities is endless, and the arm's-length standard will do nothing to clear the air since it simply does not exist. Given the general presumption under tax law that the government is correct until proven otherwise, any company faced with an allocation decision by the IRS based on some benefits test can either acquiesce and accept the allocation, or challenge it and face a long, difficult, expensive and possibly fruitless effort to prove the IRS wrong. This is the kind of arbitrary and potentially capricious tax enforcement that any country can do without. Meanwhile, companies are well advised to allocate charges for services performed in the United States on behalf of foreign affiliates according to their own best estimates of sound cost accounting practice and thereby seek refuge from IRS allocation decisions regarding services. The best defense here is a good offense. Companies should take the initiative and make allocations which they feel are reasonable. When this is done, a company has provided an a priori demonstration of its effort to allocate costs and comply with Section 482. Companies that do not take the initiative should prepare to live with the consequences, which will be IRS allocation.

As for tax policy in this area, it is essential that the Treasury clearly establish economic and administrative feasibility in addition to technical elegance as criteria for future regulations. If technical elegance and practical feasibility conflict, the latter must take precedence. This should be clearly stated. The alternative is the present state of affairs where those sections of the regulations calling for determinations which are wholly impractical, given the present state of the development of accounting theory and management science, will simply be ignored by the IRS and the courts. The result will be a tax law based largely on case decisions. This is unfortunate, for if ever a clear and feasible set of regulations were needed, this is an instance. The direction which seems most fruitful would be to abandon the arm's-length fiction and concentrate upon guidelines for cost allocations.

Use of Tangible Property. The rule is that when possession, use or occupancy of tangible property owned by one member of a controlled group is transferred to another member, an arm's-length charge must be made. If neither the owner nor the user was engaged in the business of renting property, the arm's-length charge is deemed to be the allowable depreciation on the property plus 3% of the property's depreciable basis and all expenses connected with the property. Where use of leased property is transferred by a sublease, the charge should be equal to the expense deductions attributable to the property. This section, which is similar to the first section dealing with loans and advances, does not appear to present any special problem of interpretation.

Use of Intangible Property. All intangibles which are sold, assigned, loaned or otherwise made available in any manner must be charged at an arm's-length rate, except in those cases where a member of a group of controlled entities participates in a cost-sharing arrangement for the development of intangible property. A bona fide cost-sharing arrangement is a written agreement providing for the sharing of costs and risks in return for a specified interest in the intangible property developed.

The definition of intangibles for purposes of this paragraph is extremely broad. Provided that they have substantial value independent of the services of individual persons, the following are considered to be intangible property: patents, inventions, formulas, processes, designs, patterns, copyrights, trademarks, trade names, brand names, franchises, licenses, methods, programs, systems, procedures, campaigns, surveys, studies, forecasts, estimates, customer lists, technical data and other similar items.

Although the regulations again appear to be precise and definitive, except for the bona fide cost-sharing provisions, they prescribe a method which is difficult to follow in practice. There is no such thing as an arm's-length price for most of the intangibles on the Treasury list. One observer commented: "The proposed regulations on intangible property transfers are indeed an elegant structure, but mere fluidity of language should not obscure the fact that when all is said and done little more seems to have been accomplished, as a practical matter, than a reiteration of the approach that has always been applied in Section 482 cases, viz., did the interparty transactions distort true net incomes of the affiliates to such an extent that a re-allocation is necessary in order to clearly reflect such incomes . . .

the proposed regulations deal more with matters of shadow than of substance. Their constant reference to all the facts and circumstances belies the guideline function which supposedly animated their issuance in the first place. What really seems to be their major defect, however, is a failure to understand the commercial realities of related-party dealings: in other words, the regulations attempt to pull asunder (under the guise of the arm's-length standard) that which by definition is a unitary economic enterprise; since affiliates just do not deal among themselves as they would with outsiders, and probably never will, the Treasury seems to be promulgating a complex set of rules that simply will not work in practice."[4]

The problem is simple. There is no comparable arm's-length charge for the bulk of actual cases of intangible property covered. There are transactions in the intangible property covered in the regulations by unrelated parties, but they are not comparable to the transactions of other companies. How much is a patent worth? By definition, a patentable idea is unique. Can there be a comparable patent? The same is true of a copyright. What about a franchise or method? Admittedly, arm's-length is the purest standard of value, but if it can be determined in only a trivial number of cases, we must rely on a more obtainable, if less elegant, standard, such as prevailing industry charges.

Sales of Tangible Property. This final section of the new regulations is of particular interest since it deals with controlled intracompany transfers (i.e., transfer pricing) of raw materials, finished and intermediate goods. Thus, decisions in this area will affect not only the location of profits within multinational corporate systems but the current account of the balance of payments as well.

Determining Arm's Length

The general rule which applies to sales of tangible property is again the arm's-length formula. Three methods are spelled out in the regulations for establishing its existence. They are, in order of preference, the "comparable uncontrolled price method," the "resale price method" and the "cost-plus method."

Comparable Uncontrolled Price Method. Uncontrolled sales are considered comparable to controlled sales if the physical property and circumstances involved are identical or nearly identical to the physical property and circumstances of controlled sales. The precision of this method is impressive, but unfortunately in practice it will have little applicability except in cases of companies dealing in such standard items as number 2 winter grade wheat or number 16 nails.

Resale Price Method. Of the other two methods, the resale price method is given preference in the regulations. It provides that an arm's-length price can be established by reducing the applicable resale price by an appropriate markup and making adjustments to reflect any differences between uncontrolled sales used as the basis for establishing the appropriate markup percentage and the resale of property involved in the controlled sale. The applicable resale price is the price at which property purchased in a controlled sale is resold by the buyer in an uncontrolled sale. This method must be used if all of the following circumstances exist: there are no comparable uncontrolled sales, an applicable resale price is available and the buyer has not added more than an insubstantial amount to the value of the property.

What is an appropriate markup? According to the regulations, it is the gross profit as a percentage of sales earned by the reseller or another party on the resale of property which is both purchased and resold in an uncontrolled transaction most similar to the resale of property involved in the controlled sale. The regulations specify that whenever possible, markup percentages should be derived from uncontrolled purchases and resales of the reseller involved in the controlled sale on the assumption that similar characteristics are much more likely to be found among different resales of property made by the same reseller than among sales made by other resellers. However, in the absence of sales made by the same reseller, the regulations permit markup percentages to be obtained from resales by other resellers. The regulations allow that if the controlled reseller is located in a foreign country and information on resales by other resellers in the same foreign market is not available, then markup percentages earned by U.S. resellers performing comparable functions may be used.

Pittsburgh Plate Glass Case

The resale price method in Section 482 enforcement is an innovation of major significance. Already, it appears to be the cornerstone of a major enforcement effort by the IRS. In 1967, for example, IRS examiners allocated almost $2,000,000 of income from Pittsburgh Plate Glass Company International (PPGI), first incorporated in Cuba and later in Puerto Rico, to Pittsburgh Plate Glass Company, Inc. (PPG) for the tax years 1960 and 1961. The basis for the allocation was the IRS conclusion that the PPG pricing formula for sales to PPGI (cost plus 10%) resulted in a net profit as a percent of sales (8%) for PPGI which was too high, considering the functions performed by PPGI. This move follows the traditional approach to enforcement of Section 482. The IRS examines the distribution of income and, if it does not appear to be in line, allocates income to achieve the desired distribution.

PPG went to court to challenge the IRS allocation. In court the IRS made a rough attempt to apply the resale price method by arguing that PPGI was comparable to a combination export manager (CEM) in terms of functions performed. Government economists had estimated that CEMs in general earned about 2% net on sales, and the government had evidence that a CEM dealing in products comparable to those sold by PPGI was earning approximately this amount. With the argument of comparability of function, the government asserted that the 2% net return was in fact the appropriate return for PPGI.

Interestingly, although the new Section 482 regulations were available during the PPG case, the IRS continued to focus upon net profit results rather than arm's-length prices and gross profit percentages to reach its income allocation decisions. It appears that the IRS will continue to look at results rather than at the actual prices and gross margins of operations. The new element is likely to be a partial application of the regulations by an emphasis on rates of return in allegedly comparable business organizations.

In defense of its pricing decisions, PPG referred to the new Section 482 regulations. The company argued that PPGI was not comparable to a combination export manager and that PPG's prices in the disputed years were reasonable in comparison to prices charged by an unrelated company for comparable products sold to

PPGI. The PPG case is now before the Tax Commissioner. The decision of the tax court on this important case is not expected before mid-1970.

The PPG case results in the paradox of the IRS essentially bypassing Treasury regulations which call for allocations based on gross, not net, income, and a taxpayer defending its pricing decisions before the service and the tax court by applying the methods outlined in the regulations.

Cost-Plus Method. The third and lowest priority method of establishing the existence of an arm's-length price is the cost-plus method. Interestingly, this method is easily the most relied-upon method currently in use by U.S. corporations to establish transfer prices.

The regulations specify that cost must be determined by following standard accounting practices that neither favor nor burden controlled sales in comparison to similar uncontrolled sales. The allowable gross profit percentage is that figure which is equal to the gross profit earned by the seller on uncontrolled sales which are most similar to the controlled sale in question. The regulations specify that, wherever possible, gross profit percentages should be derived from uncontrolled sales made by the seller involved in the controlled sale, but that in the absence of such evidence, appropriate gross profit percentages may be obtained either from uncontrolled sales of other sellers who perform a similar function or, failing this, from the prevailing gross profit percentages in the particular industry involved. Since the comparable uncontrolled price and the resale price are likely to find little application in practice, the "cost-plus" method could eventually be the most applicable section of the regulations dealing with tangible property.

On Being Competitive

A businessman examining the Section 482 regulations will quickly begin to wonder, with all of the emphasis upon an arm's-length price, whether it is possible under the spirit of these regulations to continue to price with regard to market and competitive factors. Clearly, if only the arm's-length standard is applied, it does not necessarily permit a company to respond to competitive factors which exist in every market, domestic and foreign. Fortunately, the regulations may provide an opening for the multinational company which seeks to be price-competitive or to price aggressively in its foreign marketing of U.S.-source products. It appears that the drafters of the Treasury regulations intended to leave a wide opening for companies that wish to respond to competitive or any other price factors which may exist in foreign markets. The applicable section reads:

"One of the circumstances which may affect the price of property is the fact that the seller may desire to make sales at less than a normal profit for the primary purpose of establishing or maintaining a market for his products. Thus, a seller may be willing to reduce the price of his product, for a time, in order to introduce his product into an area or in order to meet competition. However, controlled sales may be priced in such a manner only if such price would have been charged in an uncontrolled sale under comparable circumstances. Such fact may be demonstrated by showing that the buyer in the controlled sale made corresponding reductions in the resale price to uncontrolled purchasers, or that such buyer engaged in substantially greater sales-promotion activities with respect to the product involved in the controlled sale than with respect to other products."

The key provision in this section is the third sentence citing "comparable circumstances." This could be interpreted as nullification of what is an essential provision in the regulations. A company may properly reduce prices and increase marketing expenditures in a market through a controlled affiliate when it would not do so through an independent distributor. This would be the case when a company lowered its prices in order to gain a market position. This position is in effect an investment and an asset. A company would invest in such an asset only if it controlled the reseller. If the third sentence applies, there is, unfortunately, extremely limited endorsement of competitive or marginal cost pricing. If the last sentence applies, the regulations will permit a company to lower its transfer price for the purpose of entering a new market or meeting competition in an existing market either by price reductions or by increased marketing efforts in the target markets. Companies should have this latitude in making price decisions if they are to have any chance of succeeding in foreign markets with U.S.-sourced products.

The immediate significance of these regulations and of recent enforcement efforts by the IRS is that companies can expect that the arm's-length standard established in the regulations will be tested by attempts to identify comparable uncontrolled prices, gross margins and, most importantly, rates of return. Executives responsible for intercorporate pricing should be aware of this probability. In those few cases where a comparable arm's-length price or margin from a comparable business-product relationship exists, companies which use these prices and margins will presumably not find their prices challenged. In the vast majority of cases, companies will not have comparable arm's-length prices or product-business situations and will have to rely upon standards of reasonableness and cost-plus methods of defending their transfer pricing decisions or, in the case of competitive or marginal cost pricing, evidence that the prices charged were the basis for market price reductions or marketing expenditures.

Whatever the pricing rationale, it is important that executives involved in the pricing policy decisions of multinational companies familiarize themselves with the Section 482 regulations and that the pricing rationale utilized by the company conform with the intention of these regulations. In practice, this will not result in a massive adoption of the Treasury's beloved arm's-length pricing standard, but companies should be prepared to demonstrate that their pricing methods were not the result of oversight but of informed choice. There is ample evidence to date that regardless of the sometimes perplexing inscrutability of Treasury regulations and IRS enforcement policy, there is no intention on the part of the government to do anything other than seek to prevent tax avoidance and to insure that the income from the operations of multinational companies is fairly distributed. The company that makes a conscientious effort to comply with the new regulations and which documents this effort should have no difficulty with IRS deficiencies. In the event that there are deficiencies, it should be able to make a strong case for its decisions in court.

The new regulations herald a much more rigorous standard of review of intra-company transfer pricing. However, assuming that the IRS and the courts do not use the third sentence of the section dealing with competitive pricing to nullify the entire section, they do offer a specific opening to permit price reductions to support lower market pricing or more intensive marketing efforts. Without this, they would put a straitjacket around intra-company transfer prices and effectively erect a major, new non-tariff barrier to international trade.

Goal Is Proper Income Allocation

More broadly, the Treasury regulations begin a new era in the rapidly developing world of international business. Those executives and tax experts who have argued that Section 482 should only apply when a tax avoidance motive is possible are not happy with its expanded scope, as the regulations make it clear that the proper allocation of income is a major goal of the new enforcement effort. The alternative, in all cases where tax avoidance was not a possible motive, would permit the private corporation to establish its transfer prices and decide where it would report earnings. In effect, private corporations would be left with the power to decide which of the nation-states of the world in which they operate would receive the tax revenue on the earnings of their multinational system of operations. For all sovereign governments, this is an unacceptable state of affairs.

The proper effort should not be to fight the inevitable and the manifestly necessary development of international tax law, but to contribute to the development of an effective and reasonably efficient international tax code. Both the government and the private sector should work together to achieve this end. This is a complex task, and much study and effort will be required to achieve success. The Treasury is to be congratulated on taking the initiative to draft regulations to guide enforcement in this complex area. Still, its initial effort is a good example of what can happen when a passion for technical perfection is combined with inadequate knowledge of the operating realities of global business in order to meet the enforcement demands of the Internal Revenue Service through the tax code.

N O T E S

1. "Allocation of Income and Deductions Among Taxpayers: Determination of Source of Income (Section 482, IRC)," *Federal Register*, April 16, 1968.

2. Samuel M. Frohlich, "Section 482 and Its Effects on International Business Transactions," *Proceedings of the 13th Annual William and Mary Tax Conference*, Marshall Wythe School of Law, 1968. The history of Section 482 enforcement outlined here is drawn from this article.

3. For a more detailed review of Section 482, see James Eustice, *Tax Law Review*, Spring 1968.

4. James Eustice, *op. cit.*

CHAPTER 14

THEODORE L. WILKINSON

*As a common language of business, accounting is
failing to communicate compatible information from one
country to another. Should something be done about it?*

International
Accounting: Harmony
or Disharmony?

FINANCIAL STATEMENTS are a method of communicating information, just as are the words in this publication. In fulfilling this role both the financial statements and the written word must be in terms familiar to both the writer and the reader. Differences in accounting practices in various parts of the world are of such magnitude as to inhibit severely the communication function that financial statements are meant to perform.

When a reader in the United States receives financial statements from a U.S. company audited by a U.S. accounting firm, he has as much assurance as he can get that at least everybody is speaking the same financial language. This is not the case when a reader must make use of financial statements that, for example, reflect adjustments for price-level increases or reflect overconservative practices designed to even out fluctuations in income from year to year. U.S.-prepared financial statements are not necessarily better; they are only different.

Differences in accounting practices and the need for mitigating their effect are subjects which have drawn the attention of accountants to an increasing degree in recent times. Unfortunately, the development of accounting has had a decidedly nationalistic flavor. While accountants continue to deplore the effects of the situation and argue eloquently for uniformity (or at least less divergence) at their international congresses, there are no prescribed international standards of accounting nor is there any organization which could persuade adherence to such standards. Regrettably, there is not much visible progress toward their establishment.

How did this patchwork come about? The answer can be found in examining the ways in which accounting principles travel about and gain acceptance. The accounting principles of one country have never been "sold" to another country; no accountant, no matter how eager a proponent of minimizing differences, willingly accepts the idea that someone else's accounting principles are better than his. Accounting principles flow from one country to another when (1) the second country has no organized body of accounting principles to begin with, and (2) when large amounts of capital from the first country invested in the second enable investors to impose their own accounting principles. Evidence of the truth of this allegation can be seen in the way U.S. principles gained acceptance many years ago in Mexico. A more serious problem exists when capital is invested in a country with long-established accounting principles of its own that clash with those of the investor.

The Accounting Environment

In citing the differences in existing accounting practices around the world, it is hard to avoid giving the impression that one or another practice is considered better. The differences under discussion are on an "as compared to the U.S. practice" basis and do not imply the superiority of the U.S. practice, which is merely used as a convenient benchmark. Some of the differences include:

The concept of historical cost as a maximum valuation for assets, as opposed to replacement cost or price-level adjusted valuations. U.S. accountants have not yet been inclined to face the problem of continued inflation and its effect on accounting. It seems that their principles are based on the questionable theory that cost-of-living indices go both up and down, whereas the experience of most countries in recent decades is that inflation is a one-way street. The only recognition of the problem of accounting for inflation is the adoption of the LIFO (last in, first out) method for inventory and, perhaps, accelerated depreciation of property. It seems that acceptance of LIFO was based at least as much on the desire to save taxes as the desire for improved financial reporting. (Interestingly, LIFO is the only example of a treatment which must be booked in order to gain the related U.S. tax advantage.)

Accountants in the Netherlands and Brazil are not as confined as those in the United States by the historical cost concept. Dutch accountants accept replacement cost in lieu of historical cost, and although their acceptance is probably not guided as much by consideration of inflation as by the need not to overstate income and to protect the enterprise, the use of replacement cost is a good example of how to avoid the erosion of capital in an inflationary environment. In Brazil, the severity of inflation makes financial statements prepared on a historical cost basis virtually meaningless. Several features of price-level adjusted accounting are in common use there, including the application of coefficients based on cost-of-living indices. When income and expenses are expressed in current cruzeiros in an inflationary setting, it makes little sense to charge depreciation at historical rates. Admittedly, the inflation experience in many developed countries has not been as severe as Brazil's, but it is getting worse. Management and the accounting profession have not given sufficient thought to drawing the line between inflation which it can keep on ignoring and inflation that destroys the validity of financial statements based on the historical cost concept.

The concept of conservatism. A basic difference in concept exists between accountants in some areas, principally in Western Europe, and others with respect to the philosophical approach as to what financial statements should in essence purport to show. Most Western European accountants accept the proposition that the financial position of a company should be at least as good as that shown on its balance sheet, i.e., the balance sheet may understate but should not overstate a financial position. Compare this with the U.S. idea of fair presentation or the British "true and fair view." The effects of the Western European approach are not always apparent from reading financial statements or even the legislation which prescribes methods for valuation of assets. The Swiss Federal Code of Obligations, for example, requires inventories to be valued at the customary "cost or market value, whichever is lower" as a *maximum* valuation. There is no *minimum* valuation for financial reporting purposes. The Italian Civil Code likewise prescribes the cost or market rule, but an overconservative view of what constitutes market value is not uncommon.[1]

Income levelling. To U.S. businessmen and their accountants the idea of showing a net income deliberately adjusted to resemble that of periods gone by is abhorrent. In computing net income they prefer to "let the chips fall where they may." Accountants abroad, once again mainly in Western Europe, uphold the diametrically opposed view that fluctuations in income pose a threat to the stability of the enterprise and to its ability to provide investors with a return on their investment. European accountants are not too inclined to accept the idea of the importance of net income for any arbitrary period such as a year. If the only real net income is the one provided by the life of the enterprise as a whole, why not show it in fairly equal installments, at the same time guarding against any possibility of eroding invested capital? The close relationship between the concepts of conservatism and income-levelling looked at in this light suddenly seems more logical.

Consolidation practice. It is surprising to note the numerous areas throughout the world in which the practice of consolidating the accounts of a parent company and its subsidiaries is not prevalent. A review of the situation in 25 countries indicates that the practice is generally accepted only in the United States and nine other countries, five of which are members of the British Commonwealth.[2] In Germany, where it is estimated that something like two out of every three companies are related to other companies, the practice of consolidating accounts was not customary until it was mandated by the new German Stock Corporation Act which went into effect in 1967. In some countries stockholders must be presented with separate financial statements of all the subsidiaries in which inter-company transactions and balances are set forth separately. However, this procedure obviously cannot communicate financial position or results of operation as effectively as fully consolidated statements, especially in those cases where inter-company profits are not eliminated.

When subsidiaries are not consolidated, the investment in them is usually shown at cost or less. Presentation of investment in unconsolidated subsidiaries under the so-called "equity" method seems to be exclusively a U.S. practice.

Attitude toward disclosure. Ideas about what financial statements ought to reveal or ought not to reveal vary greatly from one area to another. One executive put it succinctly this way: "Another part . . . (of the communications problem) . . . stems from a tradition of business secrecy that prevails in much of the world. There is, we all know, a fine line between what a business can reveal publicly for the good of the public and its nation and the kind of financial information it reveals which will boomerang . . . I can't really draw that line but I do know it's a long way removed from where businessmen in many nations feel that it is."[3]

Financial analysts have been particularly vociferous in their complaints about the lack of disclosure in financial statements prepared outside the United States. For example, analysts employed by different leading brokerage firms estimated the consolidated earnings of a major French company in one year at anywhere from $2 per share to $4.85 per share, whereas the company itself reported merely that the parent company alone earned $1.15 per share.[4] More recently, the financial press reported that another large French company, after its shares became the subject of a tender offer, suddenly advised its shareholders that earnings of the previous year had increased by 35% rather than the 14% estimated earlier.[5]

It cannot be denied, however, that we are seeing progress toward fuller and more meaningful disclosure. The new German Stock

Corporation Act and the British Companies Act of 1967 contain requirements that in some particulars are more comprehensive than those in the United States. The British act requires that the directors' report must indicate the proportion of turnover (sales) and pretax profit contributed by each substantially different class of business carried on by the enterprise. U.S. firms are still largely in the talking stage on that point.

Accounting based on legal requirements. There appears to be a direct relationship between the quality of financial statements produced in areas where their preparation is guided by legal requirements and areas where their preparation is guided by pronouncements of a developed and organized accounting profession. The former situation exists largely in some of the developing countries, particularly those whose accounting is mainly under the influence of Italian, French and Spanish thinking on the subject. Attitudes toward business in general in such countries are not always positive and certainly do not encourage disclosure. In the absence of a strong independent accounting profession, governments have stepped in and prescribed the minimum requirements. As might be expected in such an environment, financial statements are prepared in a perfunctory manner with more emphasis on form than substance. Accounting becomes something akin to a form-filling process rather than a dynamic vehicle for conveying financial information.

Financial and tax accounting. Income tax laws are promulgated by countries in the light of national economic policies rather than in the light of good accounting practices. Yet in many countries these laws are applied to determine income for financial reporting purposes. Some excuse for this practice might be offered in those cases where no recognized body of accounting principles exists and income tax laws logically are substituted. Some degree of uniformity is achieved, and the accounting process is simplified, by viewing income tax laws as the authoritative expression of accounting rules. Less reason for this practice would seem to exist in many European countries (Germany and Sweden, for example) which certainly do not suffer from a dearth of sound accounting thought. There is a practical explanation, however—an unfortunate requirement that an advantageous tax treatment must be booked in order to benefit from it. The requirement is unfortunate for two reasons. First, it forces distortions into the accounts, generally in the direction of under-statement of income. Secondly, it has not in general achieved its goal of stricter compliance with the income tax laws. On the contrary, some of the countries which require book and tax conformity have gained a reputation for loose adherence to income tax laws, while others which do not have the requirement have achieved better fiscal control. At least it can be said with reasonable certainty that the case for improving compliance with income tax laws remains unproven. Perhaps the root of the problem rests in the accountant's reflexive rejection of the "two set of books" concept. However, accountants in the Netherlands have overcome that obstacle admirably. They have no hesitation about drawing up separate additional financial statements based on requirements of the income tax law.

Some Pitfalls

Property and plant accounts may be shown at revalued amounts. This is true not only in areas affected by inflation in an extreme degree, but also in many countries which enjoy monetary stability. While historical cost is certainly acceptable as the basis for valuation in countries of stable currencies, revaluation based on technically assessed value is often also an acceptable basis. Disclosure of the revaluation is generally, but not always, required. When revaluation is accepted because inflation has invalidated historical cost, depreciation for tax purposes is generally allowed on the revalued (higher) basis. When revaluation is not the result of inflationary conditions, allowable depreciation is usually limited to that based on historical cost. Treatment of the credit arising from the revaluation varies greatly from one country to another.

Depreciation may be based entirely on what the income tax allows, which may be anything from zero (as was, until recently, depreciation on buildings in Brazil) to 100% (as in the case of "flexible" depreciation in Puerto Rico). When depreciation based merely on what the law allows has to be booked to be claimed, as is usually the case, the resulting net valuation of property may bear little resemblance to what it would be under sounder accounting methods.

Charges which normally would be made against income under U.S. practice may be handled as if they were distributions of earnings. This situation is common in countries in which stockholders are required to vote on provisions or accruals for doubtful accounts, depreciation, directors' fees, legal reserves, dividends and sometimes even income taxes long after the books are closed for the year. In some cases where income tax amounts are subject to lengthy negotiations, payments may be charged as made to retained earnings.

When accounting is viewed merely as a legally required exercise, financial statements may fail to recognize the importance of subsequent events to provide for all liabilities and losses and lack consistency in the application of accounting principles. Under such conditions, the further removed an economic fact or contingency is from being an actual cash receipt or disbursement, the less likely is it to be recorded in the accounts.

The basis of valuation of inventories may not be disclosed and the term "market" in "cost or market" may have different meanings in different areas. In the United States, "market" in that context means replacement cost (by purchase or production), except that it must not be an amount higher than the net realizable value nor lower than net realizable value less an allowance for normal profit margin. "Market" in some other areas is taken to mean simply net realizable value or replacement cost.

Proper segregation of assets and liabilities as between current and long-term and as among trade debtors (or creditors), directors, employees, affiliated companies and even subscribers to capital stock may be lacking. The meaning of a "long-term" item as one not receivable or payable until after one year or the end of an operating cycle is not in agreement with the meaning applied in many other countries.

Factory overhead may be excluded from the valuation of inventories or constructed plant additions, with the cost only of materials and direct labor thereby included.

Current assets may include investments acquired for control purposes.

Treasury stock may be shown as an asset even when purchased with intention to retire it.

Valuation reserves may be shown "broad" (sometimes even in the stockholders' equity section) instead of being offset against the assets to which they relate.

Goodwill may be written off soon after acquisition despite the absence of any evidence of limitation on its life.

Income tax provisions may be based strictly on the amounts currently payable or simply on amounts as they are actually paid, without regard to deferred tax liabilities arising from differences between book and tax treatments. (Of course, this problem does not arise when the law requires conformity between book and tax treatment.)

Dividends proposed by directors may be shown as liabilities before their formal and legal declaration.

Stock distributions may be charged to retained earnings at par value rather than market value. (The U.S. practice of publicly held companies charging the market value of small stock distributions to retained earnings is at variance with that of the rest of the world.)

Pension costs may be accounted for in a variety of ways ranging from "cash basis" accounting to accrual of amounts based on actuarial studies.

Stock dividends received may be recorded as income because they are taxable income under local tax laws.

Uniformity

Some practitioners and academicians are appalled by the coexistence of varying accounting environments and practices and have called for the establishment of uniform international standards of accounting, although it is not always clear whether they argue for uniformity on a truly worldwide (international) scale or possibly for the adoption of uniform principles in each country (domestic uniformity), which may differ from country to country. In any case, the advantages usually cited are that adoption of uniform principles would facilitate:

(1) The work of financial analysts, and thereby contribute to the more beneficial use of available capital.

(2) Collection of useful data by governments and economists for

purposes of economic planning and legislation (including income tax laws), labor negotiations, etc.

(3) Administration of laws concerning businesses by supervisory authorities.

(4) Education of accounting students.

(5) Training and replacement of accounting employees.

The arguments against uniformity are perhaps less numerous but no less weighty. Opponents of uniformity frequently maintain that:

(1) The experience of financial analysts bears out the claim that U.S. practices relating to reports to the Securities and Exchange Commission and to stockholders has induced a flow of meaningful accounting disclosure considerably greater than that induced in countries in which the uniformity approach has been well-established.

(2) Uniformity, even if it could succeed, demands too high a price in that it stifles experimentation and progress. Principles that gain acceptance through persuasion rather than compulsion are more easily replaced by other more persuasive principles when required by changes in circumstances or outlook. The British view on this point has been admirably set forth:

"The more serious problem . . . is whether a standardized plan of accounts is in any event a desirable objective on a national or international scale. The danger(s) of such a project as they would appear to most British accountants . . . (are) . . . that the plan, if it was effective, would not be sufficiently flexible to accommodate varieties and changes of circumstances and . . . accounting . . . would tend to become unresponsive to . . . new ideas, new situations, and new needs."[6]

(3) Uniformity seeks to treat dissimilar matters in a similar way, thereby causing distortion, overabundance of detail, and meaningless disclosure.

(4) Uniformity is literally costly, as evidenced by the experience of Germany and France, which shows that acceptance of the respective uniform charts of accounts has generally been limited to larger companies.

The greatest drawback to any plan of uniformity which attempts to cover the endless variety of circumstances in the real world is that it inevitably produces merely the appearance of uniformity. No plan of domestic uniformity could possibly be so well devised as to contemplate all the existing and future complexities.

Harmonization

While accountants in the United States have taken some short strides in the direction of uniformity in recent years in restricting the definition of generally accepted accounting principles, the thought of over-all uniformity in the derivation and presentation of financial information, including standard formats for financial statements, is repulsive. To add to domestic complications the difficulties which would be introduced by consideration of foreign tax laws, customs, attitude toward disclosure, etc. would seem to render the task of international uniformity a hopeless one not even to be attempted.

Yet, to advocate the present situation or even to tolerate it seems somehow like resisting an inevitable trend. The present situation came about when international investment was on a scale much lower than that which is probable in the future. The capital available for investment is not unlimited; its mobility must be maximized. As the uneven development of accounting is one factor that obviously diminishes the mobility of capital, a search must be made for ways to eliminate or reduce the negative effects of that unevenness. The harmonization must be approached without compromising the high standards existing in many developed areas and without attempting to select the practices of any one area and superimpose them on the world.

As a first step, the developed countries should undertake a program of accounting aid to developing countries to provide more opportunities for people in the developing countries to obtain adequate technical training and to strengthen their societies and institutes of professional accountants. The aid should take the form of additional scholarships to promising nationals of developing countries, the establishment in those countries of educational centers for accountants, expansion of international staff exchange programs by firms in a position to do so, and the appointment of volunteer resident counselors to the accounting profession to assist universities in the improvement of curricula and guide local professional societies on a continuing basis.

There must be any number of eminently qualified retired practitioners in the developed countries who would be willing to contribute time and effort to such a "Peace Corps" for the accounting profession. The International Executive Service Corps has a program of this type directed to business firms in developing countries. Arbitrary restrictions against the practice of the profession by foreigners should be eliminated by the developed countries and developing countries alike. The opportunity for nationals of all countries to obtain a good accounting education and the international traffic of accountants must both be increased.

Relief Needed and Possible

While these suggestions are essential to the ultimate raising of standards, more immediate relief is needed to overcome the problem. Uniformity, both domestic and international, has already been examined and seriously questioned. There is, however, hope that relief would be provided by the establishment of minimum consolidation and disclosure requirements which would apply, by agreement among the capital-supplying nations, to all cases where capital is sought by any entity outside its country of domicile.

In the final analysis, there are not so many different accounting principles in existence that, assuming adequate disclosure and acceptable consolidation practice, trained accountants outside the country of issuance of financial statements would be unable to comprehend them and recast them in a more familiar mold. In other words, accountants would continue to keep their books and prepare their financial statements in accordance with practices that are normal in their respective jurisdictions. However, if the financial statements were to be used in connection with the raising of capital outside the jurisdiction, then certain agreed consolidation practices would have to be followed and certain information (principally as to methods of valuation) would have to be disclosed.

The requirement as to consolidation practice would be the only spelling out of a uniformly applicable accounting principle as such. This would be necessary, as it is hard to imagine any amount of disclosure which would be meaningful in the case of a company with numerous substantial subsidiaries which would be able to present only separate parent company statements, were it not for the proposed requirement.

No insurmountable obstacle would seem to exist which could prevent the design of a usable international companies act along the lines suggested. Present disclosure practices as set forth in generally accepted reporting standards and in the requirements of the Securities and Exchange Commission, the Companies Acts in Great Britain, and the new German Stock Corporation Act would have something valuable to contribute. For example, the German act includes the recognition that a company can be an affiliate of another for accounting purposes through contractual relationships as well as through stock ownership. While provisions to that effect in the act were introduced because the prevalence in Germany of certain types of enterprise agreements makes common management the only useful way of defining affiliation, those provisions could be considered for possible application elsewhere.

The creation of international standards for consolidation and disclosure might have great impact on the development of accounting practices around the world, even if the requirements were minimal and their application limited to international financing efforts. The standards would no doubt tend to flow down to areas where no clearly defined body of principles now exists. It would not be surprising to see eventual acceptance of them even in the developed countries.

In view of the general reluctance by accountants to accept the practices of accountants of other countries, about the best they have been able to do to minimize the effects of differences is to prepare financial statements destined for use in another country on the basis of principles of the country of use rather than of the country of origin. That is fine as far as it goes, but suppose the statements are intended for use in a number of countries? Then the profession must have either international uniformity, which seems an entirely unrealistic suggestion, or it must put the reader of financial statements in a position to interpret them through meaningful consolidation practices and adequate disclosure of essential information. This approach, together with the suggested effort to raise the level of accounting education and professional development, seems to offer the best hope of introducing a note of harmony in international accounting.

N O T E S

1. AICPA, *Professional Accounting in 25 Countries,* New York, 1964.

2. AICPA, *op. cit.*

3. Arthur K. Watson, address before the Eighth International Congress of Accountants, 1962.

4. "Lifting Corporate Curtains," *Fortune,* March 1966.

5. *New York Times,* January 20, 1969.

6. W. E. Parker, remarks at the Fifth Congress of the Union Européenne des Experts Comptables Economiques et Financiers, 1964.

CHAPTER 15

BURT NANUS

*As computer technology and the art of using it grow,
so do its capabilities. Soon it will be routing messages through
outer space to become a global medium of communication,
a medium that may make it possible for the
multinational corporation to come into its own.*

The Multinational

Computer

IN THE LAST TWO DECADES, the number, size and influence of multinational firms have been increasing at a rapid rate. Such firms typically have some form of direct investment in a number of different countries. Their managements make decisions on production, research and marketing within a global perspective—that is, in terms of alternatives that are available to them anywhere in the world. The reasons for the growth in importance of multinational operations are well documented and need not be repeated, but several specific factors that have important implications can be identified.

The trend toward the aggregation of larger units for international business operations through direct foreign investment and mergers means that many multinational firms have gained considerable financial strength. This has assisted them to achieve economies of mass production and mass marketing, but in order to do so, they must be able to coordinate their operations effectively across national boundaries.

Sharp competition among the large multinational firms is causing all of them to adopt practices in production and marketing similar to those of the most successful competitors. As a result, there is a growing internationalization of the art of management which is facilitated by the sharing of consultants, textbooks and business school courses, all of which draw upon a common pool of management research and experience.

A new breed of manager is emerging—one who is proficient in multinational operations and equally at home in a variety of countries.

If there is a single distinguishing characteristic of multinational operations, it is the necessity to accommodate to great variations in local conditions—variations in political, economic and social environments, as well as in the behavioral characteristics of workers, supervisors, suppliers and customers. As a result, many functions that are performed centrally in a national firm are performed locally in the multinational firm.

On the other hand, there are many who feel that extensive opportunities for cost savings and operational efficiency are being lost by overdecentralization and suboptimization. Clearly, the headquarters office has an opportunity to accumulate in its central staffs a great deal of business know-how collected from the experiences of all the local staffs. It should be able to apply this know-how, as well as its financial resources and specialized functional skills, to a balancing and coordination of the firm's multinational operations in a way that improves the performance of the organization as a whole. Many multinational firms would probably like to coordinate their operations more closely and would do so if they could discover coordinating mechanisms that did not interfere with necessary local initiative in dealing with local circumstances.

Decision makers in multinational firms are plagued by inadequate information at every level. At headquarters, a lack of system-wide data may force decision makers to meet problems with ultra-conservatism and costly delays. At the local level, inadequate information resulting from a lack of sophistication in management control techniques or from a poor flow of information from headquarters often reduces considerably the flexibility of local managers to respond to unforeseen shifts in the competitive environment. Hence, there is a great need for better management information systems designed to improve the amount and quality of information that is available to decision makers at every level. Similarly, there is a need to improve the skills of local managers in information collection and interpretation, problem identification and decision making.

These factors suggest that multinational corporations can benefit from the use of some of the newer management techniques involving large-scale information systems.

A Multinational Concept

To understand how these benefits could be achieved, imagine a large central computer in a headquarters office tied to satellite computers in the larger regional offices and plants in the major countries in which the multinational corporation operates. The regional offices, in turn, might be tied to hundreds of remote input/output devices located at branches and sales offices. Data would flow from the local offices to the regional computers to be assembled and used for various decision-making and performance-evaluation purposes related to current operations. Information needed by the branches would be fed back to them on remote consoles located there.

The summary data, together with special study data such as reports on economic and political conditions in the various countries, would be fed from the regional offices and plants to the central computer for storage, analysis or large-scale computation purposes. The central computer would have the capability of handling the large computational jobs and of storing the main files of the corporation. In addition, it would store historical information about corporate performance and environmental information.

Within this general framework, the multinational corporate

information system would have a number of service-oriented characteristics:

1. The system would be capable of operating in all the languages of the countries in which the corporation operates, at least with regard to a minimal set of operating codes. This implies the need for company-wide data collection and processing standards as a precondition to the implementation of the system.

2. The system would permit essentially simultaneous use by many remotely located users, each of whom could be independent of the others or could interact with the others at will. Furthermore, it would be designed to be available 24 hours per day to provide as much or as little computing service as each user wished.

3. The system would permit private priority access to data from the company's information files to authorized requesters and deny such access to others. Additionally, it would have built-in memory protection to guard against the possibility of one user affecting the files of another.

4. The system would be able to provide to each user at remote stations a range of facilities similar to that which he would have if he were the sole operator at a private computer. This includes the ability to interrupt processing; to read out memory; to change previously stored data; to introduce, monitor and debug new routines and to draw upon libraries of routines.

5. The system would be designed to provide each level and position of management with the planning and control information that it needs in the conduct of its job. The information would have to be current, easily understood and preferably in a form that is under the control of the manager.

6. The system would be able to provide many forms of analysis when needed. This includes the use of mathematical models so that the impact of management decisions could be studied and so that executives could analyze the logical relationships between the organizational units in which they are interested.

7. The system would lend itself to easy modification to accommodate corporate growth and change. Expansion might involve the addition of computers and modules to the system or the connection of the system with other special-purpose systems and data bases on either a multinational or a local basis.

The advantages of such a multinational corporate information

system are of two kinds—improved decision making and economies
of scale. The most direct and obvious way that the proposed system
could contribute to improved decision making is by providing better information for decision makers at all levels—information that is
more timely, more accurate, more convenient and more relevant.
The system would permit the decision maker to use more quantitative information and to use it more effectively by taking advantage
of the ability to correlate current data with historical data, to compare one country's operations and performance with those of another and to test hypotheses about the future effects of current
decisions through the use of simulation and other techniques.

Some multinational firms, in responding to the need for local
autonomy in certain decisions and transactions, seem to have gone
overboard in decentralization and have created a disjointed com-
posite of small businesses. They have thus deprived themselves of
some of the advantages of their size. The real strength of a multinational firm is in its ability to consider opportunities available to
it throughout the world.

Economies of Scale

There are several ways to achieve economies of scale:

1. By reducing the time delays in the information system required to detect shortages, initiate purchases and place purchase
orders, there would be less need for buffer inventories; over-all inventory levels could be reduced, and cash could be freed for other
purposes. Moreover, by being able to purchase critical materials for
the entire organization rather than having each unit purchasing
everything for itself, quantity discounts and purchases could be
arranged in those countries that have the greatest competitive
advantage for each resource.

2. With a company-wide perspective, it is possible to minimize
transportation and warehousing costs by shipping over least-cost
routes and by considering each delivery in terms of the particular
combination of demand, transportation and warehousing conditions
existing at a given time as well as applicable customs and duties.

3. The processing of orders, particularly when parts and finished goods may be arriving from several countries, often puts the

multinational firm at a competitive disadvantage when compared to its domestic rivals. Speedup of delivery with the assistance of a multinational information system may turn out to be the key competitive factor in such operations.

4. Some economies may occur purely from the point of view of computing power. A large central computer with several satellite computers permits a balancing of input-output speeds and costs by permitting a hierarchy of storage subsystems with various access times and capacities. At the same time, users would experience faster service and turnaround time than they could get if they had to use a smaller computer, even one that was located next door. In addition, the system would permit a more economical allocation of computer power by permitting so-called "production" processing (payrolls, dividends, etc.) to be run when the on-line load is minimal from a system-wide point of view. Finally, such a system would permit the economical use of scarce programmers since all programs could be made equally available to all organizational units online to the computer, wherever they are located.

For these reasons—better decision making, competitive advantages and economies of scale—substantial benefits could be derived from a multinational information system. However, costs and feasibility must be explored as well as benefits.

Feasibility

In discussing feasibility, it is necessary to examine the concept from both a technical and an operational point of view. The first is relatively easy since anyone familiar with current hardware capability will agree that equipment exists, or will exist shortly, to fulfill all the requirements for such a system. The only reservation might be in the area of communications, since the system would require a great deal of data transmission across national boundaries and perhaps over great distances with accuracy and reliability. However, with laser technology and communication satellites, this problem is unlikely to be a major technical obstacle within a few years. With regard to other aspects of hardware—power, input-output, memory, speed, reliability, etc.—there is little doubt that the concept of a large multinational information system is technically feasible. With software, there do not seem to be any unusual demands that have not been met somewhere and implemented, cost considerations aside. Thus, technical feasibility does not seem to provide any insurmountable problems, given the current and foreseeable state of the art.

Operational feasibility, on the other hand, presents problems of a different sort. To explore this subject, it is necessary first to examine the degree of computer acceptance in the business worlds of foreign countries to establish whether sufficient human resources could be assembled for such an undertaking. Next, the economic feasibility of the undertaking must be examined and then, multinational organizational considerations must be taken into account. Finally, the question of political feasibility must be addressed.

The question to be answered on computer acceptance is whether managers in various industrialized countries are sufficiently familiar with the use of large data processing systems to permit such an undertaking at the present time. The fact is that the state of the art of business data processing in most foreign countries is considerably behind that of the United States. In fact, the United States may have from three to five times as much computer equipment as all the rest of the world together, largely because the U.S. government has supported and nurtured the computer industry by means of substantial contracts in the military and space fields. In the software and business applications spheres, the United States is also considerably ahead of other countries, many of which are plagued with serious shortages in programming talent.

What does this lag in computer know-how imply with regard to the operational feasibility of a multinational corporate information system? One must conclude that the environment in many countries is simply not yet ready for it. The sponsor of such a system would have considerable difficulty finding enough programmers with the proper training to construct the system. He might also have difficulty in making arrangements for adequate international high-speed data transmission facilities, and he would be faced with a need for a monstrous training program. These problems can, of course, be overcome by money, but the costs might be so prohibitive as to make this a serious roadblock to the current implementation of the system. However, one may conjecture that conditions will change—indeed they must change if other developed nations are to retain their advanced industrial status—and these problems may very well not be serious roadblocks within a few years.

The Costs Are Large

While it is not possible to do a detailed cost analysis of a system that is defined in only general terms, one can make some bold guesses based upon other large systems currently in existence. For example, given the costs of the largest computers now installed and making allowances for the fact that hardware power per dollar has been increasing greatly with time, it may be assumed that the order of magnitude of hardware costs for the conceptualized system would be in the range of 10 to 20 million dollars, with the software costing perhaps an additional 20 to 30 million. It is clear that expenditures of this magnitude, even if spread out over several years, could only be justified by the very largest multinational corporations and not even by them unless a return on the investment of, say, 10 million dollars per year could be expected.

It may be conjectured that such savings and more can be realized by means of lower inventories, fewer warehouses, economies in purchasing and economies in data processing. Even more important, there is an excellent chance that greater returns could be realized in terms of improved decision-making effectiveness and greater coordination of the firm's operations. Although the concept appears to be economically feasible, because of the magnitude of the expenditures and the risks involved one would not expect a corporate stampede to implement large-scale multinational information systems in the near future.

Even assuming that the computer environment is favorable and an economic analysis proves the benefits of the concept convincingly, one must still ask whether executives are ready to make the kinds of personal adjustments that would be needed to benefit from a system of this type. Anyone who has traveled in other industrial countries must conclude that a multinational information system would be considered a radical innovation to most of today's executives. It might be several years before they could learn to be comfortable with and benefit from the great capability which the system could provide. However, with the growing internationalization of management and with many progressive managers attending courses at the business schools of the industrialized countries, this situation will probably be remedied in the coming decade.

One might predict strong political opposition to multinational information systems in many countries. Consider the situation from the point of view of one of the countries in which a multinational corporation is operating. It will be clear to the government of that country that control of the enterprise is being exercised from the outside in a more direct manner than has been the custom to date. The government will assume (probably correctly) that the intent of the information system is to effect economies of scale, some of which may conflict with the government's objectives. For example, economies could be realized by transferring production, employment or capital from a high-cost country to a lower cost one, but this might conflict with governmental desires in one or possibly both countries.

On the other hand, it is not clear whether a country, any more than a firm, can ever afford to permit its productive resources to be used less efficiently than its neighbor's without permanent loss of stature and power. Obviously, if some countries forbid multinational information systems operating within their borders and others welcome them, the most efficient and sophisticated producers will be attracted to the latter. The long-range political picture is a difficult one to predict in this case, but it may be safe to assume that if the economic arguments are compelling enough, considerable political and legislative ingenuity will be exercised to make the approach politically palatable.

It is also possible to take the analysis one step further and examine the implications such a movement would have for the nature of multinational organizations and for the environments in which they operate. Will the introduction of a multinational computerized management information system cause greater centralization of control in multinational firms? Those who feel that decentralization of many such firms took place only because executives at the top were unable to get sufficient information about operations will feel that once the computer makes such information available to them, recentralization will be the natural tendency.

Decentralization Effects

There are strong reasons, however, to believe that the use of computers across national boundaries will ultimately strengthen the decentralization that is needed to deal with different languages, cultures and tastes; to operate successfully with numerous governments, each with its own peculiar set of laws, traditions and patterns of interaction with business; and to cope with the differing work habits, labor practices and available skills in each country. Since most of these tasks have human, social and value-forming elements, they cannot be successfully dealt with by a centralized headquarters staff but must be handled by competent local managers who have the necessary information to relate their operations to the larger corporate picture and to act on their own initiative in a manner serving the best interests of the corporation as a whole.

This can be done by having a centralized computer collect data from decentralized sources, process them and transmit information back to the remote point for local decision making, enriched by analysis and comparison with other similar units throughout the corporation. With the informational and computational resources of the entire corporation at his fingertips, the local manager will be better equipped than he is now to make decisions on matters properly within his sphere. Thus, while one might expect to see some redistribution of decision-making authority toward the center in the multinational firm, a far more important effect is likely to be the strengthening and coordination of decision making at all levels throughout the organization.

What effects would such a concept have upon managerial skills? There are many experts who assert that the introduction of a computerized system in a large corporation leads to fewer jobs with more highly programmed content at lower levels in the management hierarchy. They feel that those who are now engaged in low-level planning functions, such as turning production decisions into parts orders or schedules, will be eliminated. There is some truth in these contentions—surely, the most programmable elements in management jobs will be relegated to the computer. However, in the case of the multinational firm, the conclusion that the lower level of management will disappear, lose its significance or decrease greatly in numbers, does not appear to be reasonable in view of the other forces at work. In addition to the critical human and social inter-actions, the dynamics of corporate growth in the multinational firm, with its emphasis upon ceaseless innovation to develop better com-petitive methods, will contribute to a greater demand for managers at every level.

Of course, these new managers will need a much greater under-standing of the role of the information system in their organization and of the various analytical tools at their disposal than is presently found in multinational firms. This need will place many demands upon the educational systems of the countries in which multi-national firms operate. It may take years to upgrade the current gen-eration of multinational managers. The gap will have to be filled in the short run by internal management-development courses. There are definite signs that multinational corporations are awakening to this challenge.

Implications for Labor

The introduction of multinational information systems would almost certainly have profound effects upon workers. In the first place, it is likely to have the short-term effect that is commonly asso-ciated with the introduction of automation anywhere—the problem of worker displacement and adjustment. A second effect would be an alteration in the work content of many jobs throughout the multinational corporation. Hundreds or thousands of people will have to receive training on how to interact with the new informa-tion system—preparing inputs, interpreting outputs, designing seg-ments of the system, etc. For the rest of the employees, the introduction of such a system might greatly decrease the amount of routine, repetitive and boring work in the corporation.

A third effect on workers is related to the degree to which each employee will be able to reconcile his sense of patriotism with loyalty to the multinational firm of which he is a part. This problem exists to some degree today, but with the virtually complete auton-omy of local management, the employee is not nearly as aware of the presence of the multinational coordinating influences as he will be when he is constantly called up to interact with an information source in a distant country and to adjust local decision making to the needs of the over-all organization.

As an illustration of such a potential conflict, an executive in the United Kingdom might be called upon to decide whether the product required to fill a Swiss order should come from an Italian plant to minimize over-all production and transportation costs or from a British plant to contribute to an improvement in the balance-of-payments situation in his own country. One might expect that as companies become more truly multinational in their operations, and staffs in each country become more international in their composition, conflicts such as these would be resolved in favor of the corporation, but the cost in terms of individual frustration might be very high.

The multinational information system would probably create a whole new framework of relationships with customers and suppliers, particularly with other multinational firms. These relationships might include, for example, more frequent negotiations at headquarters level for worldwide supply and distribution of a raw material or finished product. It might even extend to the point where large multinational customers and suppliers tie at least a portion of their information processing systems together for the purpose of coordinating shipments and production schedules for mutual benefit.

In the economic and political spheres, multinational information systems might have considerable long-term impacts:

1. There is likely to be more government involvement in the affairs of private industry. No multinational information system could be built without extensive communications linkages, and governments in most countries either own or tightly control these facilities. Moreover, every government will feel obligated to protect its citizens from at least some of the social costs of short- or long-term economic displacement caused by the introduction of computers. Governments will also wish to play a more active role in protecting national interests in such matters as labeling, advertising and financing as corporations make more of their decisions on the basis of international rather than national considerations.

2. As a result of increased integration and coordination within multinational firms across national boundaries, there will be a need for more comprehensive international trade agreements. As it be-

comes easier for multinational firms to shift resources among their plants and offices in various countries, differences in tax laws will serve to harm those countries whose rates are higher, and there will be strong pressures toward uniformity or at least agreements between countries to minimize the damaging effects of such differences.

3. Labor unions will have to become truly multinational if they are to maintain their bargaining positions with large multinational companies and protect the interests of their members. At first, unions are likely to be interested mainly in ensuring equitable treatment for their members in basic matters such as wages and seniority. Eventually they may attempt to negotiate international contracts, using the threat of an international strike as a weapon.

4. There is likely to be more government support for electronic data processing. Most governments are already aware of the need to stimulate the use of electronic data processing in their countries if they are to retain their position in the industrialized world. The implementation of multinational information systems will support proponents of this view. It can be expected that the governments of many nations will considerably expand the support they provide in the field of EDP—both directly, by providing funds for training and research, and indirectly, by improving and expanding government-owned computer facilities.

In the long run, it is to be hoped that these effects will be beneficial and will provide a powerful incentive for closer cooperation between all nations and peoples. There is already a rapidly growing internationalization of tastes, attitudes, product preferences and behavioral patterns due to the expansion of international tourism and mass media communications. The multinational corporation concept, which is likely to be measurably strengthened by the type of information system discussed here, will certainly accelerate the forces already at work in this direction. This may be the most important effect of all, as Rensis Likert has pointed out: "As managers of industrial and comparable enterprises throughout the world acquire the same basic knowledge and skills, the capacity to communicate and to interact constructively in solving complex and difficult problems and conflicts will increase correspondingly. A new and much more effective resource will become available to help in the solution of the world's international conflicts. . . . This might well become the most important contribution that the art of management will make to human well-being."[1]

The world may not have to wait until the year 2000 to enjoy the benefits of this development.

N O T E

1. Rensis Likert, "Trends Toward a World-Wide Theory of Management," *Proceedings of CIOS, 13th International Management Conference,* New York, 1963.

CHAPTER 16

FREDERICK HELDRING

*Banks are migrating all over the world
to provide clients with a full complement of services.
In so doing, they are touching the
sensitive nerves of national interests.*

Multinational Banking Strives for Identity

BANKING WAS PROBABLY the earliest multinational institution. The Rothschilds, the Fuggers, the financiers of Lombardy set up shop in practically every country of Europe and England almost without regard as to who was at war with whom.

Today, the international aspect of the institution has been resurrected and extended. The multinational corporation is one of the most interesting phenomena of the postwar period. According to an ideal concept, such a corporation produces wherever in the world it is most economic to produce, sells wherever it is most economic to sell, is owned by stockholders throughout the world and draws its management from whatever country offers the best talent.

As far as the last aspect is concerned, we are probably farthest removed in practice from the ideal. The majority of multinational entities today are companies with headquarters and a majority of their stockholders in the United States and with a U.S. citizen as president. There are also a number of companies of other nationalities, largely European, which operate under a similar set of conditions.

As long as there is no world government under whose law a multinational company can be registered, it is probable that the same condition will remain. It is interesting to speculate, however, on whether this tendency of corporations toward a multinational structure will hasten the day when a world government will become a practical economic necessity. Certainly, historically speaking, economic forces have contributed substantially to uniting provinces or counties and forging them into nations. Such forces also operate on an international scale and may eventually result in forging the nations of the world into one unit.

In banking, multinational investment has generally taken the form of U.S. banks opening branches abroad or affiliating themselves with foreign banks. The former has been likened to the growth of a rising supermarket chain, with a new branch seemingly opened week after week. The statistics bear out the substances of this observation. At the end of 1955, there were 111 foreign branches of U.S. banks in operation. Ten years later, this number had almost doubled. With 51 new branches opened in 1967, the total number of overseas branches at the end of March 1968 has risen to 308. This represents a 50% increase over 1965. The other common form —that of affiliations with foreign banks—sometimes involves majority ownership, at other times only a minority interest.

A legitimate question can be raised as to why either of these investments need be made. Probably the direct profitability of the investment has not been the major motivation. The prewar and immediate postwar world of international banking seemed to operate quite smoothly on the basis of correspondent banking. If a U.S. corporation wished to make an investment, usually the only service required was an introduction by the U.S. bank to its correspondent in the particular country. From then on, the foreign bank would take care of the financing requirements of the new subsidiary. Even then, however, a number of U.S. banks had branches abroad to which a substantial amount of business flowed. In any event, correspondent banking no longer meets the requirements of the international corporation, which expects its bank to be present in the principal countries of the world and to be able to serve it directly rather than indirectly.

There is another important reason behind this move: the continuing balance-of-payments deficit of the United States. Since the time of the Marshall Plan, the international accounts of the United States have been characterized by a trade surplus which has been more than offset by U.S. Government overseas expenditures and private investments. After realizing that a continued balance-of-payments deficit would eventually disrupt the international monetary system, the Kennedy and Johnson administrations made the restoration of equilibrium a fixed policy.

Accepting the premise that the overseas military and economic assistance programs could only be moderately tightened without jeopardizing national security interests, the administration concentrated on imposing capital restrictions as a means of realizing the desired return to equilibrium.

In 1963, the Interest Equalization Tax (I.E.T.) was introduced. Designed to reduce private capital outflows, it placed a prohibitive tax on the purchase of foreign stocks and bonds by U.S. citizens. The tax substantially reduced the ability of foreign institutions and corporations outside the less developed countries to sell stocks and bonds in the strongest of all national capital markets. Logically, what followed was a sudden swelling of bank loans to foreign borrowers. It has been estimated that possibly as much as two-thirds of all new commercial and industrial loans in New York during the 1963-1964 period were made to foreigners.

Thus, in closing one source of the capital outflow, the I.E.T. had swiftly opened another. The result was a new balance-of-payments program announced in February, 1965. Now both U.S. banks and corporations were to heed a set of "voluntary" guidelines or restraints in making new commitments for overseas loans and investments. The year 1964 was chosen as the base period. By exceeding a fixed percentage of their commitments during that time, banks and corporations would clearly invite legal restrictions.

Eurodollars the Incentive

While a fixed ceiling had been established during a time of international business expansion, one major source of U.S. capital still existed: the Eurodollar. Suddenly, this formerly ignored offspring of the U.S. balance-of-payments deficit assumed a role of great significance. Defined as dollars on deposit with banks outside the United States and used for lending to other banks and commercial borrowers, Eurodollars rapidly became a kind of off-shore U.S. capital market.

Since that time Eurodollars have become recognized as useful, valuable and prized sources of funds. If banks were to service international investments, they had to have access to the Eurodollar market. Since, by definition, Eurodollars are held outside the United States, there was a major incentive to open offices overseas in order to participate directly in this active market.

An effective yet harmless antidote had been found for the balance of payments guidelines. To the extent that they successfully bid for Eurodollar deposits, bankers with overseas operations could accommodate the capital requirements of their customers. Exempt from all Federal Reserve statutes (including reserve requirements and limits on rates of interest), Eurodollars give a distinct advantage to domestic banks with overseas branches and ultimately cause a redistribution of bank reserves within the over-all banking system.

Use of Eurodollars by U.S. banks overseas has no direct effect on the U.S. balance of payments, since the Eurodollars have already been recorded as an outflow. Nevertheless, the Federal Reserve has taken note of the new use to which banks have put Eurodollars. In times of tight money, foreign branches have made a practice of lending Eurodollar balances to their head offices in this country. Again, this perfectly legal use of Eurodollars has given an impetus to overseas expansion.

The great rush for overseas branches in the mid-1960's is not sustainable. While in raw numbers banks are unlikely to increase as quickly as before, they will no doubt substantially increase both their size and their significance in the countries where they function. The emergence of this Eurodollar has attracted a veritable invasion of U.S. bank branches, principally in London, which is the acknowledged center of the Eurodollar market.

Recently, however, it has become evident to a number of banks that the expense of establishing a branch in London is so high that other locations for branches are more desirable. In Nassau, the Bahamas, where expenses involved in such undertaking are about one-tenth those in London, Eurodollars can be handled just as efficiently. Other considerations are playing a role in avoiding London. Apart from Eurodollar operations, it is clear that London is over-banked as far as U.S. institutions are concerned. Total investment of U.S. corporations in the United Kingdom amounts to $5 billion. It is doubtful that seventeen branches of U.S. banks having total assets of more than $110 billion are required to serve that investment. At the same time, except for those banks which have been in the market for a long time, it will be difficult to build up a profitable sterling business with British customers.

The Eurodollar market may be here to stay, but then again it may not. The margin between cost of funds and lending rates in that market is much lower than those prevailing in any local market, including that of the United States. In the last analysis, banks look to that margin for the return of their new worth. The small margin in the Eurodollar market does not directly add to a bank's over-all profitability. It may actually subtract from it. There appears, therefore, to be no solid economic justification for almost any U.S. bank entering the London market at this time.

Reciprocity

The implication that the multinational bank is strictly a U.S. enterprise should not go unchallenged. Foreign banking operations in the United States have been making rapid strides in recent months. Centered in New York and California, these banks can be expected to become increasingly numerous, competitive and aggressive. A recent survey by the *American Banker*, for example, found that in New York City 13 foreign banks operate branches, 20 have state-chartered affiliates or subsidiaries, 25 have agencies, and 61 have representatives offices. What may be the start of a trend to overcome the handicap of their small size relative to U.S. banks may be seen in the formation in New York last May of the European-American Banking Corporation and The European-American Bank and Trust Company. Capitalized initially at $70 million, the new banks represent a joint venture of four leading European banks, Société Générale de Banque (Belgium), Midland Limited (England), Deutsche Bank, A.G. (Germany), and Amsterdam-Rotterdam Bank (Netherlands).

The Challenge of Global Banking

The thrust of both corporations and banks, particularly in Europe, has constituted the "American Challenge" so effectively described by Jean-Jacques Servan-Schreiber. This challenge, which has touched all the nerve centers of nationalism, has often been spoken of in terms of a technological gap. The schism has deeper roots. In banking—where technology is relatively less important—the challenge is just as great as in industry. The problem is based on differences among management men in Europe and the United States toward the handling of people. It is a management gap. "Americans are not more intelligent than other people. Yet human factors—the ability to adapt easily, flexibility of organizations, the creative power of teamwork—are the key to their success. Beyond any single explanation, each of which has an element of truth, the secret lies in the confidence of the society in its citizens."[1]

Frequently, we speak of industrial plant capacity being used only up to a certain percentage, but what of human resources? Not one human being is employed up to 100% of his capacity all the time. What of the difference between one company and another, one industry and another, one country and another? Is it possible, for example, that the Japanese utilize people to a larger percentage of their capacity than the English? Could this account for differences in economic growth and balance-of-payments performance? Undoubtedly, this is an oversimplification, but it may well be one facet of the complicated truth that is the "American Challenge" in Europe.

At the same time, it is important to say a few words about nationalism, a force which is generally underestimated in the business world. It is natural for one to be proud of his nation and to treasure its independence in economics as well as politics. It is understandable that a people, when it sees important fragments of its industrial power taken over by foreign companies or even multinational companies, should become fearful of its economic independence. It is also understandable that the investing corporation, considering its individual investment decision on a rational basis, sees no reason why it should be restrained by nationalistic sentiments. It is easy to laugh off the fear of losing one's independence as being irrational, but it is a real sentiment, and the situation will probably become worse before it gets better.

In banking, particularly in Europe, the "American Challenge" is real. Reactions in Europe range from satisfaction that some of the old staid ways of banking are being shaken by new banking methods, to fear and even resentment. Most of this is inevitable. Even if banks were to behave impeccably at all times (and some do not), there still would be the fear of the foreign, the new and the big. A branch or a majority-owned affiliation in any country should have one abiding and overriding principle: to identify itself with the progressive aspirations of the country in which the investment is located. That principle may well override the short-term interest of the parent bank.

If a foreign bank, by having branches or affiliates in most of the European countries, is able to render a clearing service useful to clients with operations in those countries, and that service cannot be duplicated by a local bank, the latter may have to accept the situation. The service is obviously helping to integrate an area, and this, in turn, is good for the individual countries. It is up to the local banks to coordinate their services among themselves to a point where they can be competitive. When that happens, every side gains.

One form of banking investment abroad which identifies closely with the country in which it is located is the minority affiliation. In such cases the equity percentage of the investing bank should be small enough for nationals to retain the voting power, but sizable enough to show that the foreign bank has serious intentions. A number of U.S. banks have made their investments on this basis.

One other form of banking presence abroad is the representative office. Assuming that the individual representative is well acquainted both with his own bank and the home market and is competent in interpreting the overseas market to the corporate client, this may be a very useful instrument. The representative office reduces the possibility of conflict with nationalistic sentiment and is frequently welcomed. In a world where intelligent advice is of increasing importance, a good representative can be of an inestimable value to the corporate client.

It is clear that banking is still removed from the multinational concept. Yet U.S. banks are coming closer to the ideal than institutions in any other country.

In the long run, multinationality in its truest forms may be one solution to the problem of legitimate nationalism. Although the nation-state could consider itself threatened even by the multinational company, at least the identification with one specific country would be avoided. In the meantime, it would seem advisable for international banks to demonstrate an increasing understanding of the problem of nationalism. Nations may appreciate the import of technology and management techniques, but pressure groups may promote resistance in the name of national interests.

The fundamental problem which must be resolved by banks operating overseas is the divergence between their over-all orientation and that of the countries in which they are located. A recent study of foreign government restraints on overseas U.S. bank operations describes the situation:

"On the one hand, the banks are profit motivated, oriented toward aggressive competition with other financial institutions and, at least in their international transactions, have no great compulsion to shape their actions primarily to preserve cultural or national identities. On the other hand, governments as representatives of people with such values are motivated both by the general economic welfare of those people, the particular welfare of special groups in their society and less tangible considerations of preserving a feeling of national unity."[2]

The extent to which the convergence of interests between banks operating abroad and their foreign hosts is understood and pursued will determine the long-term success of the multinational bank.

N O T E S

1. Jean-Jacques Servan-Schreiber, *The American Challenge*, New York: Atheneum 1968.

2. From a report prepared by the American Bankers Association for the Joint Economic Committee of the U.S. Congress.

CHAPTER 17

SIR RICHARD COSTAIN

The international construction business requires
a strong constitution and a crusading spirit.
Without such equipment, there is
precious little reason to remain in . . .

The Strange World

of the International

Construction Company

THERE IS ONE MAJOR DIFFERENCE between international contracting
and other forms of world trading: we have to make the finished
product in the place in which it is finally required. Once we have
obtained the contract, we must set up in the shortest possible time
a complex organization containing within its scope the courage,
experience, initiative, and techniques needed to engage and defeat
natural conditions, some of the earth's worst climatic vagaries, and

that deep resistance the land always shows to those trying to change its face.

Let any manufacturer who reads this imagine the problems of establishing a factory within a matter of weeks, in a location with a disagreeable climate, far from civilized amenities, lacking in power, water, and sometimes raw materials, with labor willing but largely unskilled, speaking only a foreign language and having to be housed and fed; of providing at short notice the necessary management, very often on a bachelor-living basis; of importing and assembling the plant and machinery for robust and full-time operation, with spares and workshops; of doing all this and reaching a profitable turnover, in say three months, on as much as $3 million per month—this is the world of the international contractor.

It is reasonable to ask, then, what motivates a contractor to work abroad. Although in a free enterprise society the profit motive cannot be minimized, it would be wrong to ascribe the decision to work internationally primarily to the desire to make more money, real and ever-present though this is. For a man to be a contractor, or a builder, or a civil engineer, he must have an inherent desire to change the world—a strong feeling that he can leave things in some degree better than he found them. He must believe in what he does and be ready to live the job as a part of himself, with a wholehearted and total commitment to it, for his achievement will be a permanent monument to himself, his company, and his country.

It has been said that business is made up of three activities: talking, writing, and thinking. In a world of increasing complexity, many make successful and rewarding careers without ever coming face to face with the physical problems of the processes involved. In contracting the confrontation is inescapable, and lends a sense of adventure and decision to each day's round. The pioneering spirit, which lingers in many of us, finds outlets in a civilized society increasingly restricted; in these times contractors rather than explorers are often the pioneers of new territories. So to the right kind of man, life cannot offer a more satisfying prospect than to live and work in far-off places, creating something he hopes will be indestructible.

Rapid improvements in communications and transport have made the world smaller—the magic names which invoke the spirit of history and adventure are no longer impossibly remote; transit is

measured in hours rather than weeks. The sensations of leaving the
stomach far behind, of not knowing what day or what time it is, of
being momentarily unsure whether one is in Baghdad or Bangkok
are well known to our people. We travel at short notice and our
passports are always at hand, our injections up-to-date, and our
wives resigned. It is not uncommon for senior staff to spend three
months or more of the year abroad, and this makes severe demands
on stamina, digestion, and endurance. Often important decisions
must be made after a sleepless night on an aircraft, far from the
intricate consultations and wide-ranging experience of Head Office,
and involving an assessment and judgment of factors outside the
normal scope of the industry. Above all, senior executives must
know and believe that they have the full confidence and support of
their company and that it will stand firmly behind their decisions.

The "Mysterious Alchemy"

So we have the will to work abroad, and we have the men, but
how do we get the jobs? What mysterious alchemy, what deeply
plotted behind-the-scenes activities lead contractor A to be awarded
the prize, while contractors B and C go away empty-handed?

Contractors must either sponsor, design, invent, and foster activities which can be sold directly to and negotiated with those who
require them, or bid competitively on a predetermined basis against
their fellows in the open market, under recognized conditions of
international bidding. The ground rules of competitive bidding are
well understood and are on the surface demonstrably fair—the bids
are opened and unless there is some strong reason to the contrary,
the lowest is successful. There are, however, very few other forms
of selling a single product, often worth very large amounts, comparable to this: in other fields it is a rash assumption that the cheap-
est article is the one to be preferred, even if descriptions and specifications make them apparently equal. In the field of international
contracting, it is equally hazardous to proceed on the basis of price
alone. It is difficult for clients to assess all the applicable factors
when asking for bids, and the contractors' appreciation and understanding of them may differ in each individual case. Even when the
design has been fully detailed by consultants and the applicable

conditions have been defined, each bidder must carry out a technical study in depth, to determine the method and sequence of operations, the number and status of site staff, the types and quantities of plant required and the way in which it will be employed.

It can be observed from a study of published bid results that there are wide divergencies in prices—wider than might be thought possible, for in addition to variations arising from different methods of approach, further differences may result from the following:

1. Firms that are not competent to do the work often put in foolishly low bids. (Fortunately, the larger and more complex projects are at present beyond the powers of more than a relatively few international firms, although this situation is changing, as a study of the names of bidders for large contracts shows.)

2. Some companies are subsidized to operate at a loss by their governments and deliberately underbid in order to acquire foreign currency or infiltrate politically.

3. Some contractors may have much work in hand, and while not wishing from the point of view of good relations to decline to bid, do not really wish to be successful, except at a higher than usual return. Others have insufficient outlet for plant and resources already owned, and are therefore prepared to accept lower margins.

4. A contractor may bid low, but with certain conditions or qualifications. If his bid is accepted, he may be invited to discuss these qualifications, withdrawal or clarification of which would enable him legitimately to increase his price.

5. In addition to the practical difficulties of estimating accurately what the work will cost, a number of management decisions must be made each time a bid is submitted. These decisions frequently relate to the political and financial stability of the client country over a period of years, the possibility of labor unrest, of sudden increases in costs arising from events outside the contractor's control, and many other factors that may prevent timely completion of the contract. It is axiomatic that these judgments will vary with the individual bidder.

Since a given work opportunity may attract a wide range of bids from firms of varying competence and seriousness of purpose, it may be thought that a reputable contractor will be unable to put in the lowest bid and still work profitably. Such is not the case, for at least two reasons.

In asking a bidder to submit a firm price, the client is accepting the implication that he will pay for the contractor's assessment of the risks, whether they become real or remain imagined, so that provision for contingencies which do not arise may well increase profits.

The second factor relates to the value which the contractor puts upon the plant and equipment which he proposes to use; this may be purchased new or it may already be in his possession, but in either case the contract must bear some proportion of its cost and depreciation. How much is charged to the contract depends on what future use or disposal is calculated for the plant—for example, if the contract is the first one of a possible series, having the plant available and working in a distant location may well give an advantage in securing further contracts.

The Inevitable Extras

Before leaving the subject of bidding, a word might be said about claims. Anyone who has arranged with a builder to build a home knows that it is unusual for the cost of the work to be within the initial estimate, and on larger ventures this is likely to be true to an even greater extent. For variations arising from changes of design, intent, or predetermined conditions, it is for the contractor to claim and for the client, after assessment and verification, to pay. A contract, basically, is an agreement between two parties by which something is done for a consideration; if any variation arises between the original concept and the execution, it is reasonable to expect the party benefiting from the difference to pay for it. Nevertheless, resentment is often caused, although recourse to arbitration is infrequent. It is rumored that there are certain contractors who, when bidding, include the profit they expect to make from claims in the price they submit, with teams of legal experts studying the contract for loopholes. As in most other forms of business activity, however, a reasonable line must be drawn between what is illegal, unethical, or simply inadvisable. There is a code of ethics in contracting which is truly international in application, and violations soon become known, for contractors, although rivals, are seldom enemies and the competitor for a contract in one case may well be the joint-venture partner in another.

There are numerous heartening examples of Anglo-American cooperation on international projects by means of joint ventures, and my own company has been singularly fortunate in this respect. Disagreements between partners are rare, for they have a joint, easily definable, and limited target—the profitable completion of the contract—and experience has shown that in these circumstances different nationalities work happily together, each learning from the other. Contracting is a sphere of international activity in which politics, nationalism, or dogma play little part.

Although no truly international contractor objects to bidding against genuine competition, most prefer negotiation to tendering, and employ worldwide intelligence systems to keep in touch with future work opportunities. The target is to find a client who will in the future need what they have to sell, and in order to be able to fulfill this need, most major contractors are prepared to undertake design-and-build, or "turn-key," projects. However, the expense and effort required to design and price a large project, and the difficulty of ensuring that the client will go through with the deal once the design is in his hands, restrict this approach generally to medium-sized projects. So far as the clients are concerned, particularly those in developing countries, the approach has advantages and in the final analysis, is not likely to be more expensive than competitive bids, although this is not widely believed.

In order to undertake design-and-build projects, the contractor must have the ability to arrange satisfactory finance over a period of years, and even the most powerful contractors need help from their governments in doing this. A contractor must keep his own financial resources for the necessary lock-up of his business, and will rarely invest in a project simply as a means of obtaining negotiated contracts. There is a saying in the industry: "we can work anywhere in the world if we put up the money," but if a contractor is to invest in a proposition—for example, building a hotel, or the development of a township—it must be in itself profitable, considered purely on an investment basis, apart from the comparatively minor aspect of profit on the construction work.

So the contractor's world is one in which he must produce a

different product, in a different location each time, without knowing precisely what the product will cost, or how much profit he will make when he has sold it, or where he is going to sell it next! A world in which the pitfalls are many and the talents needed wide-ranging and diverse; in which each single venture involves the will to commit, in places far from day-to-day control, large resources of technical skill and finance without any real certainty of the outcome. A world of achievement, of tangible results, benefiting and improving the lives of many, and calling for courage, determination to reach the objective, a spirit of adventure, and at times a strong and rebounding sense of humor.

CHAPTER 18

DONALD M. BARRETT

*Multi-flag airlines operate in a milieu
of nationalistic diversity. Their structures may have
meaning for others in the same situation.*

Multi-Flag Airlines:

A New Breed

in World Business

BUSINESSMEN AND GOVERNMENT OFFICIALS who seek to liberate international business from the restrictions of excessive nationalism and commercial conservatism are looking to the emerging multinational corporations for fresh ideas. Commercial aviation, which has always demanded a high degree of managerial skill and innovation to meet the challenge of explosive growth, is developing creative new business structures in one of the most competitive arenas of world business.

The term "multinational" as applied to aviation must be strictly defined. It covers only those international air transport enterprises jointly owned and operated as national air carriers of two or more nations. The four principal examples of such companies operating today are: Scandinavian Airlines System (SAS), Air Afrique (RK), East African Airways Corporation (EAA) and Malaysia-Singapore Airlines, Ltd. (MSA). While certain aspects of these companies may appear similar, each one has developed special features suited to its own environment. SAS, for example, is not a corporation but rather a consortium of three national airline corporations. Each of the other multi-flag carriers has a separate legal personality in the corporate form but is organized along different lines.

The selection of these examples from among more than one hundred airlines operating scheduled international air services excludes those companies in which equity interests are held by foreign airlines, governments or individuals, and which are the national carriers of a single country. Also eliminated as "multinational" are the dozens of airlines which have pooling arrangements to share traffic and revenues among partners of different nationalities. Thus, it is the "multi-flag" aspect of the enterprise—the diversity of nationality with respect to ownership, control and representation—which constitutes the really distinguishing feature of the multinational airline.

The special politico-legal environment in which all international commercial airlines operate must be understood in order to appreciate the accomplishments of the selected examples.

The Conventions

The legal framework for international operating rights was basically laid down by the Paris Convention on the Regulation of Aerial Navigation in 1919. This Convention enunciated the principle that each nation has complete and exclusive sovereignty over the air space above its territory. This principle was incorporated into the national laws of many countries before World War II and was reaffirmed in the Convention on International Civil Aviation signed at Chicago in 1944. The "Chicago Convention," as it has come to be known, specified that no scheduled international air service may be operated over or into the territory of a contracting state, except with the permission of that state.

Consequently, every airline operating scheduled international air services must obtain the requisite authorization from the government of each country along the route it seeks to operate, as well as from the government of the country where it is incorporated or established.

On the other hand, the Chicago Convention specifically authorizes member states to participate in joint operating enterprises through their governments or through an airline company or companies designated by the governments. The companies may, at the sole discretion of the states concerned, be state-owned, partly state-owned or privately owned. Thus, provision for multinational air enterprises is embodied in the Convention itself which has been ratified by 116 countries. Operating rights, however, are negotiated on a bilateral basis between states, and this presents a special set of circumstances for governments negotiating on behalf of a multinational firm.

The concept of joint ownership and operation of international air services by two or more nations is not a recent one. Among several early proposals was a bold plan offered in 1944 by Australia and New Zealand for a single international corporation, with participation by any interested state, to operate major international routes. Several schemes to integrate air transport in Europe followed approval of the Schuman Steel and Coal Community plan in 1951. The much publicized "Air Union" project for a consortium of major European airlines was a more recent effort. Proposals for multinational airline enterprises have been advanced or are currently being considered in almost every region of the world.

While none of these many plans has really borne fruit, due primarily to changing political and economic circumstances, and, in some cases, to commercial rivalries, there were a few short-lived experiments. Australia and New Zealand, with the participation of the United Kingdom, established a joint airline in 1946 under the name "British Commonwealth Pacific Airlines" (BCPA), which operated services between Australasia and the United States from 1948 to 1954 when the Australian airline Qantas took over most of the operations. BCPA outlived its usefulness as a going enterprise primarily because of the national interest of each member country in developing its own independent service. The dissolution of another brief experiment—Central African Airways Corporation (CAA)—which operated international long-haul routes on behalf of Rhodesia, Zambia and Malawi from 1964 to 1968, was due principally to political and racial antagonisms.

Scandinavian Airlines System

Certainly the best known example of multinational cooperation in the air is the Scandinavian Airlines System (SAS). Established in 1946, it is the oldest continuously operating multinational carrier. Unification of Scandinavia's air transport was discussed for more than a decade before the three partner companies finally agreed on a plan for consolidation and cooperation.

In the post-World War II climate of aviation, the three Scandinavian airlines were faced with the choice of operating on a very modest regional scale or venturing for the first time into intercontinental service. Each airline was too small to go it alone, and each country was in a weak position to bargain for commercial operating rights on a bilateral basis with larger countries.

After initial success in the joint operation of North and South Atlantic routes, the original consortium agreement was revised in 1948 to include European services and again in 1950 to encompass all international and intercontinental services. Under the present 25-year agreement, approved by the respective governments, Sweden's Aktiebelaget Aerotransport (ABA), Norway's Det Norske Luftfartselskab A/S (DNL) and Denmark's Det Danske Luftfartselskab A/S (DDL) provide flight equipment and ground facilities for use in the joint services and divide the net proceeds of operations in the following ratios: ABA 3/7, DNL 2/7 and DDL 2/7. Each member airline is owned 50% by private individuals or enterprises and 50% by the respective national governments. The three companies are jointly and severally liable for any obligation or liability of the consortium.

In essence, the consortium agreement establishes relationships much like those of a partnership of the three member limited liability share companies. The arrangement provides unique approaches to two special requirements: registration of aircraft and negotiation of operating rights. Under the Chicago Convention, dual or multiple registration of aircraft is prohibited. The consortium meets this condition by providing that the ownership of each aircraft operated by the consortium is retained by one of the parties and is registered in its country, but all aircraft are regarded "internally" by the members as owned by them in the 3/7, 2/7, 2/7 ratio. It has been said that the SAS agreement succeeds in obtaining the substance of ownership while renouncing the form.

In negotiating operating rights with foreign countries on a bilateral basis, the Scandinavians have been largely successful because of the goodwill of other nations. A Scandinavian country, party to a bilateral agreement with another nation, has generally been able to insert a so-called "SAS clause" in the agreement, under which that Scandinavian country designates its own national airline to operate the agreed-on services. This airline, however, is expressly permitted to do so with aircraft and crew belonging to either of the two other members of the consortium. Even where such a clause has not been explicitly incorporated in an agreement, its application has been generally accepted in practice.

Arrangements with the United States are handled on a somewhat different basis. The United States has separate bilateral agreements with each of the three Scandinavian countries without any "SAS clause." But the routes exchanged are compatible so that a single entity, the consortium, can provide service over the routes on the basis of a single foreign air carrier permit issued by the United States Civil Aeronautics Board to SAS rather than to each of the three national airlines.

The SAS management organization presents an interesting model of balance and flexibility. Under the 1950 agreement (for which, incidentally, the English language was chosen as the original and official version), the affairs of the consortium are managed by a Board of Directors, an Executive Committee and several Managers, one of whom is designated "General Manager (President)" and acts as chief executive officer. The Board of SAS consists of the persons who from time to time are members of the Boards of ABA, DDL and DNL. At the meetings of the SAS Board, however, only six representatives from each party may take part as voting members and are named by the parties for each meeting.

Board decisions are taken by majority vote on most matters. In appointing the various management personnel, the Board and the General Manager are obligated to make every effort to achieve an organization which is as "rational and efficient as possible." Appointments, furthermore, are to be made "with due consideration of achieving a reasonable proportion between Swedes, Danes and Norwegians."

This unique balance between the interests and powers of the three partners has apparently worked well in practice and achieves the unity of purpose and harmonious operation intended by the organizers. Of course, it is almost impossible to avoid all criticism, and there has been agitation in some quarters from time to time to dissolve SAS. Certain elements in Norway, for example, have suggested that Norway pull out of the consortium and set up its own international air services. These critics allege that SAS's domestic operations in Norway are inadequate and that SAS employment in that country is inequitable in relation to Norway's capital participation.

In this connection, the agreement wisely sets forth the policy that operations shall be governed by "sound business considerations, practice and policy." Another guiding principle is that "The Consortium shall make every effort towards allocating in a reasonable way the business activities of the Consortium between the three countries." However, in case of conflict, an *Aide Memoire* states that "the business principle in certain cases must yield in order to preserve and enhance the Consortium's Scandinavian character and in order to consider the national interest."

SAS has proven to be, on the whole, a successful enterprise, enjoying an excellent reputation for service and dependability. It would seem that the strong motivation of the Scandinavian countries to cooperate closely and the carefully worked out relationships of the partners have produced a viable organization flexible enough to handle problems of growth, financing and the occasional cries of "go it alone." Instead of using the restrictive practices of international aviation as competitive weapons against each other, the Scandinavian airlines have combined to mutual advantage and will probably survive new stresses so long as cooperation based on sound business principles continues to be the guiding philosophy.

Air Afrique

Air Afrique represents the most daring of the new approaches to joint air transport endeavors. This unique airline is the product of the Treaty of Yaoundé, signed in the capital of Cameroon on March 28, 1961 by the heads of state and governments of 11 West African nations: The Republics of Cameroon, Chad, Congo (Brazzaville), Dahomey, Gabon, Ivory Coast, Niger, Senegal, Upper Volta, the Central African Republic and the Islamic Republic of Mauritania.

These 11 nations (joined by Togo in 1964) agreed to form a single, multinational airline operation, known as Air Afrique and designated as "the instrument chosen by each of them for exercising their rights in respect of international traffic and air transport rights." The Treaty of Yaoundé is a model of clarity and simplicity. In only 18 brief articles it established Air Afrique as a private, limited-liability, joint-stock company, with ownership divided equally among the parties, having a unitary structure with a registered head office and full legal powers in each of the capitals of the member states, and enjoying the status of the national airline of each state.

The Air Afrique concept grew out of the need of the newly independent nations of West Africa for rapid communication internally and with other nations. Air transport was seen as the best method to achieve domestic unification and to foster beneficial international contacts. After examining existing forms, planners rejected as inappropriate the SAS consortium formula, since the problem in West Africa was not how to unite existing enterprises but how to create an enterprise having at the beginning no resources, no equipment, no facilities and no personnel. Creating individual companies in the several states and joining them in a consortium would have meant formation of empty structures at considerable cost. Erecting separate national entities would have emphasized the diversity (or even potential opposition) of national interests.

The first basic principle adopted was, consequently, that of a unitary organizational structure, which would be the direct owner of the equipment and facilities, the direct employer of all personnel and responsible for the operations and obligations of the joint enterprise. The second fundamental principle adopted was that of multinationality. Various existing unitary organizations were studied, especially those in Europe such as Euro-Chemical. But these forms of organization, when adapted to international aviation, would produce encumbering consequences attendant on the question of nationality, i.e., ownership and registration of aircraft, negotiation of landing rights, etc.

Optimum utilization of air traffic rights of member states dictated a joint approach to bargaining with outside nations. In this regard, Cheikh Fal, the Chairman and General Manager of Air Afrique, has observed: "In the case of new states, only one thing counts . . . because they have nothing else . . . taking advantage of their traffic rights. . . . New countries cannot afford to throw away their rights which form the basis of their operations and their sole valuable possession." At the bargaining table, the whole is greater than the sum of the parts! For these reasons, the joint corporation is vested with the nationality of each of the contracting states.

Civil aviation laws and regulations of partner states were relatively easy to bring into harmony because of pre-existing general uniformity of legal codes and practices. This has minimized bureaucratic entanglements, which could have strangled the nascent enterprise. The Treaty envisages multiple registration of Air Afrique aircraft, and a ruling on this is pending before the Council of the International Civil Aviation Organization pursuant to a special provision of the Chicago Convention. Meanwhile, the corporation's aircraft are registered in a single member country.

Creation by international treaty signed by heads of state has assured Air Afrique of strong domestic political support within member states. While direct action by governments launched Air Afrique on the soundest possible political basis, the founders did not neglect the practical side. They astutely chose to involve friendly, experienced, commercial airline organizations. Two French airlines, Air France (AF) and Union de Transports Aériens (UTA), were invited to participate in the new venture through a holding company called "SODETRAF" which would have a minority equity interest. Experts from the two airlines contributed valuable ideas and encouragement during the formative stages of Air Afrique and continue to provide vital administrative and technical skills as department heads while African personnel are trained.

A committee of Ministers of Transport establishes common policy and promotes development of commercial aviation. In this way the Treaty anticipated a crucial need. Each state is obligated to submit to the Committee for its opinion any draft air traffic agreement and to be guided by the Committee's opinion.

Air Afrique enjoys exemptions from certain taxes, customs duties and other charges within member states under the terms of an Annex to the Treaty which obligates the states to harmonize their respective laws on these subjects. In addition, parties facilitate the transfer of funds and currencies required by corporate activities.

The Articles of Incorporation, annexed to the Treaty, delineate the organization and legal powers of the corporation and its management. The General Assembly of shareholders appoints a Board of Directors, which is the decision-making body. Thirty-four members chosen in direct proportion to the shares held serve for a period of four years. The Board has full powers to act in the name of the corporation. Management consists of the Chairman and General Manager, who is chief executive officer, several other officers, and four functional divisions: commercial, financial, technical and operational. Cheikh Fal has described the management philosophy of the corporation as requiring "decentralization on the administrative side, but recentralization at the decision-making level."

It is a tribute to the founders of Air Afrique that the Articles of Incorporation have been amended only twice: in 1962 to eliminate the separate position of General Manager and to combine the functions of this office with those of the Chairman; and in 1963 to amend the provisions on the division of capital so as to guarantee "SODETRAF" representation on the Board when new states become associated with the enterprise.

There were many in 1961 who predicted complete failure for Air Afrique. They charged that it was impossible to make constructive and mutually acceptable decisions with a single structure; that the problems of international ownership it posed were insurmountable; that such a corporation would not be recognized by third countries because it was too original and would pose too many problems for them. It should be noted that some of these predictions came from the same people who had foretold the failure of SAS.

Air Afrique has not failed. True, there have been many difficulties, one of these being the pace of Africanization. But today Air Afrique's network is already the longest in Africa—over 60,000 miles —and covers 23 countries on the continent. It is first in carriage of cargo in Africa and second in terms of passenger mileage. In less than eight years, Air Afrique owns a fleet of four DC-8's, two jet Caravelles, four DC-4's and a DC-3. Its flights serve France and Switzerland in Europe, and, under a "blocked-space" agreement with Pan American, Air Afrique leases passenger and cargo space on PAA aircraft operating between West Africa and New York.

Air Afrique's eight-story building in Abidjan, Ivory Coast, serves as administrative center, housing 500 employees, and as headquarters for the more than 3,000 employees of the company, 86% of whom are African. Revenues in 1967 exceeded $58 million, and investments in that year in aircraft, materiel and facilities totaled over $48 million, or more than eight times its authorized capital.

Though Air Afrique has not yet paid dividends, neither has it received a subsidy from any state. The management of Air Afrique regards the company, like the African nations themselves, as still "too young," and not in a position to distribute profits when the demands for consolidation and expansion are so urgent.

East African Airways

Following the independence of Kenya, Uganda and Tanzania in 1963, East African Airways Corporation (EAA) was reorganized the same year under an Act of the Central Legislative Assembly of the three nations as a public, statutory corporation jointly and equally owned by all three. EAA services have grown from the original company's East African operations, begun in 1946, to the present regional African, European and Asian operations.

On December 1, 1967, in a major step to strengthen East African unity, the three partner states signed the Treaty for East African Cooperation, creating an East African Economic Community of 30 million people. Common services, such as railways, harbors, post offices and airways, hitherto operating wholly or partly under the direction of the superseded East African Common Services Organization (EACSO), were reconstituted as corporations and made institutions of the East African Community.

Since it has long been the policy of EAA under its previous charters to plan and act on an East African basis and to view its operations as a whole for the benefit of all East African peoples, the new set-up should not prove burdensome. EAA remains essentially what it was before—a self-contained corporation.

For over-all policy guidance, EAA looks to the East African Authority, consisting of the presidents of the three member states. Civil aviation matters come under the Communications Ministerial Council composed of the Ministers of Communications from each member state and certain other representatives. Decisions of the Authority and the Council must be on the basis of unanimity.

Although EAA receives strong support from the Community, it has been wrestling with three difficult internal problems: decentralization, Africanization and expansion. To decentralize some of the facilities, an engine overhaul shop may be established at Entebbe Airport in Uganda. Sensitive to demands for more rapid Africanization of EAA's personnel, management is spending substantial sums on training programs aimed at rapid replacement of expatriate flight crews and technicians, while constant political pressures continue to challenge sound business practice.

On expansion, Chief Fundikira, the Chairman of EAA, has said, "No airline can stand still. To live it must expand and we are expanding." EAA developed new routes to West Africa in 1967 and extended the Asian service from India to Hong Kong in 1968.

In spite of an enviable earnings record—EAA has operated for 12 years at a profit and without subsidy—there has been criticism that EAA's foreign-exchange earnings do not cover the payment of overseas purchases for expansion. EAA management contends that the cost of new aircraft (three VC-10's are in operation, with a fourth to be delivered in 1969 and an option on a fifth) is being met on a pay-as-you-earn basis.

While justifiably optimistic for the future, Chief Fundikira is also realistic. He has recently said, "We have not allowed ourselves to be influenced by prestige. We are a commercial proposition and the governments (of East Africa) are very alive to the need for us to remain as such." With that kind of hard-headed attitude, EAA management may well continue its profitable record while making a major contribution to East African unity.

Malaysia-Singapore Airlines

Unlike the formation of SAS by consortium agreement, Air Afrique by formal treaty, or EAA by joint legislative act, Malaysia-Singapore Airlines, Ltd. (MSA) evolved from an agreement signed on May 14, 1966 by the governments of Malaysia and Singapore to acquire joint control of an existing airline, Malaysian Airways, Ltd. (a regional carrier based in Singapore with a history of operations in Southeast Asia going back to 1947). The two governments each now hold 42.5% of the shares of MSA, while the British airline BOAC and the Australian airline Qantas hold small interests, along with the government of Brunei and Straits Steamship Co., Ltd.

Mounting political differences between the leaders of the predominantly Malayan peoples of the mainland Federation of Malaysia and officials of the ethnically Chinese community on the island of Singapore resulted in separation of Singapore from the Federation in August 1965. The joint airline is now one of the few remaining effective links between the two countries.

MSA is managed by a 14-member Board of Directors, a Chairman and a General Manager, with five staff Directors, 11 managers of functional departments, together with various overseas and area managers. Malaysia and Singapore each have four representatives on the Board, which gives the two governments effective joint control, but there is no special, formal intergovernmental entity to coordinate decisions on vital policy questions. Today, there is open discussion about a possible break-up of the airline. Political and economic differences between the countries may cause increasing internal stresses in the airline's administration.

Serious division over MSA's activities has arisen from a contradiction in the policy objectives of the MSA partners and over such matters as allocation of services between domestic and international routes, employment practices and replacement of expatriate personnel, distribution of foreign-exchange earnings, the location of facilities and related benefits to the respective economies.

Another policy question dividing the partners is the exchange of air traffic rights with third countries. Malaysia's principal airport at the capital of Kuala Lumpur is, in design, the most attractive in Asia today. Malaysia would prefer to encourage international airlines to use the "K.L." airport without exacting reciprocal landing rights from foreign countries—thus sacrificing strict reciprocity in order to secure a bigger share of the tourist market for the mainland—and to help pay for the investment and operation of the new airport and facilities. Singapore, however, has so far taken a more restrictive attitude toward foreign-carrier landing rights at both "K.L." and Singapore to protect MSA from feared excessive foreign competition.

Perhaps the most difficult problem confronting the parties is the allocation of the airline's services between domestic and international operations. Malaysia needs convenient and reliable communications with the far-flung cities and towns of the mainland and island territories of the Federation. On the other hand, Singapore's geographical position at the crossroads of Southeast Asia, its preeminence as a trading hub and its expanding industrial and tourism interests lead Singapore to seek development of an air service that will connect the island via major international routes with distant trading and tourism centers in the Pacific area.

An official of the Malaysian Ministry of Foreign Affairs recently remarked: ". . . having an equal share in the airline, Malaysia cannot afford, any more than Singapore, to minimize the importance of running MSA on sound commercial principles. . . ." He added: "Our concerns will sometimes differ, but there is a clear need for us to understand each other and to accommodate each other. . . ."

These difficulties must be overcome to avert the break-up of a respected company which is capable of becoming one of the most successful and profitable airlines in Southeast Asia.

What will be the role of the multinational airline in the difficult years ahead when the new generation of super-jets and supersonic aircraft come into use? Knut Hammarskjold, Director General of the International Air Transport Association, recently observed: "Most nations—large and small—feel a determination to participate in international air transport. . . . With latest types of aircraft now being contemplated costing upward of $20 million each, and with the prospect of the ultimate SST costing between $40 and $50 million apiece, the problem of these countries finding economic resources to enable their own airlines to remain fully competitive is becoming an overwhelming one.

"I think most people will agree that the solution of this problem in the future will lie in the expansion of cooperative arrangements between countries, either through jointly owned airlines or equipment-interchange schemes. The example already set by, for instance, SAS and Air Afrique, will, I believe, become more and more the norm of the smaller countries."

Experience to date would appear to support Hammarskjold's view. However, it should be recognized that a workable multi-flag enterprise requires solid agreement on the following essentials:

(1) Compatibility of interests and commitment to common objectives;

(2) Strong support by participating governments with some sort of intergovernmental machinery to coordinate policy from inception;

(3) Freedom of management to operate on sound commercial principles and practices (especially in the face of political pressures); and

(4) Flexibility of administrative structure to provide constantly balanced representation of the parties and to meet changing conditions.

Experience also suggests that for a multinational airline to survive the centrifugal forces inherent in diversity of nationality, the form of organization is less important than a mutuality of goals and benefits.

CHAPTER 19

WILLIAM H. HANNUM

Regardless of product, the by-product is knowledge.
To survive in poor countries, the multinational company
must upgrade employees, suppliers, even customers—
work at which it is uniquely fitted to excel.

Profit Maker by Design, Educator by Circumstance

RECENT LITERATURE ON THE multinational corporation emphasizes its social-engineering as much as its capital-supplying function. The global company is seen as catalyst and irritant, diffusing knowledge, uplifting incentives and changing habits of thought and action by example. Indeed, to many observers this is its most significant contribution. Writes Arthur K. Watson, the chairman of the 1964 Advisory Committee on Private Enterprise in Foreign Aid: "While capital is scarce in the less developed countries, the more subtle and difficult shortcoming is human and institutional. The most basic problem in the whole development effort is that of transferring skills and technology, and to some degree attitudes, to individuals and institutions in the less-developed countries."[1]

What skills and attitudes is a private multinational enterprise able to impart; how does it convey them, and why is it a more effective transfer agency—if indeed it is—than other vehicles? This article explores some of these questions.

Perhaps the most basic skill imparted by the foreign multinational company is the ability to perform a specific job. Global companies strive to train as many foreign national personnel as possible to take over positions at all levels of the organization—from production and clerical through top management. While overseas operations are usually begun with a large proportion of expatriates, international companies have had enormous success in reducing their number over time.

Training is both formal and informal. Formal instruction assumes many aspects, ranging from highly structured classroom sessions on basic operations or processes to special seminars and institutes on methods and concepts of management, often conducted in the home country of the multinational firm. A typical example is that of a Far Eastern subsidiary of a U.S. fruit and vegetable packing company which provides formal middle-management training for its younger nationals at its installations in the United States and at management institutes and special scientific meetings held throughout the world. Normally, two nationals at a time are involved for periods of from three months to two years per person. The company also sends a top-level supervisor to its U.S. branches each year. In addition, it has extensive in-plant training programs for a wide range of employee skills.

On-the-job training and other informal methods of education, such as visits to installations and conferences, are also an important part of the total employee development programs of private firms. A Latin American branch of a U.S. appliance manufacturer has developed an on-the-job training program to emphasize the importance of proper tool making and tool maintenance. The employees also learn about productivity and product quality both for the company's and for their own well-being.

Financial support and time off for job-related training outside the firm are other company-offered inducements to change. Typical is the approach of a textile firm, a joint venture of Latin and North American firms, which wants its workers to take part in tuition-paid training at public vocational centers of the national management association. The goal of the company is to develop top-level supervisors from within.

Beyond job-related skills, companies make available technical services and information to subsidiaries and divisions or to local customers and suppliers in developing countries. The supplier emphasis is particularly important: the expatriate firm insists on securing local people who can guarantee high production standards and product quality. To help them meet these standards the company often has to furnish technical assistance. Sears Roebuck and Company, in its Latin American operations in Mexico, Brazil, Venezuela, Peru, and Colombia, provides a prime example of a firm that has developed its lines of supply locally, and in so doing has accomplished an enduring transfer of technology. In the typical case, company technicians write the specifications and operating requirements for the products they need and then act as consultants to prospective local suppliers to help them set up shop.

A North American processor of food products maintains a technical services group located in Western Europe which dispenses advice to various units of the company on development and marketing of both consumer and industrial products, information on engineering and other technical problem areas, and guidance on business practices, such as importing and exporting procedures. A company branch in South America, however, is engaged in spreading knowledge in areas that are completely independent of the corporate technical services group. The branch furnishes research findings to farmers and government agricultural agents and disseminates information on high-altitude, cold-weather crops and hybrid seeds.

Companies sometimes go to great length to guarantee that their products are properly used and maintained, in the process circulating an immense amount of knowledge. In some cases special programs are set up to provide product and service-related information both in the country of the parent company and on the local scene.

U.S. firms dealing in agricultural equipment and supplies have managed to promote modern farming techniques in various parts of the world through what is really social engineering. Typically, the firm suggests to participating farmers that they divide their plots of land into two parts. On one part farmers can follow their usual cultivation methods and on the other part they must use techniques laid down by the firm. The company guarantees a return to the farmers on the second part of their land so that they risk nothing in following the company's advice. Farmers quickly find that the productivity of the second half of the land exceeds that of the first half and in this way are induced to abandon deeply ingrained methods.

Product promotion is another knowledge-diffusing technique. In some cases, promotion is limited to printed matter, mass demonstrations, or radio and television communications. Even these methods, if properly used, can have an invigorating impact on the social system. Formal training and demonstrations, which in the United States are limited essentially to complicated industrial products, are applied overseas to a multitude of products and services, both consumer and producer. A large portion of a company's promotion budget may be spent for this type of market development, which can have an enormous influence on the consuming public's way of life.

Not for Profit, But Good Business

The foregoing activities are for the most part closely profit-oriented; there are other transfers that are less immediately tied to gain. Companies may consult with governments and the general public on the planning and completion of public projects or cooperate with public agencies in training programs, supplying instructors, physical facilities, and even scholarships.

An agricultural-implements company in one developing area operates a fully staffed training center near its headquarters. A typical course covers use of tropical equipment, lasts five weeks, and is designed for agricultural advisors, development officers, and farm managers as well as dealer employees in various countries. Dealers are urged to sponsor the attendance of teachers, major customers, or influential farmers in their communities. The course of instruction covers a full range of cultivation equipment, and it's two-way: participants and company staff are encouraged to exchange knowledge.

Companies also get involved in joint research projects with local agencies. And though these ventures may be unrelated to product lines, findings frequently are broadcast through company media, either in technical reports or even in the company newsletter.

Then there is the whole area of general education. A number of international firms design broad educational programs, with invitations issued both to employees and their dependents. Local language and literature, English, mathematics, social sciences, and home economics are popular subjects. Literate, resourceful, and confident employees, it is felt, eventually become more efficient than illiterate, unresourceful, and despondent ones, though this doesn't happen overnight.

A lumber company operating an installation in the form of a community compound finds that its isolation necessitates a broad educational effort. It has established training programs not only in academic and company skills, but also in personal hygiene, home medical aid, child care, home economics, and basic carpentry skills. Some firms in plantation compounds focus special resources on child education. They recognize that children could become a "drag" on the community and company operations unless they are adequately educated in a healthy environment and equipped to seek work elsewhere in the economy.

Although these nonprofit-related activities are considerable, they are less important than the profit and product-tied efforts we have just discussed. What makes the latter so vital to the have-not country is that company problems in these areas are virtually identical to national problems. If in its self-interest, the company makes a dent in the wall of ossified and traditional practices, national goals are correspondingly advanced. If foreign companies inculcate key work skills, habits of analytical thought, respect for property, awareness of the need for regular job attendance, and appreciation of the value of a team effort, the spillover effects can be considerable.

But why is the private multinational company a more successful "teacher" than the indigenous firm or the public agency? What special leverage is available to this entity and unavailable to the local people?

Status, Secrecy and Stagnation

In some developing countries, status considerations and many social customs and values encourage local private businessmen to cling to traditional methods and to forego the benefits of greater productivity or increased activity. Local firms are often family owned and operations may be circumscribed by the need to protect the status of a family member. Moreover, activities within local companies tend to be conducted secretly, which may effectively bar the flow of knowledge. One segment of a company does not know what another is doing. Periodic reports and other means of disclosure of activities necessary to proper managerial control are not used. If decisions affecting resource allocation are generally made by groups most interested in maintaining wealth positions and family interests, misallocations and misdirection of resources may occur throughout the economy.

The problem is aggravated by the fact that local executives and owners in developing countries are untrained in the requirements of modern management. Their backgrounds are legalistic, not analytic. So even if secrecy and parochial interests were no problem, the executive resources necessary to establish proper procedures could not be called upon. Nor are these managers eager to uplift themselves: there is a tremendous resistance to mid-career training, and going back to school is very embarrassing in many societies. Lacking internal executive resources and classically unwilling to delegate authority to professionally trained managers outside the ownership group, local firms are often condemned to drift and ineffective performance.

Now enter the international corporation, buttressed by a history of successful operations in a variety of national environments and furnished with a formidable inventory of management skills and experience. It is able to hold out the carrot of permanent career opportunities to those foreign nationals willing to adjust, remold and modernize. It is able to soften the resentment of individuals at being forced to relearn or unlearn, by means of powerful economic incentives unavailable to public agencies. A colleague spent two years without success on a publicly sponsored project designed to develop management courses and train professors to take them over.

Yet an American personnel manager during the same period was able to train a person in the same country to take over his job simply because the American manager was in control of the process and could provide material incentives and the promise of a career. Neither of these could be offered by the professor or the sponsoring agency.

In carrying out its educational work, the multinational company often moves by indirection and the unobtrusive but insistent posing of questions. A New York-based director of Latin American operations for a company recently located in Peru offers an example. From daily production records of individual employees as reported to New York from Peru, the director would select an employee whose production was consistently low and ask the Peruvian management to explain the employee's substandard level of performance. The executive was not really concerned about particular employees, he simply wished to direct the attention of the Peruvian managers to productivity as an aspect of managerial control. This technique, along with requests for reports from supervisors and local managers, was successful in focusing attention on the need for formal control of operations. The process helped improve production levels satisfactorily within a few months. It also generated attitudes and perceptions which were not in evidence before but which were nonetheless vital to the successful operation of the plant.

Formal control of operations means job descriptions, but this is an area of grave deficiency for the developing country. The lack of interchangeability of individuals at lower and middle management levels has made it difficult to develop effective organizational patterns. Typically, there are no job descriptions; the nature of jobs changes as individuals become entrenched in the organization. Under these conditions, as a company ages, its flexibility often declines. The multinational firm changes this. It insists upon formal organization in terms of jobs and tasks to assure effective and continuous operation. In this manner it promotes an important transfer of modern organizational concepts.

The international company's preoccupation with long-range planning and unlimited time horizons offers another plus for the developing economy. For example, a U.S. manufacturer of electrical equipment and appliances began operations in a developing country by first shipping parts to its local branch, where it conducted an assembly operation. Later, it began local manufacture of component parts for its products. Now, it makes many of the components at its branch and buys several others in the local economy. In the course of developing its local manufacturing activity, the company had to train employees in the necessary skills and make arrangements for local supply. Thus, over a period of time, the company was able to upgrade the skills of the local people and its contribution to local needs.

Still a further advantage of the multinational firm is its ability to direct managerial and technical skills accurately to the precise level of the needed assistance. Such companies are able to command the services of technical experts and the skills available from personnel and research operations located in diverse parts of the world at varying stages of development. Thus a joint venture of a Colombian and a U.S. firm was able to send a team of Colombian engineers to a project in Peru. Since the Colombian engineers had skills appropriate to the level of technology in Peru, it is likely that they could make a better contribution to the effective diffusion of knowledge and the training of Peruvians than would have been made by U.S. engineers.

Of course, most global corporations do not aim their activities at, nor assemble staffs exclusively for, operations in developing countries. However, the nature and variety of technical problems facing a multinational firm require a degree of flexibility and a reservoir of talent that can seldom be mobilized as easily by other agents of technical assistance. The benefits which accrue to host countries come as by-products of a firm's global operations. A United States processor of food products recently assembled an entire management team in a Middle Eastern country and brought it to Canada to be trained in operating a specific installation. When the training was completed, the management team returned home to the Middle East to direct an installation that was constructed along lines similar to the Canadian one. The total training time was approximately eight months per man. This is an example not only of the injection of technology through the introduction of a production facility, but also of the ability of the multinational firm to route trainees to the appropriate level of technology within its own organization.

A Technology for Every Occasion

There is another case to be cited, on a somewhat more ambitious scale. The technical director of the international division of a U.S. chemical company, a European, assembled a group of scientists and technicians from various countries with training and experience at levels of technology appropriate for operations of this firm in countries *at all stages of development*. This director thinks of his company as a seller of the technology embodied in its products. Applied research done by the company has led to the development of a food compound which was found to be especially suitable for large flocks of domestic fowl. The result appears to be an innovation in the culture of domestic fowl as a source of protein. While this development is not suited to the back-yard culture of food fowls typical of developing countries, it illustrates the innovating capabilities of a multinational company carrying on applied research on problems of countries in which it hopes to develop a market. Similar research in the future may result in innovations applicable to a developing economy.

So much for the strengths and advantages which private foreign enterprise can claim in its role as diffuser of knowledge. There are debits to be mentioned, of course—limitations and disadvantages which result when private enterprise is the change agency. For example, diffusion may be limited to persons living within a geographical region or enclave in which the firm is located; or transfer of knowledge may be checked by cultural or language differences among the territories of a given country. Alternatively, diffusion may be limited to a single industry. This can occur, for example, if a country has a very narrow range of industrial and technical capabilities. Third, transfer of knowledge may be confined to the job behavior, with little fallout in social areas. For example, standards of cleanliness and dress required on the job for health or safety reasons may be ignored at home or away from the job, even though life would be more comfortable or healthful if the standards were accepted.

Some of these restraints may be counteracted by the deliberate efforts of global firms to develop sophisticated suppliers and customers; others must be offset by more intentionally designed channels or means of technical assistance. Such channels are usually public. How far the diffusion of knowledge by private companies as a form of motivated social change can be expected to extend beyond the activities and areas immediately controlled by these firms is not easily forecast or measured. It depends partly on the technical nature of the local environment and partly on the openness of the society in which the global enterprise operates. Obviously, it is also a function of the subtlety, skill and commitment of the enterprise itself.

The development of quantitative measures of the economic significance of the technical-assistance activities of private firms is a fruitful area for research. Methods of cost-benefit analysis have not yet been developed to evaluate the effects of private knowledge-diffusing activities within a country. But even if cost-benefit analysis were feasible, it would be difficult to derive estimates of costs or volumes of resources devoted to the transfer of knowledge. In the way of data, companies would generally be able to provide estimates of the cost of training programs and activities of central staff units. However, the information would cover only a fraction of the total knowledge-diffusing activities which actually take place. The bulk of the diffusion occurs as a by-product of activity in pursuit of other goals: production, direct sales effort, and so on. In general, transfers of knowledge are not centrally planned nor are accounting reports and information-flow procedures set up to provide a break-out of cost data on the technical assistance content of normal operations. Thus it is difficult—even through a careful study of entire company operations—to obtain estimates of the magnitude of corporate activity in this area.

The difficulty of portraying, in quantitative terms, the significance of overseas-company contributions to the diffusion of knowledge has undoubtedly been a factor in the lack of attention devoted to these efforts. But it is not the only reason for neglect; basically current models used to study the needs of developing countries do not treat the diffusion of knowledge by private or public agencies as a factor. Instead emphasis is overwhelmingly on the capital component: existing capital stocks and the role of external capital in closing two types of gap: (1) between exchange earnings and foreign-exchange needs and (2) between domestic savings and total capital requirements.

If there is little awareness of the nature and significance of private activity in technical assistance, it stems in part from the failure of some elements of the business community to draw attention to this aspect of operations. Companies seldom are motivated primarily by a desire to improve socio-economic conditions in the countries where they are located. Instead, as has been mentioned, technical assistance and social engineering are achieved by private firms as by-products of their search for other, more specific corporate goals. And while businessmen are generally aware of their ability to induce changes in attitudes and behavior within their operational environment, the diffusion of knowledge is not, in and of itself, of interest to those who evaluate the performance of the company.

To recapitulate: (1) By way of their normal operations, global firms operating overseas become effective agents of technical assistance and knowledge-diffusion to developing countries. (2) Effectiveness in this role flows from certain aspects of private enterprise —primary among these are a system of control over key aspects of operations and a system of incentives which encourages persons to acquire skills and change behavior patterns. (3) Under the pressure of international competition, global firms offer career opportunities which require persons to attain modern perspectives and perform within the framework of effective modern organizations. (4) Among other special characteristics of private enterprise conducive to knowledge-diffusion is the ability to carry on long-range planning with unlimited horizons and to direct managerial and technical talent with swiftness, flexibility, and precision to the levels at which assistance is needed.

N O T E

1. Advisory Committee of Private Enterprise in Foreign Aid, *Foreign Aid Through Private Initiative*, Agency for International Development, Washington, D.C., July, 1965.

THE ROLE OF EQUITY

CHAPTER 20

DONALD M. KENDALL

*Management may soon be reporting
to a new variety of stockholders,
with far-ranging implications.*

Corporate Ownership:

The International

Dimension

IT IS SOMETHING of a modern article of faith to look with favor on internationalism generally, and particularly on those efforts that appear to be directed toward greater international understanding and good will. Yet, somehow, the mantle of broad approval does not seem to cover the international operations of business in the same way that it does those of governments, universities, foundations and other public and private agencies. Because the activities of business are profit-directed, the assumption seems to be that a business enterprise subscribes to a more suspect code of morality,

257

or even to venality, and that it therefore cannot participate in such lofty ideals and world amity.

What is most curious about these attitudes is that business today seems to be pointing the way toward a more meaningful and effective brand of internationalism than any that has been tried before. And it is doing this in its customarily pragmatic manner—by becoming more international than governments or most institutions or individuals, and by bestowing the fruits of its industry and enterprise with little or no regard for geography or national boundaries. Indeed, the fastest-growing brand of enterprise in the most enterprising nations may well be what has come to be called the multinational corporation.

Such growth, it might well be argued, represents no more than the quest for greater profits. And perhaps it does. But, motivations aside, it also brings substantial international benefits that might otherwise be hard to come by. The multinational company can get capital that may be out of reach of local business. It can take greater risks and in this way contribute substantially to the economic growth of the countries in which it operates. Its greater efficiency can lower the cost of products, expand payrolls and local trade, and in other ways contribute to higher living standards. By working with and through local people, it can promote broader understanding—day-by-day understanding—and help the cause of peaceful relations.

The benefits of freer world trade are not hard to demonstrate, and despite many barriers and restrictions, a remarkable amount of business is being done by companies that regard the world as their market and that reach almost everywhere for customers, capital, ideas or people. Nevertheless, the benefits of multinational business would be far easier to achieve if, in the mounting tide of world trade and the world's growing economic interdependence, additional measures were undertaken.

A Case of Pepsi

First of all, it would be helpful to define what we mean by the multinational company. An example is PepsiCo, operating in 114 countries. Its most familiar product is bottled in 512 plants outside the United States. Production and distribution facilities in almost every country are owned by nationals of those countries. Regional managers may come from the area in question—or from some other part of the world—Frenchmen, Englishmen, Latin Americans—not necessarily from the United States. In the Philippines, where PepsiCo is about the twelfth largest taxpayer, the whole operation has only two persons from the home office. The company is multinational as far as employment, operations, manufacturing and marketing are concerned, and a good part of the operating management and plant ownership abroad is also multinational.

An essential of multinationalism is a corporate philosophy that takes in the whole world. Such a philosophy is necessarily reflected in corporate planning. PepsiCo's financial department, for example, now looks at every facet of world finance. Its industrial relations department studies labor problems throughout the world, and the long-range thinkers are making five-year plans on the basis of the socio-economic problems of each country in which the company operates or hopes to do business. That is the extent of PepsiCo's multinationalism. But even that is not enough.

There will be no truly multinational companies until there is multinational ownership. And there will be no multinational ownership in any real sense until there is some worldwide sharing of ownership in the parent company. Investors from every country where the company does business should become PepsiCo stockholders so that they would have a vested interest, not alone in the company of which they own a part, but in the operation of a free global enterprise system and a free global market economy.

It would not then be too long or difficult a step to move toward worldwide corporate management. Such management usually reflects the nationality of the directors, and they in turn usually reflect the nationality of the stockholders. A truly multinational company would be one in which there would be no national bias in filling these roles.

Parent or Subsidiary Stock

Stated in these terms, multinationalism sounds only slightly more idealistic than the solutions to world problems being put forward by campus undergraduates today. The pragmatic businessman tends to suspect idealistic solutions that sound too pat or too easy to come by. And indeed there is a detour or two en route to the ideal of truly multinational businesses.

One question is whether people abroad really want the stock of parent companies headquartered elsewhere or whether they prefer the stock of local subsidiaries. Another problem is how to get the stock widely distributed in significant amounts. Still another is how to get it to stay widely distributed.

As to the first question, there are arguments—with varying degrees of validity—on both sides. Those who favor distribution of the stock of a local affiliate point out that it is usually more familiar and may already be broadly held and therefore more easily traded in their countries than the stock of parent companies. Furthermore, dividend and earnings retention policies tend to match local desires and interests, including tax laws in their own countries. And finally, growth prospects may be better because of the more rapid expansion rate of the local subsidiary (usually the case when the acquisition by the parent company has been a good one from its viewpoint).

But the more compelling arguments, at least in a large or longterm sense, appear to favor the parent company's stock. Often the local company is in a developing stage or needs large amounts of capital for other reasons; this in itself could severely restrict nearterm dividend prospects. Or local company profits might be hurt by the shifting of resources or inventories for the over-all benefit of the larger corporation. Moreover, local political and economic crises would have a minimal effect on the earnings of stockholders in the parent firm.

The net effect of international distribution of the parent company stock is to give people a piece of the action on a worldwide basis, rather than confining their interests to only what happens in their own countries. Multinational companies, like common markets, have moved giant steps toward achieving relatively free interchange of people and products. What parent stock distribution would accomplish, in addition, might be called "free interchange of profitability."

Nevertheless, it is not always easy to convince the local investor that his interests would be better served by a stake in the entire international enterprise than by one in the far more visible local company. Particularly in the less mature and sophisticated economies, it is difficult to see the value of stock in an international company, based as it is on assets, product lines, sales and earnings that are diversified throughout the world. It is therefore important that the parent company be profitable, that it show a good growth record and further growth potential, and that it be prepared to distribute a substantial dividend year in and year out.

Because these are not necessarily the objectives of the larger company, or the order in which they would be given, a great many companies involved in international enterprise seem totally indifferent to having their stock owned and traded abroad. A recent study turned up some salient facts in this respect. One company said it would be delighted to have all its shares that were being traded overseas come back to the United States, because it would then have no problems about maintaining the value of shares traded on foreign exchanges. Another said a listing abroad was made only for public relations reasons, and it therefore made no effort to have the stock traded actively. And very few sought to take full advantage of the range of possibilities in worldwide ownership of their shares.

On the other hand, restraints on direct foreign investment from the United States have compelled several companies to find alternative techniques to finance acquisition and expansion overseas. Some of them are using debentures, fully convertible into parent company stock, to achieve these purposes. The Chase Manhattan Bank reports that from 1965 to mid-May 1969 there were 79 convertible Eurobond issues by 75 U.S. corporations. Their dollar total amounted to $2.509 billion.

These elements of multinational ownership of multinational companies are not entirely new or revolutionary. One of the recommendations of the Fowler Report in 1964 was that "U.S.-based international corporations should consider the advantages of increased local ownership of their parent company shares in countries in which they have affiliates." It is the kind of proposal that must be urged over and over again until it is adopted in practice.

Indeed, it would appear short-sighted to do otherwise. The widespread sale and distribution of stock has been used for years to raise capital, to finance acquisitions without depleting resources, to secure the loyalty of shareholders, to recruit and hold able workers and managers through stock purchase plans and options, to enhance the corporate image and, in general, to increase sales and profits. All these advantages somehow seem less evident abroad. With rare exceptions, widespread ownership of the parent stock has not been used to expand sales and profits in world markets—a neglect that seems inexplicable.

For the most part, the mechanics of getting the stock distributed presents no difficulties. It can be listed on various foreign exchanges, it can be swapped for shares of a local company, it can be distributed to local executives and employees by means of options and purchase plans. In his Columbia-McKinsey lectures, Frederic Donner described the committee he organized in General Motors to study its overseas policies. One recommendation was to increase worldwide ownership of the company's common stock. Stock awards were made in 1965 to nearly 850 executives outside the United States and Canada.

But merely getting the stock initially distributed abroad does not solve the problem. Even—or especially—when there is a large exchange of parent company stock for that of a locally owned subsidiary, it does not necessarily mean that the shares will remain in the hands of the original recipients. Investors tend to be loath to tie up large amounts of their capital in a single business enterprise, particularly when that enterprise is based outside their country. What happens, then, is that the stock drifts away from the public toward large institutional investors or sometimes into the hands of local governments. Frequently, in negation of the real purpose of the distribution, the shares return to the home country.

Much of the National Dairy stock listed in Australia after a 1959 swap returned home via the arbitrage route when the stock began to sell for higher prices in New York, because the Australians were disappointed in the dividend. It is believed that many of the 3M shares traded for Ferrania stock will be converted into cash, with the stock moving either back to the United States or to Switzerland. From the standpoint of achieving true multinationalism, then, the simple distribution of parent company stock abroad is not an effective measure.

How To Control "Stock Drift"

In some of the early postwar efforts by U.S. firms to participate in the expanding economies and growing markets of other countries, the companies moved to help catalyze the growth through a more direct and intimate involvement than merely exporting goods to them.

Various governmental and quasi-governmental agencies and committees questioned whether a U.S. company should have partners abroad, or whether all its plants and facilities should be 100% U.S.-owned, or whether a minority interest might be held by either the overseas partner or the U.S. partner. There were debates about expanding a business, for example—whether to do it rapidly, with no dividends, or more slowly, or whether to finance acquisitions with cash.

That is when it occurred to a number of businessmen that an interest in an over-all world enterprise would obviate the problems of conflicts in local management philosophy. But it was necessary to make this a continuing and relatively stable interest, rather than one that disappeared with the vagaries of local market conditions. One way in which to do this would be the creation of a kind of "blocked stock" that could be traded only in a limited geographical area and in no circumstances could come back to the United States.

According to this proposal a U.S. corporation could go abroad, acquire a local company and use parent company stock for the acquisition. This stock would be the same as that traded in the United States, except that the back of the certificate would be stamped so that it would be negotiable only in the country for which it was issued, or in a limited region that might represent the country's natural trading area for equity interests.

Thus, stock used to acquire a company in Malaysia could thereafter be traded only in Malaysia, or perhaps in Singapore and Indonesia as well. If such a stock were tied to a dollar dividend, it would help overcome for the holders such problems as runaway inflation or local currency devaluations. It would help to have some kind of agreement with the country whereby enough profits could be taken out to pay the dividends on that stock, if there were such profits.

The total ownership of such stock would necessarily be cumulative within a country or trading region. As other subsidiaries were purchased with parent stock in the same area and as bonus or option shares were distributed, holdings of the "blocked" stock would build up. A country might develop a substantial position in a multinational corporation, perhaps eventually to the point where it would be invited to elect a director or two.

Governmental and Other Obstacles

The obstacles to be overcome in bringing about such a system of special stock ownership are substantial, even as are the present barriers to ownership of stock in multinational companies. Some countries, for example, go so far as to prohibit their citizens from acquiring or holding foreign assets, including stocks. Many make it impossible for their citizens to own foreign stock on the same basis as they can hold local stock. The interest equalization tax makes the United States one such country. Tax problems are among the most discouraging to contemplate and the most intricate to negotiate. A great many new tax treaties would have to be worked out, particularly those affecting double taxation of dividends, to make the plan viable.

U.S. tax laws bear a good deal of the onus for discouraging foreign ownership of stock in U.S. corporations, despite some amelioration in the Foreign Investors Act of 1966. Except where specific tax treaties provide otherwise, foreigners not resident in the United States find that dividend and interest income derived from U.S. securities is subject to a 30% withholding rate. U.S. estate taxes, although at a maximum rate of 25% rather than the previous 77%, are levied on securities even when they are held abroad. The 1966 Act increased the estate tax exemption for nonresident aliens from $2,000 to $30,000, but U.S. estate taxes are still a deterrent to foreign ownership of the securities of U.S. corporations. The Fowler Report recommended that these estate taxes on intangible personal property held by aliens be eliminated.

In addition, there is a veritable obstacle course of currency problems, differences in accounting and reporting procedures, and technical questions involving stock splits, warrants and rights, voting rights, and even multilingual stock certificates—which no company has seen fit to issue to date. But possibly the major barrier to multinational ownership of multinational companies is still the simple fact that the investment habit has not yet taken deep root in most countries, as it has in the more developed.

Barriers notwithstanding, nothing could provide a greater spur to multinational stock ownership than a single good example of how it could work to everyone's advantage. So perhaps the best and quickest way to overcome the obstacles is simply to move ahead and establish a sound base of multinational stock ownership wherever it can be done without paying too great a penalty. Some of the larger corporations would have to be convinced that this is the way to move, both in their own interests and in that of the economies of other countries.

Listing on local exchanges could be helpful. A good stock often creates its own demand, regardless of nationality. Such blue chips as General Electric, General Motors, Eastman Kodak and others are already actively traded on European exchanges. Governments, unions and national institutions are less likely to interfere with the operations of a company if there is a meaningful financial stake in it locally. Listing may also carry with it the suggestion that the company is essentially locally owned—as Singer is thought to be by many in France, Germany and even Italy, and as Nestlé is often deemed to be in the United States.

Multinational stock ownership could be given a major psychological boost through some form of official recognition by such organizations as the International Monetary Fund, the World Bank or the United Nations. One of these organizations, for example, could offer a worldwide incorporation facility (since corporations are already subject to all the laws of the countries in which they have operations) and thus become the first international or neutral site of incorporation, a supranational state of Delaware.

A corollary might be the establishment of an international stock exchange (although the New York Stock Exchange might already be regarded as filling such a role, listing, as it does, 261 securities issues of 69 foreign governments and 23 foreign corporations).

More deep-seated, perhaps, than any of the other obstacles to the growth of multinational enterprise is the still-rising tide of nationalism. Granted, it is chiefly political nationalism, but it has

inescapable economic overtones. Governments tend to guard jeal-
ously their prerogatives with regard to investors from other countries. When they offer incentives that purport to attract risk capital,
they hedge them with provisions for local equity participation or
control. Such conditions are not always fatal to the effectiveness of
the foreign investment, but they certainly limit the flexibility with
which the investor can adapt to rapidly changing markets and
technological developments.

It is not surprising, then, that some observers abroad are becoming increasingly conscious, if not suspicious, of their multinational
guests. Jean-Jacques Servan-Schreiber, in *The American Challenge,*
shows quite correctly that the economically strong countries always
make direct investments, thus gaining control, while economically
weak ones simply make portfolio investments abroad, watch their
savings get drained off and rarely get control of anything. There is
nothing especially new in all this. Nearly 70 years ago a book called
The American Invaders was published in England, and it described
the threat to British enterprise posed by such companies as Singer,
H. J. Heinz, and McCormick Harvesting Machine.

What is new, as Servan-Schreiber makes clear, is that U.S. business has been successful mainly because it has put the forces of
reason to work in the field of management and organization and has
concentrated on the most advanced and fastest-growing industries.
If this continues, he says, it will force Europe out of the running in
the international business sweepstakes. "This would be unacceptable for Europe, dangerous for America, and disastrous for the
world."

Whether or not the fear he expresses has any sound basis, it is
nevertheless a very real fear. One of the more obvious features of
direct investment by a foreign company is that it moves control of
a local business outside the country, and this may tend to impede
the development of a more independent national economy. How
important this is to the country, however, may be judged from the
report of a special task force studying foreign ownership in Canadian industry, one of whose conclusions was "that the economic
benefit exceeds the cost of having no direct investment."

Whatever may be thought or felt about the motives of business
and businessmen, it seems clear that in those conflicts that have
already arisen between nations and multinational businesses, one

fact stands out. While a truly multinational company tends to take a large view of the whole world and to make its decisions accordingly, this is not always a usual stance for a nation—or even for its statesmen—to assume. Indeed, the ultimate debate between corporations and nation-states may boil down to the pursuit of international interests by the former and of narrowly national interests by the latter.

The coming struggle for power between these two important elements in contemporary life may be bloodless, but its portents are very real. The differences between countries and corporations—in size, influence, capabilities, even in the number of people whose lives they directly affect—are no longer as great as they once were. If General Motors were a nation, it would rank 14th among the countries of the world in gross national product.

By 1975, 1980, 1985, the muted conflict promises to raise its decibel level. In 15 or 20 years, it is not at all unlikely that a large portion of the world's economic activity will be systematically organized by a relatively few huge economic units able to mobilize people, technology, capital and management far more efficiently than has ever been done before. The increase in their international character will be inexorable. In a very few years, many of them will have multinational top management, as Shell, Olivetti-Underwood, IBM World Trade Corporation and others do now.

These observations may easily prompt challenges that they constitute a proposal for economic imperialism. On the contrary, this is a plan in which any party may one day become dominant, on the basis of merit. What it may foreshadow is that at some future date commercial arrangements may help do away with economic boundaries all over the world. In helping this come to pass, the real strength of the multinational enterprise lies in its ability to disregard old forms and manners and conventions that have long hampered international cooperation. It is an important strength. National identities, which seem to become accentuated in such forms as the United Nations, tend to disappear in the multinational company. In that sense, multinational business has already started to build an effective world community.

CHAPTER 21

RICHARD D. ROBINSON

*Transfer controls of capital may
shift company attention from cash outflow to skills
outflow. It's a kind of investment the "haves" are equipped
to make and the "have nots" are prepared to assimilate.*

Who Needs Equity?

THE WORLD is literally being pulled apart. The gap in material well being, however measured, between the relatively rich and the relatively poor nations continues to widen. This, despite the annual flow of something like $6 billion in economic aid to the lesser developed countries from the United States, Europe, the Soviet Union, Japan, and the international institutions. This flow is patently inadequate and, as B. K. Nehru of India points out, it is actually declining as a percentage of the donor countries' gross national products. Sooner or later, one suspects, something must give way. One has the feeling that acts of utter desperation may follow. Perhaps we are already witnessing them in China and Southeast Asia and elsewhere.

If this be true, not only is the growing disparity in wealth and skills likely to create a *two-class* world, but due to human deprivation, we will in fact create superior and inferior societies in terms of disparate *biological potential*—thus, a *two-caste* world. Pile on top of that possibility the demonstrable brain and skill drain flowing from the poorer to the wealthier countries and the long-run prognosis for the kind of world in which one cares to live seems dim indeed.

Nor is business doing much to solve the problem. On the contrary, the bulk—perhaps 75 to 80% of *private* capital flowing internationally (a possible $4 billion)—moves among the rich nations. The net transfer of resources from rich to poor countries is simply inadequate to start closing the gap, despite the economic-aid effort. Yet, if there is anything to international investment theory, a dollar invested in capital-starved India or Turkey should yield a substantially higher return than a dollar invested in the relatively capital-rich United States, Western Europe, or Canada. Where capital is relatively scarce, returns should be higher. One should take cheap capital and invest it where it is expensive. Figures suggest that in the aggregate such investment does, in fact, yield a higher return. Clearly something is wrong.

What is wrong is the apparent fact that though returns in the poor countries are greater, they are not great enough to offset the Westerner's well-developed sense of risk. After all, if a businessman feels 50% sure of a 20% return in, say, India, and 90% sure of a 12% return in, say, West Germany, he is likely to invest his dollars in Germany. Why does the investor discount earnings from India at such a high rate? The discount rate used for these returns is not based on historical record; it is a subjective judgment, rarely quantified in any way. However, the rate is usually high. The investor has less direct experience with poor-country enterprises than he does with rich-nation ventures. The market is difficult to measure adequately. The environment is less familiar generally. There is fear of political upheaval. The list is familiar to businessmen and scholars alike. But often inadequately expressed is a basic structural difference between operating internationally and operating domestically.

All business activity is directed to the end of selling something to somebody else at a profit—to both parties, one might add. Domestically, the symmetry of the transaction is assumed. The seller—and society—assumes that the buyer buys a product or service at a given price because he feels that its value to him is somewhat greater than what he is giving up. We have a few laws about fraud and deliberate misrepresentation, and sometimes safety standards, but these are limited. In world markets the protection—for both buyer and seller—is even more limited. This is because in all cases imported products and services imply a commitment of local resources—including the foreign exchange earned by the national market with which to buy the import—and the relevant authorities may decide that the tradeoff is not to their national advantage. Hence, barriers are erected. These barriers may block imports, whether in the form of commodities, services, or raw capital (either in debt or equity form), or the barriers may block the realization of profits from these transactions, the extreme case being the loss of control of assets, up to and including expropriation.

The added difficulty or risk in international business is therefore explicable in simple terms: The ultimate consumer, an individual, is not given perfect freedom in the marketplace. Some authority— generally political—interposes its own consumption preferences for those of the ultimate consumer, ostensibly in the interests of a better society.

Can the international corporation operate in such a world? I leave aside the question of whether it should. Unless it is prepared to accept that *two-caste* world I spoke of, it must. In order to flourish, the international corporation must (1) satisfy the demands of the various governing elites that it serve national ends and (2) satisfy its own needs to maximize earnings and minimize risk.

Let us concentrate on point 2, the internal preconditions for multinational activity. Clearly the global enterprise cannot push levels of return high enough to overcome the heightened risk factor in poor countries. This would run the very real risk of being charged with exploitation by sensitized elites. On the other hand, even with various investment guarantee schemes, it is unlikely that the sense of risk can be sufficiently reduced in the near future to make such investment competitive with that in the Western world. The alternative, I suggest, is some combination of return maximization and risk minimization. But, one may say, that is precisely what business tries to do now. Or does it?

Send Skills, Not Money!

The first question a U.S. or European business firm going international might well ask itself, if it were to pay attention to the conventional investment theory I have alluded to earlier, is: "Are we exporting our most capital-intensive output?" Bear in mind that high-level knowledge and skill, R & D, modern technology, etc., are the most capital-intensive outputs of all. Consider the capital invested by society in individuals who embody such knowledge and skills. It is the sale of such services or skills in capital-poor countries that is likely to generate the highest return on investment. Another way of putting it is that the capital-intensive services and skills are precisely those in which Western firms have the greatest comparative advantage. Certainly a capital-poor country in which average life expectancy may be half that of ours cannot afford this sort of investment. We would all be better off if they traded their more labor-intensive consumer products for our capital-intensive skills.

Consider some of the other implications. If one is to supply a rare and useful knowledge or skill, one is in a position of virtually no risk. Not only is one in a powerful bargaining position, but the major investment to exploit the foreign market in these terms is made within the country that develops the exportable technology and skills. Furthermore, the asset carrying the commodity being sold—namely people—can be withdrawn fairly readily from a foreign market without serious loss. Physical assets may be expropriated or control over them lost, but technology is soon obsolete and little value remains. With but rare exception, individuals carrying knowledge and skills of commercial value can be withdrawn and the R & D flow stopped. I have heard of cases in which such persons were held as hostages. Indeed, I was involved briefly in such a situation, but such cases are very infrequent. Human rights tend to be better protected than property rights, a situation incidentally that did not always prevail.

The point is that just because a firm is a manufacturer of goods within the domestic market does not mean that it should necessarily manufacture on its own premises abroad. In fact, one suspects that many direct foreign investors are not maximizing their return on investment to the extent that they would if they limited themselves to the export of rare skills and technology via long-term contract. At the same time, by making investment in physical assets abroad, an investment that often cannot be withdrawn without heavy loss, the businessman increases the risk factor. His firm not only fails to maximize return on investment, but also fails to minimize the amount by which such return must be discounted because of risk. It may be true—ironical as it is—that our present restrictions on foreign investment are pushing some firms to more nearly maximize return and minimize risk. They are discouraged from exporting capital with which to buy foreign assets. They also find it difficult and expensive to lay hands on funds abroad. Hence, there is pressure to limit investment to domestically produced capital equipment, technology, and skills.

Everything but Equity

A lively business has grown up in the marketing of foreign skills in the developing world. Everywhere firms specializing in the international sale of industrial services are opening their doors. If a host government or private investor wants a paper mill engineered, constructed, equipped, and staffed with trained personnel, perhaps managed as well, it is no longer necessary to become involved with a paper manufacturer. If one wants oil areas explored and developed, it is no longer necessary to turn only to the petroleum companies. It is the same for steel mills and textile plants—and the list is growing. Increasingly the skills required to build, equip, and staff and manage modern industrial plants are available *without turning over partial or total ownership* to a Western manufacturing firm.

Instead the local group makes the major capital commitment and assumes actual ownership, perhaps assisted by externally generated debt financing, public or private. The Western promoter in turn may supply some of the debt financing to cover all or part of the foreign capital-equipment purchases; but his principal profit-earning activity over time will be the sale of skills and technology in plant construction, training, continuing R & D, and perhaps certain aspects of management. If the associated indigenous firm produces an exportable product, the Western firm may sell its marketing skills as well.

Some of these international service firms are subsidiaries of manufacturers of capital machinery for particular industries, though not all. Technology is now being separated from production as management was from ownership earlier in the century. Of course, if a manufacturing firm has a real lead in technology or design, particularly if adequately protected by patent or trademark—or *if* it enjoys a brand preference in the target foreign market and if that preference will be allowed by the authorities to work in the market (a large "if" in some cases)—in these circumstances the manufacturing firm may maximize its return by investing in its *own* manufacturing facilities within the target market. But perhaps not. Certainly it will not know unless the alternative is considered.

Clearly the service alternative carries less risk. Investment in skills or technology is more readily transferable than are outlays for plant and equipment. Contracts and debt financing are less likely to be attacked than direct investment. Where the relevant foreign currency is in short supply, repayment of debt is likely to be given priority over repatriation of equity capital even if one were able to sell the relevant assets. Also, interest payments, fees and royalties are generally accorded precedence over dividends in the allocation of scarce foreign exchange. And written contracts for the sale of skills and technology are seldom broken so long as they are adequately serviced.

Nationalism Is Important

One can look at the problem in another way. Even as Europe moves hesitatingly toward some form of unity, much of the rest of the world is charged with a highly emotional nationalism as new nations appear and people find new identity with them. This is as it should be. Identity with a national political state, as distinct from tribe, religious sect, or region, is probably a necessary step in finding an eventual identity with some supranational ideal. But nationalism means that alien ownership of a substantial share of a nation's economy will be resisted, if not specifically outlawed. This may be as true for Canada, France, and the United Kingdom, as for Mexico, Argentina, and Pakistan. It is also true for the United States, though our sheer size makes us somewhat less sensitive—and vulnerable—to foreign control over important industrial sectors. Even so, we prevent by law foreign control of some activities, such as communications, power development, and agriculture.

It is generally true, I think, that unless a foreign firm makes a continuing contribution to its local overseas enterprise, a contribution valued as highly by the host society as the profits the alien firm extracts, the desirability of foreign ownership is lost. Certainly if someone else stands ready to provide similar services at less cost, particularly if he is a *local* national, the interest of the original firm is in jeopardy. Someone has suggested that a firm owning physical assets abroad should really view its ownership as a lease that must be revalidated periodically in terms of the benefits flowing to the lessor, i.e., the host country. Mere ownership is not enough to justify a perpetual return. There must be some continuing input that cannot be purchased for a comparable price locally or more cheaply from another alien. Take note that increasingly the industrial *service* firm of which we have spoken is providing a source of needed technology and skills attractive to the potential manufacturer overseas. The monopoly of the present *manufacturers* is thus being broken; they have competition.

It should also be noted that the elites of many of the less-developed countries have reached, or soon will reach, a level of independence, sophistication and national responsibility that makes possible honest and sound evaluation of the relative gains or losses to the national society arising from a foreign firm's activities. No longer can many of these governments be bought out or pressured politically to secure acquiescence. It is transparent that the elites of these societies have set as their targets a catch-up rate of development, however foredoomed to failure we may feel this effort to be. Anything other than this is seen as committing oneself to perpetual inferiority. Everything tends to be increasingly subordinated to this end, including ideology—whether socialism or capitalism—up to and including the concept of private ownership. Nothing is sacred. As the gap between rich and poor nations widens, one can anticipate an even closer scrutiny of the relationship between an owner's continuing economic contribution and profit, particularly if the owner is foreign and the profit is being taken out of the country.

One suspects that the foreign firm repatriating profits generated from the use of locally available assets—such as land, buildings, labor, power, raw materials, skills—is not likely to be tolerated in the long run by a poor country committed to a catch-up growth policy, possibly not even by Western Europe. On the other hand, repatriation of profit that has been generated by assets *not* available locally —such as technology, skills, continuing R & D, international market organization—is another matter. Hence I feel that many U.S. and Western firms now relying on wholly owned foreign manufacturing plants overseas may be in for real trouble.

Communications May Not Help

Paradoxically, the trouble is increasing in a period when the growth of rapid, cheap communication is for the first time making international management control look viable. But as a matter of plain fact, the technical improvement in communication facilities does not necessarily imply an improvement in the *quality* of communication. Faced with nationalist demands that skill transfer be speeded up and faced, additionally, with the high cost of compensating Western executives for overseas service, international corporations have been employing a higher percentage of local nationals in their foreign operations. A by-product is that—in *relative* terms— fewer and fewer Western nationals are gaining any real overseas operating experience. A decreasing proportion of home-country employees are equipped to communicate effectively with associated foreign managements or with the overseas marketplace.

To communicate effectively, one has to be sensitive to the social context within which the other party is acting—the so-called "silent language." Otherwise, there is no common ground of implicit understanding. Words and behavior become inexplicable. Yet everything is rational—within a context. The secret is to determine the context. When another's behavior is inexplicable to us, it is because we do not know the circumstances in which the observed behavior makes sense. When we call an act rational or irrational, we are assuming a context. If not, the terms rational or irrational carry no meaning. Where are the bicultural communicators likely to come from if the process of nationalizing business management continues? I suggest that the answer for the businessman lies in the *international* recruitment of top management of the international corporation itself. One already sees this process at work in New York. International *ownership* of the international corporation would seem a natural next step.

Admittedly I have been addressing these comments to business conditions in the less-developed countries because we are speaking of the future. It seems clear that the great markets of the future lie in Africa, Latin America and Asia, wherein dwell more than two-thirds of the world's population. By 1980, the proportion will be roughly three-fourths, and per capita incomes in these areas are likely to double by that time. Europe, Australasia, Canada, and Japan are of interest to the international businessman in the long run, I suggest, primarily because of the possibility of using them as base points from which to penetrate these large future markets more easily. For a variety of reasons they may provide a useful transmission belt for the U.S.-based international corporation.

To sum up, one can, I think, get a glimpse of the private international corporation of the future—if private business has not just become a quaint old North American and Western European custom. The highest net return on investment is likely to be generated by the firm that invests principally in R & D, in the international recruitment and training of skilled technical and managerial personnel, in the organization of interrelated global markets which result in marketing economies, and in the capability of engineering and starting up modern plants, farms, mines, fisheries, schools, hospitals—whatever is needed, so long as ownership is not a precondition. It will probably sell its technology, its skills, its distribution services on a contractual basis to largely locally owned firms. Whether the latter are owned by a government entity or a private group may be wholly irrelevant. (An interesting recent development along this line is the international joint venture in Yugoslavia which involves foreign capital and managerial-technical skills in return for a share in profits.) In some instances the international corporation may place a foreign firm under a manufacturing-managerial contract, particularly during the latter's start-up phase, or if it is to supply a third market in which the international corporation has a distribution system.

If the international firm's skills—distribution, managerial, technical—are competitive, breach of contract is very unlikely. The international corporation will justify itself because of the economies of scale in (1) high-level staff work, including R & D; (2) the international recruitment of able people; and (3) the international organization of the market, whether on the supply or selling side. Note that I have omitted the actual process of production, in which *international* economies of scale are probably much more restricted than in these other areas. Hence, global ownership is less justified in the area of production if the technology, marketing, and managerial skills are separated out. Perhaps ultimately, these international service organizations will come to be managed and owned by nationals of many different countries.

The result may be that the flow of direct investment abroad as measured by current statistics (i.e., via equity) may level off; but, in fact, the flow of investment abroad embodied in high-level skills and technology may be vastly increased. Heavy investment may be made in the more developed countries to service this foreign opportunity. The tendency in this direction is already revealed by the rapidly increasing flow of fees and royalties to the United States, West Germany, and other relatively developed countries.

AMBIGUITIES
OF THE LAWS

CHAPTER 22

HENRY P. de VRIES

*Multinational enterprises create
multinational problems. Executives
find themselves in a new and
strange legal environment.*

Legal Aspects
of World Business

The Legal Climate for Investment

THE INCREASING INVESTMENT abroad in manufacturing and service industries and the need for massive transfers of private capital and technology to developing countries require preliminary appraisal of the legal climate of the country of investment to assure a minimum level of certainty and stability.

Questions of investment incentives, repatriation of profits and capital, requirements of local majority ownership or compulsory use of local nationals and materials, tax policies and guaranties against non-business risks, all are important elements of the investment climate. Capital financing of a foreign enterprise needs the formal structure of laws and legal institutions relating to business organization, banking and insurance, commercial contracts and credit instruments, labor relations and business taxation. Transfer of technology and product identification depend on legal effectiveness of contracts—turn-key, technical assistance, management, licensing—and on remedies available for defense of industrial property rights—patents, trademarks and know-how.

Beneath this formal structure necessary for economic regulation and protection of foreign direct investment, a favorable legal climate must contain an infrastructure of attitudes, beliefs and assumptions expressed in legal norms. A first element is a developed legal system at least national in scope, a well-defined and organized body of rules relating to governmental as well as private activity with established institutions, and a professional class and procedures for administration of those rules. It is difficult to conceive of a developed country without a developed legal system. It is easier to point to developing countries with developed legal systems (in the Western Hemisphere) or to developing countries with developing legal systems.

An essential element is a minimum degree of acceptance of the legal system by the country's population. The anchor of a legal system is not its inherent excellence but the extra-legal factor of a people's civic or social consciousness implying a willingness to abide by collective decisions.

Perhaps the discernible gap between the developed legal systems in Latin American countries and effective administration of justice may be explained by the emphasis on *individualismo* and *personalismo*. A substitute for this social trait was formerly found in the Crown, the Church or some other symbol of legitimacy—an article of faith which, by remaining unquestioned, furnished the pivotal connection for acceptance of law by society.

Closely related to the issue of civic consciousness is the literacy rate of the population. As pointed out by the President of the World Bank, "Four or five thousand years after the introduction of the written word, more than a third of adult mankind still remains illiterate." Many countries in Latin America, Africa and Asia have "received" a developed legal system without the literate capacity necessary to participate in any of its processes, particularly outside of urban centers. In such countries law tends to become the exclusive province of a small group and even the most advanced legislative enactments remain dead letters on the books. Modern codes and laws written with the assistance of foreign technical experts await years of infrastructure development to become truly effective.

Other Factors

Numerous other factors affect a country's legal climate for private foreign investment: exaggerated nationalism leading to discrimination against the rights of aliens; a mixed economy strongly oriented toward public ownership of productive facilities and generally cool toward the protection of private property rights; political instability, creating uncertainty in long-range investment planning. These factors, however, as well as determination of the stage of development of the legal system, the population's rate of literacy and willingness to accept collective decisions, point to the key issue of appraisal of a country's legal climate: the effectiveness of its legal institutions, professional class and procedures.

Aside from a few Stone Age aboriginal territories, every part of the world today has access to and the opportunity to import the latest models of legislation. By treaty or by internal enactment, a developing country can buttress its incentives for investment with freely available shipping laws, mining codes, patent laws and negotiable instrument legislation. The problem of their practical application remains.

In view of the range of governmental participation in economic activity, a vital issue of contemporary legal life is the extent to which administrative authorities are or can be subjected to procedures for review of their actions. With the emphasis on exhaustion of domestic remedies as a condition to diplomatic protection, the adequacy of internal protection against arbitrary executive acts in the country of investment is a continuing problem.

In the United States, it is a court, and normally a court of general jurisdiction, which will review governmental action. By the logic of history the judicial power in the United States has developed into the ultimate decision maker of the legal system. No other court system in the world has the gamut of powers ranging from that of annulling legislative enactments to compelling performance by public officers under threat of fine or imprisonment.

As in other countries of the common law system, the judiciary in the United States is conscious of its responsibility for definition and development of the legal system. The legal climate created in the United States by the judiciary is unique in that it does not merely reflect a technique of deciding cases by referring to past decision; it embodies a political acceptance of the courts as final interpreters of the Constitution and of legislative acts. The social and economic status of the judge is commensurate with the importance of the role assigned. The identity of the individual judge is emphasized, and the views of particular judges are constantly examined and evaluated. They have absolute immunity from damage suits even for intentional violations of individual rights. By elaborate reporting methods court decisions are widely disseminated. The legal climate, Roscoe Pound's "taught tradition," is determined by judicial behavior.

The lawyer trained in a common law system quite naturally assumes that supremacy of the judiciary is a logical and inevitable characteristic of any legal system based on separation of governmental powers. He is troubled and even dismayed at times to discover the different attitudes of foreign legal systems.

In the numerous countries of the world usually described as belonging to the "civil law" system—based on Roman legal idiom and tradition—the judiciary plays a lesser role than in countries of the "common law." Though the status of the judiciary varies in the countries of Western Europe and Latin America, the characteristic of executive dominance is more pronounced. In Latin America, it is not the court decision which gives life to the statute, but the *reglamento*, the executive implementation of the legislative act. In countries that follow the French system, the tendency is to deny the law courts the power to pass on executive action and to maintain separate administrative courts. The German system places greater emphasis on departmental review. Both systems rely on the prestige of a career civil service as a counterpart to the Anglo-American judicial power.

In the modern world of international business, vital decisions will often be made in reliance on the estimated degree of protection afforded by the country of investment. It is not the legal facade of investment incentive laws, tax exemptions and guaranties of repatriation that govern. It is rather the infrastructure of attitudes, institutions and remedies that determine the long-range legal climate.

The Problem of Identity

The expansion of business enterprise abroad has been accompanied by increasing complexity of legal problems and a correspondingly greater degree of collaboration between the international executive and specialized counsel.

Legal staffs attached to international divisions have become the rule. Individual corporate counsel specially assigned to a company's international operations have become familiar faces in present-day planning. For the thousands of smaller business units operating abroad legal guidance in international operations is furnished chiefly by outside counsel. In the areas of greatest importance to U.S. private enterprise—Western Europe, Japan, Canada and Latin America—the volume of legal business has justified the establishment of foreign offices of U.S. law firms. In Paris alone, more than 22 U.S. law firms are represented by resident partners.

In foreign operations the distinction must be noted between international trade and foreign investment. International commercial and maritime relations generally have tended for centuries to be conducted by merchants or businessmen without calling on lawyers except for litigation. Even in the event of disputes, in the traditional area of trade operations arbitration without lawyers participating is frequently preferred. International trade is based chiefly on the use of standardized forms and practices, a world in which a lawyer, despite his training, is considered more of a layman than his business counterpart. In the area of international trade, in contrast to that of foreign investment, the standardized instruments which contain most of the rules governing the parties, sales memoranda, brokers' notes, bills of lading, charter parties, marine insurance policies, letters of credit, all embody familiar clauses which shipping clerks and foreign tellers can be trained to follow.

In those areas of international business activity, particularly developed since World War II, involving the transfer and exchange of technology and direct investment abroad, the reverse is true. Here the individualized rather than the standardized transaction is the rule. While the import or export of goods can be, and usually is, arranged so as to involve the law of a single country, the transfer of technology and direct investment normally involve foreign as well as domestic legal factors.

The presence of the same enterprise in many countries necessarily subjects it to differing laws. Manufacturing, financing and
marketing abroad, often involving regional rather than bilateral
planning, require the confidence and the ability to handle the laws
of more than one country as well as skill in the essential techniques
of analysis of legal climate and relevant rules. The businessman or
lawyer at home only in a single country's law becomes inadequate.
The multinational enterprise demands the multinational mind.

Despite the barriers of language and habit of thought, the U.S.
lawyer accustomed to the complexities of interstate conflicts of rules
of law, and the U.S. business executive accustomed to think in
terms of regional markets have an advantage over their foreign
counterparts in projecting into the international area. The solution
of multistate problems is excellent initiation to the consideration of
multinational problems.

Corporate Forms

The primary step in the approach to foreign business operations
is a re-examination of familiar legal-business institutions and conceptions. A look at the corporate forms of business organization will
provide some examples of the three-dimensional aspect of international legal planning.

The business world and its legal advisers normally seek the
limitation of personal liability of the investing company or individual, accomplished by creation of a separate legal entity. Domestically, the corporation is relied on as the normal and dominant
form of doing business, whether giant or small, publicly owned or
held by a close few. The "Inc." is ever present in national life. Since,
in the U.S. view, corporations are created by state law, by grant of
the sovereign rather than the contract of the members, it is a truism
that they are identified with the state or territory of the Union
where organized. Thus businessmen and lawyers speak of a Delaware corporation, if it was organized pursuant Delaware law,
although all its corporate and business activity are outside that state
and the stockholders are non-residents.

In Europe and Latin America, where a single body of national
law creates or regulates corporate activity, one can refer to the nationality of a corporation. And because a corporation in many countries abroad is not considered created by grant of the sovereign but

by the contractual intent of the members, its nationality is not necessarily defined by that of the country in which it is constituted. Thus a French court has recently held that a corporation organized under Panama law by U.S. stockholders with central management in New York was not a Panamanian national. A corporation not validly constituted opens the path to personal liability of stockholders for corporate debts.

In a case before the German courts suit was brought against the U.S. stockholders of a corporation organized in the State of Washington to conduct mining operations in Mexico with its central management meeting in Hamburg. The stockholders were held personally liable for corporate liabilities on the ground that since the corporation was administered in Germany and not constituted pursuant to German law, it was an unincorporated association. The Supreme Court of Belgium also held recently that where a company organized under English law transferred its head office to Belgium, it became subject to Belgian rules, such as that limiting the duration of a corporation to 30 years, despite the provisions of English law and the terms of the articles of association.

Pursuant to Italian law if the corporate center of administration or the main business operation of a company is in Italy, even though created abroad, the corporation is subject to Italian law even as to the legal requirements for incorporation. Similarly in Latin America, Venezuela for example, a corporation organized pursuant to a foreign law and with its principal business in Venezuela is considered a Venezuelan national.

Thus the question of the nationality of a corporation is neither academic nor theoretical. Like an individual a corporation may have dual nationality; on the other hand it may be "stateless," a condition affecting its very existence and exposing the members to individual liability. Determination of the nationality of a corporation may have serious tax consequences as well as subject the entity to burdensome regulation or even expropriation of its property, as in the case of the Suez Canal Company.

No Pattern

In determining the law applicable to corporate existence and internal relations, no consistent pattern can be discerned. Some countries, such as the United States, the United Kingdom and

Brazil, look to the place of incorporation. Others, such as Morocco, look to the place of the registered head office. France, Belgium and Greece look to the center of management. Italy and Egypt apply the test of main business activity. In contrast to domestic practice in the United States, multiple incorporation in various countries of the world may be necessary simply to protect stockholders from personal liability.

In foreign operations it cannot be assumed that ownership by a single person—the one-man corporate entity—is authorized. Even in the United States, some states have specifically refused to recognize the validity of a corporation owned by one person. The North Carolina Supreme Court recently held that where all the stock of a corporation was acquired by one individual, the corporation ceased to exist. A similar rule has prevailed in France, Belgium and other countries following French legal thought. Acquisition by one person, whether an individual or a legal entity, of all the shares of a corporation causes its automatic dissolution, leading to personal liability of the stockholder for the corporation's liabilities. The Supreme Court of Belgium has gone so far as to hold that even though a foreign corporation was organized pursuant to a law that authorized the one-man corporation, such a corporation could not have its existence recognized in Belgium so as to permit it to sue in Belgian courts.

Assuming that the corporation is identified as foreign and that it is validly existing in its home country, the problem remains of its recognition as a legal entity in the country of operations. There is no rule of international law, in the absence of treaty, obligating a state to recognize foreign-created juristic persons. The capacity to sue and be sued as a separate legal entity is the most important incident of recognition. In some countries today, a foreign corporation selling goods may not be able to bring an action in the courts of the buyer in the event of non-payment. Shortly before World War II, when the owner of the Palmolive trademark, a Delaware corporation, attempted to sue an infringer in Mexico, the Supreme Court upheld dismissal of the action on the ground that the Delaware corporation, as such, had no existence in Mexico. The view that "a company can have no legal existence out of the boundaries of the sovereignty by which it is created," expressed in U.S. interstate relations over 100 years ago, still survives in some countries abroad, particularly the developing countries fearful of foreign economic penetration.

In the Western Hemisphere it has been found expedient to draft a Declaration on Juridical Personality of Foreign Companies. Parties to the Declaration, in addition to the United States, are Chile, the Dominican Republic, Ecuador, El Salvador, Nicaragua, Peru and Venezuela. The Declaration provides for recognition of foreign "companies constituted in accordance with the laws of one of the Contracting States and which have their seats in its territory." In a similar fashion Article 58 of the Rome Treaty organizing the European Common Market provides that "companies constituted in accordance with the law of a Member State and having their registered office, central management or main establishment within the Community shall, for the purpose of applying the provisions of this Chapter, be assimilated to natural persons being nationals of Member States."

Business enterprise operating abroad must choose a legal form of organization. This brief glance at Pandora's box of international legal problems would indicate that questions of identity, valid existence and recognition of a legal entity operating extraterritorially are not merely theoretical but, often unnoticed, can have serious consequences in foreign operations if not properly resolved as soon as it is possible to do so.

The Form of the Affiliate

Attention to the composition and form of the business unit which will conduct manufacturing or marketing activities in a foreign country will make a significant contribution to its ultimate success. Tax considerations both at home and abroad play an important part, but in general a major objective is to insulate the parent organization or investor from direct liability for the obligations incurred in the local operation.

To be considered at the outset is whether the business undertaking will be jointly owned with a local interest. Financing and control may depend on the choice of business form. Without discussing their merits, joint ventures, even with both parties ever present, are difficult relationships to maintain. An international joint venture, with the parties widely separated to begin with, is much more difficult to consolidate. Particularly in developing countries, stresses and strains of the simplest business operations tend to result in discord.

Often overlooked, but vital to full protection of the investors' interest, is a detailed study of the problems of eventual liquidation and dissolution. If the joint venture company has been authorized to use an internationally known firm name as well as trademarks and has received patent licenses and know-how, the severance may be far more complicated than the creation.

In some countries—Mexico, Japan and India—the impact of legal restrictions may compel organization of jointly owned companies with a minimum percentage of local equity capital. The problem then becomes one of retaining at least veto powers over important decisions and providing sensible procedures for dissolution.

Joint Venture Forms

A joint venture need not necessarily take the form of a jointly owned enterprise. It may be contractual, the type called in French the *société en participation* and in German the *Stille Gesellschaft*. Again, subcontracting components of the manufacturing process may be a more desirable form of joint operation. As defined in the new French Company Law, the *société en participation* "exists only as between members and is not disclosed to third parties."

It does not have a separate legal existence and can be established by oral agreement. Each party can retain its name and industrial property rights and in the event of difficulties can terminate the agreement in a manner previously agreed upon without need for formal dissolution of a separate legal entity.

Normally, with limitation of members' liability as a prime objective, the choice of form of doing business abroad will center on creation of an entity with legal existence separate from that of the parent or investor. As Justice Holmes pointed out, "the tradition of the common law is to treat as legal persons only incorporate groups and to assimilate all others to partnerships. The tradition of the civil law is otherwise."

The Corporate Concept

In U.S. law the term "corporation" embodies the notion of a group treated in law as a person different from its members. Though derived from Latin, the term is not directly translatable into continental law terminology. In French it corresponds to the idea of guild or a professional corps. At common law, a grant from the public authority was necessary to "incorporate." Limitation of liability of members of a corporation was dependent on a concession by the legislature. The civil law countries start from the root concept of *société* or *Gesellschaft*, "the *contract by which two or more persons agree to plan something in common ownership for the purpose of dividing the profit which may arise therefrom.*" Forms of business organization abroad are therefore varieties of *société*. The general partnership is a *société en nom collectif;* the limited partnership is a *société en commandite.* The classical distinction developed in continental law and in Latin America is between the *sociétés des capitaux* emphasizing the pooling of capital resources and the *sociétés des personnes* in which reliance is placed on the identity of the members. The partnership, general or limited, is the typical *société des personnes.*

In most cases the choice of foreign business organization to operate as a subsidiary or affiliate will be between two forms, both akin to the U.S. corporation. In the European Common Market countries (with the exception of the Netherlands, which has only a single corporate form), direct investment for manufacturing operations or intensive marketing will be channeled through a *société anonyme* (S.A.) or a *société à responsabilité limitée* (S.A.R.L.); in German-speaking countries it will be *Aktiengesellschaft* (A.G.) or the *Gesellschaft mit beschränkter Haftung* (GmbH). Like the private or proprietary company in British Commonwealth countries, the S.A.R.L. (often referred to as *Limitada* in Latin American practice) requires fewer formalities for formation and operation. The S.A.R.L. has a simple structure with management often centered in a single person (*gérant, Geschäftsführer*), lacking a board of directors or other supervisory bodies required in the case of an S.A. As international businessmen and counsel have become more knowledgeable and sophisticated, the trend of choice toward the S.A.R.L. or the

Limitada has become more definite in contrast to the earlier period when the S.A. was regarded conservatively as the most direct counterpart of the U.S. "Inc."

S.A.R.L. Preferred

The change in attitude has come from the realization that large corporations, operating as public companies domestically with shares listed on stock exchanges, function abroad through closely held companies. The S.A.R.L. gained in favor as international business found that controlled companies as well as joint ventures with a local interest could operate more effectively through the contractual details inserted in the charter of an S.A.R.L. than through more cumbersome mandatory provisions of law governing an S.A.

The relatively new institution of the S.A.R.L. originated in Germany in 1892 as an answer to the difficulties encountered by colonial business ventures in complying with the strict German corporation law of 1884. Since then it has been adopted in almost every country of Europe, Latin America, the Near East and North Africa. In each country, however, it has its own distinctive features and varies as much in important details as do the laws in different countries relating to the S.A.

In some countries, the S.A.R.L. is treated as a partnership rather than as a corporation. Thus in Panama, the preferred form is the S.A. because of the partnership nature of the Panamanian *Limitada* and because the S.A. law modeled on Delaware law is extremely simple and inexpensive to organize and operate. In Colombia the Supreme Court has held the Colombia S.A.R.L. to be a partnership, not a corporation, for tax purposes. The organizational documents of the Brazilian *Limitada* can be drafted so as to make it resemble a partnership.

For the true sophisticate, German practice has developed the "GmbH & Co.," one of the newer and increasingly utilized German forms, particularly as the non-corporate business instrumentality for joint ventures. Despite the misleading designation, the GmbH & Co. is not a GmbH at all. It is a German limited partnership, a *Kommanditgesellschaft* (KG) in which a GmbH acts as general partner and manager. As managing partner of the KG, the GmbH's liability to creditors is unlimited. But since the GmbH is itself a corporate form, members in turn are not liable beyond their investment in the GmbH. The analogy in U.S. business forms would be a limited partnership with a corporation as general partner.

A European Company

Another new form is the proposed European company. This would be a company subject to uniform rules throughout the European Common Market if established in a Common Market country. The proposal is presently being considered by the Common Market authorities following the French government initiative in 1965. It is significant that no one has advocated any form for a European company other than the S.A. In the Europe of the future, it would be as if the United States had a Federal uniform law for corporations in interstate commerce in addition to the state-law entities now used. An example may be found in the Dominion Company of Canada, a form organized under Dominion law which exists side by side with companies created under Provincial legislation.

Since creation of a European company would require either a uniform law enacted by all the countries of the Common Market or a treaty independent of the Rome Treaty, a certain degree of skepticism is warranted with respect to early adoption. However, as a result of Common Market thinking, a movement to revise company laws is making headway in Europe. Germany and France have recently adopted new laws. In Italy, Belgium and the Netherlands, reforms are in preparation. Harmonization of company law in Europe is being effected at this stage more by internal changes than by any strong urge to create a new and perhaps unnecessary superstructure of business organizations. The organizational alternatives are all complex, but a thorough understanding of their implications by responsible executives is essential to any multinational operation.

The Language Barrier

To the international business executive and his legal adviser the language barrier poses a constant and elusive problem. At critical points in the management decision process, the area of uncertainty resulting from language differences remains an effective circuit breaker in the transmission of ideas. In formation of contracts, in preparation of corporate documents, in negotiation and settlement of disputes by arbitration or court proceedings, in any reference to foreign laws or concepts, the language factor is ever present.

The international business community has found various ways of assisting the meeting of minds. An example that readily comes to mind is the increasing use of standardized international instruments containing their own definitions in various languages or referring to uniform definitions of terms. Perhaps the most universal solution in our contemporary world is found in the tremendously expanded development of English as the international language of commerce, diplomacy and science.

In this century English has become the most widely spoken language on earth. It is only fifty years since English was first accepted as the authentic language counterpart of French in the Treaty of Versailles. Today, it is the language medium of exchange used in trade agreements between Peking and members of the Soviet bloc and in cultural agreements between Egypt and Indonesia. Nearly one in ten of the world's people use English as their primary language and nearly one in four understand it to some degree. The American abroad may be forgiven for assuming that the language problem is simply one of spreading even more the use of a language already so widely accepted as a means of communication.

In practice, the chief problem today is in the area of transference of legal ideas. To the businessman a contract or a corporate document is essentially a set of operating rules to be followed as a matter of mechanics in arranging details of delivery, payment, place and date of meetings and similar details. The lawyer views the same instrument from the moment of its creation through the lens of a judge's or arbitrator's eyes. When foreign legal elements are involved, the lens will have to be at least bifocal. For operations, the contract must be understandable in the language of the personnel who must be guided by it. For settlement of disputes, the same contract or written communication must be presented not only in the formal language of the deciding body, but must be so translated as to carry a maximum burden of persuasion. In counselling on the meaning of a contract, in contrast to the advocacy necessary for litigation, the lawyer will rely on the least favorable translation for his legal opinion in order to minimize the scope of the calculated risk.

Translation Problems

To mention the language barrier is to refer to translation as the channel of communication. The importance of understanding the purpose of a particular translation is evident. A routine translation, merely to have a preliminary notion of the contents of the foreign letter, may be completely justified, while reliance on an "official translation" of a foreign law or governmental document may be a major blunder.

The businessman is often unaware of the special problems raised by translation of legal instruments. To translate is always to interpret, that is, to embody an opinion as to the legal meaning of the contents. Disputes as to the meaning of words invariably arise in marginal situations when more than one meaning is possible. Translating from legal English is usually more difficult than to express oneself directly in the foreign language. Though English may have become an international language, legal English is the product of a unique set of historical circumstances. As Professor Keeton, a leading English historian, has remarked, "Even today the language of the law is so completely permeated by Norman-French terms that it is impossible to imagine the legal system without them."

To the normally complex problem of ascertaining meaning in a single language, the addition of the foreign language factor multiplies the variables of selection and expands the area of uncertainty. Translation of legal language in contrast to scientific information is not a mechanical matching of words. With the aid of computers, over a million words a month are being translated into English from Russian technical works. In contrast to words which embody physical descriptions, most legal concepts leave room for value judgments. As stated by Professor Philippe Kahn, in fairly extravagant terms, "In translating from the foreign language into that of the court, there is a transfer of concepts, expressing the intellectual life of two peoples, the assimilation of a civilization."

In litigation, a point to be noted results from differences in court procedure. In U.S. courts and arbitration tribunals, generally speaking, the emphasis is on presenting the facts to the judge or jury through the oral testimony of the parties or witnesses in open court. Foreign language documents or laws are normally presented through the oral testimony of experts retained by the parties. In noncriminal cases abroad, parties are generally barred from testifying and translations are most often admitted only when made by "official translators," with knowledge of English as well as their own language tested by the simplest of public examinations.

Use Court's Language

The vital point to bear in mind is that the process of translation to be properly controlled must be effected during the period of drafting of the instrument. From the point of view of potential litigation, legal instruments should be written in the language of the decisional body which will settle the disputes arising in connection with the instrument. The legal language of that body will govern, regardless of the law chosen by the parties or the language actually used in the instrument.

The German Supreme Court has held that a translator is not the agent of the party who employed him at the time of preparation of the original contract but merely a conduit. If he commits an error so that the contract as signed does not correspond to the real intention of the party who signed it, the latter can rescind the contract. The Supreme Court of France has held that a French judge can disregard the translation of a court-appointed expert translator. The instrument involved was a licensing agreement in the English language, calling for royalties calculated on the basis of a percentage of "gross income." This was translated by the expert as "revenus bruts" and by the lower court as "revenus de toute nature" and "montant brut du chiffre d'affaires." The French Supreme Court held that the lower court's own translation, even if erroneous, could not be reviewed. "The translation of a contract written in a foreign language involves an exercise of the lower court's sovereign power to interpret written instruments."

Bilingual or multilingual instruments in various counterparts normally contain a choice of language clause, indicating which text is to prevail in case of divergence. Such a clause is truly effective only if the controlling language chosen is that of the decisional body. In the French case just mentioned, only a French language contract would have been binding on the court as evidence of the intention of the parties as to the meaning to be given to the term "gross income." This conclusion is not limited to foreign courts. When the 1819 Treaty with Spain was first applied by the Supreme Court of the United States in litigation involving the status of private land grants after acquisition of Florida by the United States, the Court faced the problem of translating the Spanish "las concesiones quedarán ratificadas y reconocidas." The authentic English text of the Treaty read: "The grants shall be ratified and confirmed." As so read, the Treaty would have left in doubt the ownership of substantial tracts of land. Disregarding the authentic English version, the Supreme Court applied its own translation to find the meaning to be "the grants shall remain ratified and confirmed."

The Translator

Arguably, a critically important translation of a foreign legal text should not be the work of a single person. Julian Green, the American author who wrote in French, has been quoted as saying, "I am more and more inclined to believe that it is almost an impossibility to be absolutely bilingual." A leading research manual insists that "one can translate faithfully only from a language one knows like a native into a language one knows like a practiced writer." In truly critical and decisive issues of translation and interpretation, the process should be bilateral, from one language by the lawyer familiar with that language and that country's law into the language of the law of the decisional body by a lawyer trained in that legal system.

Finally, it should be observed that just as no contract can be drawn to foresee every contingency, so no translation can eliminate all future disputes as to meaning. Particularly in international business relations, where most disagreements tend to be channelled into the language area to avoid implications of improper motives for non-performance, the translation should be carefully analyzed. There is no simple solution to the language barrier. The need is to examine both sides to determine when a language other than English should be the language of the parties and to be aware of the means of controlling language transference.

Diplomatic Protection

In sharp contrast to the laissez-faire period prior to World War I, the changes in ideology and social realignment of the twentieth century have vitally affected the legal framework of international life. In the classical nineteenth-century view, with its concept of private property derived from the image of tangible things owned by individuals, the definition of ownership in the French Civil Code—"the right to enjoy and dispose of things in the most absolute manner, provided that they are not put to a use prohibited by laws (*lois*) or by regulations (*règlements*)"—served as a model for the codes of many other countries. In contrast, the view of ownership as a "social function" found in many codes enacted since World War I reflects a rejection of absolute property rights and challenges the distinction between private and public ownership.

At the end of the nineteenth century, the Supreme Court of the United States could say: "In the memory of men now living, a proposition to take private property, without the consent of its owner, for a public park, would have been regarded as a novel exercise of legislative power." Today, the "nationalization" of private property—its transfer to public ownership—is a common phenomenon throughout the United States and elsewhere.

In international legal relations a similar change of emphasis has occurred. In the traditional view, any taking of foreign property, even for a public purpose, was suspect. Indeed, an echo of this view is found in the attitude of the Soviet High Commander in Austria following World War II. He contended that the Austrian law nationalizing the Soviet-held Austrian oil industry violated an alleged rule of international law which bars a nationalizing State from applying such measures to any foreign-owned property.

When throughout the world the public sector of enterprise has expanded with an accompanying broadening of the notion of public use or purpose, the question of whether a government's taking of private property is for such use or purpose has become of minimal importance. The issue today centers not on the power or right of a State to take private property but on whether the taking is subject to indemnification. The measure of compensation is as difficult to define in international relations as in the United States.

Prior to World War I, there was general approval in the West of the view that international taking of an alien's property required payment of prompt and adequate compensation. Such a view could persist unchallenged until met by counter-thrusts from developing countries. Today, the U.S. Supreme Court decides that our courts cannot pass on issues of Cuba's right or power to expropriate U.S. property because "there are few if any issues in international law today on which opinion seems to be so divided." At a moment when the risk of expropriation is an important factor in management decisions, the executive and his counsel find few legal pillars of support or guidance. Yet foreign investment continues to expand—when permitted by balance-of-payments problems—and the ultimate solution may well lie in the political and economic facts of particular situations rather than in piously hopeful verbalizations.

Type of Activity

It is essential to consider the need for governmental protection of multinational enterprises in terms of the nature of their activities. In the extractive industries, for example, affecting a country's natural resources, operations must be conducted where supplies are available. The risk of expropriation must be countered, but the existence of even a sizeable risk cannot act as a deterrent if the supplies are available and a market exists for them. This type of enterprise touches directly the most sensitive spot of developed and developing countries' political consciousness: foreign ownership or control of a national asset to be depleted within a fairly short historical period or alien occupation of a substantial part of the national territory. Whether it is Switzerland barring alien ownership of land, aimed particularly at the West German penetration following World War II, or Peru removing an oil enclave, the sensitivity to foreign dominance is evident.

A second type of enterprise which raises special problems is the foreign-owned or -controlled public utility. Like the extractive enterprise, its legal relations with the host country are normally governed by a concession agreement, a contract-law of the parties. The risk of expropriation in the utility field is due less to sovereignty-sensitivity than to a belief that public ownership is the only alternative to the overwhelming pressures against a fair rate structure dictated by the forces of inflation and popular resentment against rising prices. In the United States the free enterprise system has accepted regulation of public utilities by government agencies as a means of reconciling private return with public service. In other countries, for many reasons, public ownership becomes inevitable.

These are not the only factors inviting expropriation. Where foreigners come to own or control a substantial proportion of a nation's economy, an "occupation" mentality develops within the country which often finds release in measures of strict regulation of existing and new investment if not outright expropriation. It is significant that in the case of Mexico in 1911, when Mexico's decade of revolution began, foreigners owned about two-thirds of the aggregate Mexican investment apart from agriculture and handicraft, a proportion that may have set all-time records for any country claiming political independence.

The Calvo Doctrine

The Calvo doctrine, named for an Argentine jurist, is generally regarded as expressing a special Latin American attitude barring diplomatic protection of aliens by their governments, with Mexico its most devoted supporter. Its fundamental thrust is rejection of any minimum international standard of protection of foreign investment, and assimilation of the alien to a country's nationals, on the assumption that by entering the country the alien tacitly agrees to be treated as a national. The Mexican Constitution includes a Calvo clause which requires aliens who wish to acquire lands or concessions for working mines or for use of waters or mineral fuel to agree "to consider themselves as Mexicans in respect of such property, and not to invoke the protection of their governments in matters relating thereto, under penalty of forfeiture of the property acquired."

It may seem surprising to the U.S. business community that Latin American countries attach such importance to diplomatic representations. The U.S. business executive normally finds less reason for close relations with his diplomats abroad than his English or West European counterpart. Despite the popular conception in other parts of the world, including Latin America, that U.S. foreign policy is dictated by the business class, the business community displays a marked skepticism toward the effectiveness of diplomatic protection of private business interests. This skepticism is compounded by their legal advisors' preference for legal rather than political channels for settlement of disputes. Anglo-American lawyers are by tradition and training biased toward equating law with what judges do. The U.S. legal profession generally is unaware of the legal rules which guide the process of governmental negotiations and agreement in the protection of private property.

On issues of discrimination, unfair taxation and generally in matters of "creeping expropriation," the diplomatic channel has been more effective than generally realized, particularly in adjustments with non-communist countries. The protest to the United Kingdom against threatened nationalization of Ford Motor Company facilities in England is a recent example. Even with communist countries diplomatic negotiations have resulted in lump-sum settlements compensating for confiscated property of U.S. nationals.

A deeper understanding of the circumstances in which diplomatic protection is extended is necessary to international business management and their counsel. The vital point is that diplomatic protection must be initiated by the private enterprise which has suffered loss as a result of foreign governmental action. In deciding whether or not to espouse the claim, the State Department must make preliminary determinations of fact and law. In the case of multinational enterprise, a preliminary issue of major importance is one which involves the very use of the term "multinational" since a government can protect only an enterprise with a defined nationality. In matters of foreign private investment, disputes between governments usually involve a corporation. Nationality of a corporation defined by the place of incorporation is not sufficient. Thus a Delaware corporation entirely owned by non-U.S. citizens will not be considered a U.S. national for purposes of diplomatic protest by the United States. A substantial national beneficial interest in the corporation is required.

U.S. Practice

The present practice of the United States is to consider a claim on behalf of corporations organized in the United States if 50% or more of the voting shares are owned by U.S. citizens. Where a corporation is organized under laws of any country other than the United States, the Department will consider a claim on behalf of the U.S. shareholders if they represent 25% or more of the voting shares. That the United States will espouse a claim under these conditions of beneficial interest by its citizens does not mean that the country to whom the diplomatic protest may be directed will follow the same tests.

In a case presently pending before the International Court of Justice, a central issue concerns the capacity of Belgium to represent a company largely Canadian-owned in a proceeding seeking compensation for alleged expropriation of the company's assets in Spain. The International Court has indicated that the issue of nationality of a person, if raised before an international court or arbitral tribunal, will be decided not under the law of the claimant state but pursuant to customary international law requiring a "real and effective" or "genuine" connection between the private individual or corporation and the claimant State.

Type of Claim

A second issue involved in the State Department's decision is the type of claim it is requested to espouse. A claim of the taking of property by foreign governmental act without prompt, adequate and effective compensation is the classical basis for U.S. diplomatic protection. There must be a taking and it must be of property. Before the 1930s, repudiation of the public debt at times led to forcible intervention in Latin America, particularly in the Caribbean area. Since that period, forcible unilateral action by the United States has not been considered, except in situations involving national security. The United States will not act as a "collection agency" for its nationals. Yet it will espouse claims of arbitrary annulment of concessions or repudiation of vested rights acquired by U.S. nationals, particularly when such action is accompanied by taking of tangible assets. Aside from the question of protecting property, in contrast to contractual expectations, the problem remains of defining "taking."

Not even all direct takings of property will be protected—for example, seizure and confiscation for violation of customs laws. A direct taking assumes destruction of the property or transfer of possession or control from the private owner. However, many forms of state interference with foreign property rights stop short of a direct taking though they severely limit the investor's ownership rights or impose new and burdensome obligations. Thus enforcement of tax laws, currency devaluation, rate regulation or governmental intervention in company management may in effect be tantamount to a taking. The decision to espouse such claims will be decided by the Department's determination as to their being "discriminatory," "unreasonable," "an abuse of power" or similar phrases for shedding heat as well as light. Each situation will necessarily be adjudged on its special facts.

Local Redress

A third requisite to the State Department's decision to protect U.S. nationals involves the extent to which the national must first seek redress in the courts or agencies of the expropriating country. This is a central issue in the view of Latin American countries and their insistence on exhaustion of domestic remedies forms the basis for their unanimous rejection of the Convention on the Settlement of Investment Disputes drafted by the World Bank, providing for arbitration of such disputes. It has also been a reason for the refusal of those countries to participate in Friendship, Commerce and Navigation treaties with the United States which provide for diplomatic negotiation and reference to the International Court of Justice. Before the State Department considered diplomatic protection for the claims of owners of property nationalized by Castro's Cuba, it required evidence that "the American national exhausted such legal remedies as were available in Cuba—or that the laws of Cuba do not provide a remedy or, if provided, that it would be futile to attempt to exhaust such remedy."

In summary, diplomatic protection of property interests abroad has been and will continue to be a normal method of channeling negotiations between foreign governments and private enterprise. It is not, as often assumed in some developing countries, a prelude to gunboat tactics or naked power display. The formal legal aspects indicate the restraints accepted by the capital-exporting countries in determining whether to transmute private claims for protection into international disputes. Political and economic realities will, of course, govern timing, manner and effectiveness of presentation. Once the claim is espoused, however, the preliminary adjudications which led to its becoming a governmental claim insure long-range commitment and establish the legal basis for ultimate settlement.

CHAPTER 23

CORWIN D. EDWARDS

*Governments the world over are imposing
antitrust regulations on international business.
Autonomous interpretations become precedents.
Multiple liability is the order of the day.
Is harmonization possible?*

The World of Antitrust

DOING BUSINESS in more than one country, a multinational enterprise is exposed to more than one system of national law. Although this fact is not new, it currently receives increased attention in the United States because more firms are multinational and have exposed themselves to a greater variety of national laws by widening the territorial scope of their operations.

The problems raised by more than one system of national law are likely to affect many aspects of a firm's activities. There are numerous differences in corporation laws, laws about sale of security issues, laws about ownership of natural resources, laws about labels for hazardous products, laws about currency and credit, tax laws, labor laws, patent and trademark laws, and even laws of tort and of contract. National differences in any of these may require modifications of the international firm's structure and conduct in ways that hamper the coherence of its operations.

In most of these fields little or no effort is made to harmonize laws by relaxing those of the United States. Minor problems are shrugged off; ad hoc diplomatic intervention is sometimes sought; and where problems are numerous and important, the U.S. government is urged to promote uniformity by international agreements such as that for the protection of industrial property. The antitrust field is peculiar, however. Spokesmen for U.S. firms have recurrently proposed that their international problems be reduced by softening U.S. antitrust law, and they have more often opposed than supported U.S. efforts to promote international agreement about antitrust policy.

At the close of the Second World War, the U.S. government took the lead in proposing that provisions for international cooperation in curbing restrictive business practices be included in the draft charter for an international trade organization. Largely because of opposition by U.S. business, this charter was not ratified by the United States, and, primarily because of this fact, the international organization was not established. Subsequently the United States took the lead in proposing to the United Nations Economic and Social Council that a program of international action concerned solely with restrictive business practices be developed. A proposal for such a program was developed by a committee of the Council; but again, largely because of opposition by U.S. business interests, particularly the Chamber of Commerce, the United States withdrew its support from the proposal and thereby ended the matter.[1]

This unusual response can be understood only in the light of history. Before the first World War there was substantially no antitrust legislation except in the United States and Canada. Elsewhere U.S. firms could disregard legal problems that might be raised by their own restrictive conduct abroad and had no possibility of legal protection from restrictive conduct by others. Though there were beginnings of antitrust legislation in some other countries in the period between the two World Wars, they were overshadowed by government-supported cartelization in Italy, Germany, Japan, the Netherlands, Belgium, and in important industries in England and France. Until the Second World War, however, it continued to be roughly true that U.S. antitrust laws forbade business firms to engage in restrictions that were either permitted or positively required in most countries outside North America.

Although the foreign legal situation has changed, business appreciation of its problems has lagged behind the facts. Comment by spokesmen for business about the effect of U.S. antitrust laws upon companies doing business abroad still rests typically upon two premises: first, that these laws inconveniently restrict U.S. activities overseas and, second, that the foreign competitors of U.S. firms remain unrestricted. Today this is not true. Twenty-four countries (including 13 in Europe, four in Latin America and seven others) now apply laws designed to curb restrictive business practices. In nearly every instance these laws were enacted or significantly strengthened following the close of the Second World War. In more than half of these countries, the legislation is broad and vigorous enough to merit consideration in the plans of a firm that does business in the country.

National laws have been supplemented by the treaties under which six countries established the European Economic Community and the European Coal and Steel Community. In addition to these treaty provisions, which establish rules of law and means to apply them, two other international arrangements about restrictions by business have come into effect. One provides that when a government that is a member of the European Free Trade Association sponsors a complaint about a restrictive practice by one or more firms located in one or more other member countries, the interested governments will negotiate informally and, if they agree that there is a practice incompatible with the Association's treaty, member countries that have jurisdiction over the parties will provide a remedy by administrative or legal means. What is done under this arrangement is kept confidential; but the Association has reported, in general terms, that the procedure has resulted in informal corrective action in a few cases.

The other arrangement, added in 1960 to the General Agreement on Tariffs and Trade, provides that at the request of a party the other parties will consult bilaterally or multilaterally about the harmful effects of restrictive practices and, if they agree that harmful effects are present, will take such measures as they deem appropriate. No such consultation has yet taken place.

These programs are ill-suited to action against restrictive practices. Neither of them has had or can be expected to have impact important enough to be considered in business planning.

Nevertheless, the relative position of U.S. business and foreign competitors has become considerably more complex:

(a) In parts of the world in which there is no effective antitrust legislation, U.S. firms curbed by antitrust must still compete with firms that are not thus curbed.

(b) In other parts of the world, antitrust problems that confront U.S. firms spring not from the contrast between law and absence of law but from that between U.S. law and a particular foreign law that differs in stretch, standards and procedures.

(c) For firms that do business in several foreign countries, all of which have antitrust legislation, problems created by differences in the antitrust laws of these countries may be as important as problems created by differences from U.S. law.

(d) For firms that operate so widely that they encounter numerous foreign antitrust laws, the great variety of legislation applicable to their activities may create greater problems than are due to the contrast between the laws of any two countries.

The problems that arise in these situations are four in number: (1) operation where there is no curb; (2) operation under a U.S. and a foreign curb; (3) operation under different foreign curbs; and (4) operation under a multiplicity of curbs.

Absence of a Curb

The problem that arises when operations are not locally curbed appears most clearly in the so-called "developing" countries. Among major developed countries, Italy alone lacks an antitrust law; but the provisions about restrictive practices that appear in the European Community treaties are municipal law in Italy as a member of the Community. Antitrust legislation now exists in nearly all of Western Europe and North America, in Japan, Australia, New Zealand, South Africa, and (with less effect) in four other countries.

Even though uncurbed by antitrust, U.S. firms in developing countries are often subject to limiting legislation more formidable than antitrust laws. Such laws may control mineral concessions, investments, technological assistance contracts, prices, profits, exports of profits and proportion of capital controlled. Some laws apply to foreign and domestic firms alike; some have been devised for and applied to foreign firms only. The basic presumption of a contrast between a firm that is subject to antitrust legislation and a firm that is not—that both firms operate in other respects as free private enterprises—is so far from true in many developing countries that the question of immunity from U.S. antitrust becomes a minor matter. Nevertheless, private enterprise is sufficiently characteristic of some developing countries to make discussion of the country that does not curb operations worthwhile. In this situation the extent of applicability of U.S. antitrust law assumes importance.

The problem of the uncurbed competitor arises in some of the relationships between U.S. and foreign firms in countries that have antitrust laws. Because of differences in the scope of antitrust legislation in different countries, industries and practices that are subject to U.S. law may be wholly exempt from a particular foreign law. A number of U.S. business complaints in Western Europe were apparently directed toward situations of this kind. In these situations, the fact that the foreign country also possesses an antitrust law is not relevant to the opportunities of the different firms.

One should not forget, however, that just as the foreign law may exempt what is curbed in the United States, so U.S. law may exempt what is curbed in the foreign country. To assume that the typical problem here is that of the uncurbed competitor would be to distort the effect of the foreign legislation. In examining the problem of an operation that is not curbed by the foreign jurisdiction, the nature of the curbs that limit the U.S. firm without limiting its foreign competitor must be clarified.

This is not easy to do. Specific examples, with firms, products, practices, countries, competitors and dates identified, are not available in business complaints. According to antitrust officials, such specific examples have not been presented to them.[2] In analyzing the problem, therefore, one must study examples of difficulties that appear in public criticisms of U.S. antitrust policy. Since these are brief, meager in relevant detail, anonymous as to the identity of firms and even of industries and often vague as to the precise nature of the conduct involved, they do not provide a firm basis for analysis. The nature of the curbs upon the U.S. firm is also obscure, partly because of vagueness as to the conduct that is in question and partly because of uncertainty about the bearing of U.S. law upon this conduct.

When U.S. Law Applies

Applicability of U.S. law can be analyzed in two ways, either by inference from the few proceedings pertaining to conduct in foreign countries or from the far more numerous proceedings pertaining to conduct in domestic markets. Either way, the inferences are of uncertain value. Most of the few proceedings that covered conduct abroad have pertained to collusive activities, carried on partly in the United States and designed to restrict flagrantly either trade within the United States or imports into it.[3] These cases throw little light upon the problems that confront a firm when, in a less lurid setting, it considers the bearing of U.S. antitrust upon such activities abroad as exclusive dealing, joint sale, patent licensing, or participation in mergers or joint ventures.

The numerous proceedings that have involved similar activities in domestic markets are unreliable precedents for conduct in foreign markets. A practice that is clearly unlawful in the United States may not be clearly so in a foreign country because U.S. commerce is not significantly affected by it or because it is required by a foreign government or for some other reason. What is unlawful per se in domestic markets may be decided under the rule of reason in foreign markets. The principle that the law permits restrictions ancillary to a nonrestrictive purpose may have a broader application in foreign trade than in domestic trade.

With standards of legality thus uncertain, much of the conduct that is described as unlawful abroad appears to be not clearly illegal but of uncertain legality and hence hazardous. Criticism by careful lawyers tends to make the point that antitrust hazards are often great enough to inhibit desirable action. Criticism by laymen, usually less precise, often brings together and describes as illegal conduct that bears different degrees of legal risk.

To understand the nature and the limits of the antitrust risks that may arise for a firm in its activities outside the Unietd States, one must bear in mind the broad characteristics of U.S. antitrust laws. Resting on the constitutional power to regulate commerce, these laws apply to activities that affect the interstate or foreign commerce of the United States. They forbid unauthorized private concerted restraint of that commerce, private monopolization of any part of it (or attempt at such monopolization) and various acts or practices that create a reasonable probability that competition in that commerce will be substantially reduced. Except for certain particular acts and practices, the applicability of the laws depends not on the question whether or not what is forbidden took place in that commerce, nor on the question whether or not the persons involved were engaged in that commerce, but on the question whether the relevant commerce was (or was likely to be) adversely affected in the specified way. Thus, the laws apply widely to intrastate enterprises and activities if interstate commerce is restricted by them. They may also be and have been applied to activities outside the United States by U.S. or foreign firms that have the forbidden effects upon the domestic market or the country's imports or exports. Conversely, activities devoid of restrictive effects upon U.S. commerce are beyond the reach of the antitrust laws even if they severely restrict the trade of a foreign country or U.S. intrastate trade.

Broadly speaking, then, activities and agreements outside the United States by firms operating there are subject to U.S. antitrust laws if they affect U.S. commerce in the prohibited ways.

Descriptions of the handicaps typically attributed to the antitrust laws are similar enough that two or three may be used to illustrate them all. Illustration is provided by testimony given before the Hart committee in 1964 by William Persen, vice president and editor of *Business International,* and by Arthur H. Dean of the law firm of Sullivan and Cromwell,[4] plus a report on antitrust aspects of export expansion included in a report to the President in September 1963.[5] Mr. Persen's testimony briefly described 20 "disguised cases" in which firms had forgone profitable business opportunities because of possible antitrust difficulties. Mr. Dean's testimony described seven hypothetical situations, characterized as "real and recurring types of problems which confront American businessmen abroad and on which antitrust counsel are frequently called upon to advise." The report to the President included six "typical examples" of antitrust problems that confront U.S. companies in foreign markets.

Areas of Restriction

The 33 problems of restriction described in these documents pertained to three types of situation: cartel agreements, restrictive licensing of patents or know-how and ownership relations with other firms.

Two of the examples in the report to the President, three in the statement by Mr. Dean, and two (possibly three) in the statement by Mr. Persen pertained to cartelization. One of the seven clear cases had to do with the inability of a U.S. firm to condition the sale of its product to a French firm upon agreement by the latter that when the purchased article became a component of the French firm's products, these should not be shipped to the United States in competition. The second involved inability by U.S. chemical firms in Belgium to join a cartel that controlled exports from Belgium (presumably including exports to the United States). The third pertained to the need for a U.S. firm to refrain from becoming party to one or more cartels that restrained U.S. trade by acquiring an interest in an Italian firm that was party to the agreements. The fourth was concerned with the jeopardy that a U.S. firm would incur if, for a type of mineral that it produced from a concession in a foreign country, it were to take part in a scheme to raise profits on such minerals by means that included material restrictions on U.S. commerce. Though the restrictions were not specified, the statement about them implied that they might include such schemes as price fixing on an international scale or allocation of world markets. The fifth and sixth examples had to do with risks that a U.S. firm might incur if, in a particular foreign country in which it did business, it joined a cartel that applied such restrictions as price fixing or joint use of facilities to forestall construction of additional facilities. The seventh example involved the inability of several U.S. firms to agree that their subsidiaries in the European Economic Community should limit their product lines.

The types of restriction on free markets involved in this sample of cartel agreements are those characteristic of the hard core of U.S. antitrust cases—price fixing, allocation of territories or of types of goods and limitation of future supply. They are like those in the cartel cases that evoked, during and immediately after World War II, a popular outcry against international cartels and a series of

Congressional anticartel riders to foreign aid agreements and bilateral treaties of commerce.[6]

The argument for modifying U.S. law and policy to tolerate such restrictions rests initially on the point that the alternative to restriction is loss of a business opportunity that might otherwise be available. It is important, therefore, to note the nature of the forgone opportunities in the different examples.

These differ greatly in magnitude. In the fourth and fifth cases cited, the argument for permitting cartelization rested on a foreign government's desire that the U.S. firm join the cartel, expressed by pressure falling short of legal compulsion. One of these cases involved the possibility that refusal might result in loss of a mineral concession; the other appears to have involved only the subtle effects of being considered noncooperative. In the sixth case, the difficulty for the U.S. firm was that of entering a tightly controlled market without coming to terms with the business group that controlled it; in the third case, that of losing the advantage of an ownership interest in the Italian firm as a means of promoting exports to Italy; in the second case, that of competing alone in export markets against the group efforts of cartel members; in the seventh case, that of not attaining the economies which might have been achieved if each producer had made a shorter line of goods; and in the first case, merely the inconvenience of having to choose between loss of a good foreign customer and the risk that this customer might be strengthened as a potential competitor.

Four types of restriction relating to patents or unpatented know-how are also involved in the examples: (1) exclusion of the foreign licensee from the U.S. market; (2) exclusion of the U.S. licensor from export markets that are reserved for the foreign licensee; (3) use of the combined power of cross-licenses to exclude third parties (as well as each participating party) from markets assigned to a particular participant; (4) requirement that the licensee obtain from the licensor such accessory equipment and materials as he needs in using the licensed product or process.

When what is licensed is unpatented technology, the antitrust laws are fully applicable to whatever restraints of U.S. commerce take place in these ways. When patents are licensed, the applicability of antitrust law must be considered in the light of the monopoly right conveyed by a patent. But this right does not include the right to restrain trade beyond the territory covered by the patent grant, to restrain products that are not patented nor to impose restrictions based upon the combined power of two or more patentees. Where a patentee possesses a U.S. patent and counterpart foreign patents, he can keep the products of his foreign licensees out of the United States by retaining and using his monopoly right under his U.S. patent. Similarly, he can use his ownership of a foreign counterpart patent to keep both U.S. exporters and licensees under other foreign counterpart patents out of the country in which he retains exclusive patent rights. Such action needs no exclusionary contract. The use of one is likely to raise the question whether more restriction is not being obtained than is obtainable by enforcing the patent.

The arguments offered in these statements for greater leniency toward international licensing than would be applied to domestic licenses are two: First, a U.S. firm that cannot agree to grant a foreign licensee exclusive rights to a certain export territory may find that the prospective licensee chooses alternative technology available to it from a foreign firm that is not precluded from granting such rights. Second, the profitability of foreign licensing is reduced. The U.S licensor loses the benefit of potentially profitable trade restrictions: (a) markets protected by allocative cross-licensing; (b) monopoly in selling unpatented accessories to licensees; (c) ability to get license fees from unpatented technology without incurring the risk of competition from licensees in markets where they have no license. The prospective U.S. licensor of unpatented technology may face an inconvenient choice between acceptance of the risk of competition by foreign licensees and relinquishment of the benefits from foreign licensee fees.

Joint Venture Problems

The most numerous examples presented in these papers pertain to joint ventures among firms. Though some examples are presented as if mere participation by a U.S. company in a foreign joint venture is legally vulnerable, other examples make no such presumption, nor is the presumption persuasive. Even in the United States, no legal challenge has been offered to joint ventures as such, and in foreign countries joint ventures presumably operate in many instances without restrictive effects on U.S. trade. A joint venture is capable of restraining U.S. commerce, however. This possibility may arise in two forms. First, the joint venture itself may undertake restriction. For example, it may use discriminatory dumping to drive competing U.S. exporters from certain export markets. When restriction is thus overt, a question may arise whether the U.S. firm that participates in the joint venture is thereby part of a combination in restraint of trade. The same question may be raised about more subtle restrictions. The joint venture may refrain from exporting to the United States, preferring not to compete with one of its owners. If so, the capital that is withheld from such competition is not only that of the U.S. owner but also that of the foreign participant, and a question may arise whether the joint venture does not inherently include an implied undertaking by the foreign firm to stay out of the U.S. market.

Second, supplementing the joint venture, the U.S. firm and the foreign firm in which it has participating ownership may agree upon restrictions that would be, if there were no joint venture, clearly a cartel agreement. The agreement may provide that the foreign joint venture will not ship to the United States, or that the U.S. part-owner will not ship to the territory of the joint venture, or that both will maintain the same prices, sell through the same distributors, buy from the same sources or take similar restrictive action. If the substance of such an agreement restricts U.S. commerce and thus is vulnerable under the antitrust laws, the question posed by the existence of a joint venture is whether the ties of ownership between the parties remove this vulnerability by converting the agreement into mere managerial decision by a single firm.

The problems involved in joint ventures are among the most difficult that arise in applications of the antitrust laws, whether to domestic or to foreign commerce. Involved are the circumstances under which restrictive agreements are implied by conduct that might have nonrestrictive explanations, as well as the boundary beyond which a corporate complex should be regarded as a single enterprise rather than two or more. The difficulties that arise for U.S. firms abroad are similar to those at home—the ambiguity of laws that are still evolving. The relevant question raised by the examples is whether joint ventures in foreign countries are so desirable that such ventures should be treated more favorably than other joint ventures, either by more cursory examination of the inherently difficult issues or by more permissive rules of substantive law.

In the aggregate, these examples indicate that wherever operations abroad have significant effects upon U.S. commerce, U.S. firms need to consider the effect of their action upon such commerce and that, in operations abroad as well as at home, they may find that antitrust considerations make it wise to avoid conduct that, in other respects, would be profitable. However, the sacrifices involved seem to be neither so frequent nor so severe as to be of major importance for the success of U.S. trade in foreign countries. They consist in avoiding participation in international cartels that include restrictions upon imports into the United States, limiting the trade restrictions that accompany licenses of technology to those that are authorized by patent laws, and eliminating restraints of U.S. commerce from business practices associated with joint ventures.

Some Relief

Although these limitations may be inconvenient, there are mitigations and offsetting advantages. Two of these are worth noting.

First, foreign as well as U.S. firms are subject to the U.S. antitrust laws when they deliberately restrain U.S. trade, and, like U.S. firms, they enjoy no immunity because their restrictive conduct took place outside the United States. The British Imperial Chemical Industries as well as the U.S. du Pont were subjected to orders by a U.S. court in a case involving a worldwide allocation of chemical markets; the Dutch Philips as well as the U.S. General Electric were subjected to orders in the case involving international cartelization of incandescent lamps. In neither case was the liability of the foreign defendant limited to what it had done within the United States.

The effect of application of U.S. law to foreign firms is to mitigate whatever disadvantage U.S. firms may incur but not to eliminate it. In several respects the impact of the law upon foreign firms is less severe than upon U.S. firms. Unless a foreign firm does some business within the United States, proceedings in U.S. courts cannot take place for lack of jurisdiction. When U.S. trade is restricted by a foreign firm's conduct outside the United States, the proof needed for application of the laws is more difficult than in the case of U.S. firms. Either type of firm is vulnerable if what was done abroad was part of a pattern that included action in the United States. In the National Lead case, the decision acknowledged that "conduct abroad, on the part of foreign nations, relating to the commerce of foreign nations" would not be subject to U.S. action, but pointed out that "a conspiracy was entered into, in the United States, to restrain and control the commerce of the world, including the foreign commerce of the United States. The several agreements relating to manufacture and trade within the European markets are but some of the links in the chain which was designed to enthrall the entire commerce in titanium."

Foreign action is also vulnerable if its effect on U.S. trade was intended and clear. In the aluminum case, the test applied in determining whether cartel agreements made abroad by foreign firms violated U.S. law was that "both were unlawful, though made abroad, if they were intended to affect imports and did affect them." The court held that proof of intent to restrict imports was sufficient to place upon the defendants the burden of proving that the purpose was not accomplished. But, provided the foreign firm is not party to a cartel agreement with U.S. firms, the fact that its interests and operations lie chiefly abroad means that foreign restrictions by it are more likely to lack demonstrable purpose to influence U.S. trade than are comparable restrictions by U.S. firms.

When a foreign firm violates U.S. law, corrective orders against it are likely to be more limited and less effective than orders against comparable conduct by domestic firms. In the incandescent lamp decree, the general injunction against agreements that restricted U.S. exports or imports was applied to the Dutch defendant Philips only with respect to agreements with U.S. manufacturers, whereas the U.S. defendants were enjoined from restrictive agreements (more inclusively defined) with anyone. Moreover, Philips was exempted from the decree for any action abroad that was unlawful under the applicable foreign law. The Netherlands thereupon enacted a law that forbade compliance with decisions by a foreign state about restrictive conduct except after permission by the Dutch government.

In the case involving Imperial Chemical Industries, the U.S. court's efforts to subject British patents on nylon to the decree's provisions for nonexclusive licenses were defeated by a suit filed in Britain by the exclusive licensee, a firm in which Imperial Chemical Industries had a 50% stock interest. From the limits imposed by U.S. jurisdiction, limits of proof as to purpose and effect and limits of effective corrective action, foreign firms may derive considerable opportunity to continue to do what U.S. firms cannot do.

Second, the duty for U.S. firms to comply with the antitrust laws can be a source of advantage for them in cartel situations. When the law keeps them out of cartels, one possibility is that abstention makes establishment of a cartel impossible. U.S. firms like others, may dislike the resulting competition, but in being exposed to it they suffer no handicap, since their foreign competitors must compete also.

The other possibility is that foreign firms can and do establish the cartel without U.S. participation. When foreign firms agree to fix prices, limit output or sales, allocate markets, or limit new capacity, U.S. firms that do not join the agreement find advantage in their independence. So far as the agreed restrictions improve their prices and profits and reduce the intensity of the competition to which they are exposed, these benefits are theirs without action by them. While their foreign rivals are bound, they are free. They can "woo the customers that the cartel will not make, or engage in the price competition from which the cartel abstains."[7] Unless a cartel can effectively use exclusionary restrictions to keep independent firms out of cartelized markets, U.S. firms are helped when they remain independent.

U.S. and Foreign Curbs

Nearly all the major industrialized countries and a few others now apply antitrust legislation. The members of the European Communities also apply the antitrust provisions of the Community treaties. When doing business in these countries, U.S. firms find themselves subject to at least two systems of antitrust law and their foreign competitors subject to at least one. The foreign laws, however, differ substantially from the law of the United States, as well as from other foreign laws.

In some of the foreign countries, antitrust legislation covers only restrictive activities that are carried out within the particular country, as in the case of New Zealand. For a U.S. firm and for its local competitors, liability for acts in such a country might also exist under U.S. law if the activities there had direct effects upon U.S. trade. Where legal relationships between foreign and U.S. laws have this character, the foreign laws are likely to be more permissive in some respects, less so in others. Where they are more permissive, they may permit, for example, concerted agreements for exchange of technology that include prohibition of exports. Where they are less permissive, they may make it necessary for a U.S. firm to abstain locally from practices that are permissible in the United States. Thus, in particular countries, resale price maintenance by an individual supplier, which is permissible in the United States where authorized by state law, may be forbidden unless it receives special exemption.

In other foreign countries, national laws are so broadly applicable that a U.S. firm may face two-sided extraterritorial liability. Like U.S. law, these other laws endeavor, in varying degrees, to curb restraints that affect domestic trade, no matter where these restraints are imposed. The German cartel law is applicable "to all restraints of competition effective in the area of applicability of this law, even if they result from acts done outside such area."[8] The Austrian cartel law covers "cartel agreements made abroad, insofar as they are to be implemented in the territory of the Austrian Federal Republic." Under the British Monopolies Act, orders "may be so made as to extend to acts or omissions outside the United Kingdom," but only if those subjected to such orders are British subjects, British corporations or persons doing business in the United Kingdom. Though the Swiss Act on Cartels and Similar Organizations does not explicitly convey jurisdiction over what is done outside the country, a Swiss federal court decided in 1967 that the law "also applies to actions in restraint of competition which take place abroad and have effects in Switzerland." The laws of Spain and Denmark cover restrictions that have effects in domestic markets and hence may be reasonably interpreted as applicable where domestic effects spring from acts that occur in foreign countries, though neither statute makes this application explicit. Even under Dutch law, though the agreements covered are only those applicable to domestic trade that include at least one enterprise established in the Netherlands, nonresident participants have a duty to register the agreement. Since registration by one participant terminates the duty of the others to register, the obligation on the nonresident is significant only if resident participants fail to comply. In such a case, however, theoretically the nonresident could be prosecuted for noncompliance and convicted in absentia.

Application of the provisions of the Treaty of Rome that forbid restrictive agreements affecting trade between members of the European Economic Community is not limited either by the nationality of the enterprises involved or the place in which the restriction takes place. In applying this treaty, the Community's Council has made registration of agreements a prerequisite for grant of the exemptions that the treaty authorizes; and the agreements registered have included agreements made outside the Community by firms in other countries. Thus important jurisdictions have adopted for trade regulation the principle that their laws apply where their trade is affected.

The spread of this so-called "extraterritorial" principle of jurisdiction is not surprising. Incentives to adopt it are provided by contemporary business structure. Firms that operate internationally through establishments located in different countries can make individual or collective decisions in any country in which they choose to place their executives or hold their business meetings. They can restrain the trade of any country in which they have substantial operations or into which they make substantial shipments, by agreements made elsewhere: (1) to curtail the flow of their shipments to the country, (2) to raise the prices of what they send there, (3) to limit what they export from the country, or (4) to limit what they invest in it or the use that they make of facilities they already possess within it. The vulnerability of a country to restraints of trade that are executed beyond its borders differs only in degree, not in kind, from the vulnerability of a state in the United States to trade restraints that are executed in other states. As international trade has increased in volume and importance and as international firms have become more important in that trade, this vulnerability has increased.

The impact of reciprocal extraterritorial claims of jurisdiction has been minimal thus far. There are two reasons for this: the recency of the foreign laws in which such jurisdiction is asserted and the tendency for the foreign governments that assert such jurisdiction to concentrate their attention initially upon their own domestic restraints. In the United States, proceedings that involved international cartels and overseas activities were negligible for decades after the Sherman Act became law. But the potential of the reciprocal concepts is there and even today has some slight operative significance for U.S. firms that operate in the Common Market. Since U.S. firms are prominent and feared in international trade, this potential is likely sooner or later to express itself in foreign countries in action as vigorous as in the United States.

Where this happens, U.S. firms that do business internationally are likely to find that in so doing they incur significant dual liability. So far as the substance of control over restrictive activities differs in the United States and another country, acts that are permissible in one country may be unlawful in the other if they have a restrictive impact there. More importantly, restrictive agreements and actions in export trade from either country, though exempt in the exporting country for lack of domestic effect, may be unlawful in the importing country as restrictions related to that country's imports and domestic sales. Moreover, in each country firms with dual liability are likely to encounter competitors that have liability only under one country's laws, because they do business only in that country or do business abroad only in countries without antitrust laws. Since these competitors enjoy greater freedom of action than the firms with dual liability, problems of competition with uncurbed competitors are likely to appear.

It is conceivable that in a particular instance the problems thus created for U.S. business might be eliminated by unilateral change in the antitrust laws of the United States. To abandon U.S. principles of control merely on the ground that they conflict with the principles applied by another country is not inviting. But this is not the only difficulty. There are two others. The first is that, since most countries with antitrust laws are indifferent to restrictions that take effect abroad, there is no way for the United States, without gross discrimination against its own citizens, to relax its control of restrictions on its imports in toleration of reductions that are permissible in other countries and, at the same time, tighten its control of restrictions on its exports to prevent effects that are unlawful in the countries to which the goods are sent. The second difficulty is that U.S. law would have to be changed to conform to the laws of several countries whose laws do not conform to one another.

Foreign Curbs

U.S. firms that operate in several foreign countries, including one or more that assert jurisdiction where domestic effects are due to action abroad, potentially encounter problems from the differences among foreign laws. The effects of their action, lawful in one foreign country, may produce antitrust risks in another country that asserts extraterritorial control. If they operate in two or more foreign countries that assert extraterritorial control, they may encounter dual liability. The extent of these possibilities increases with growth in the number of the countries that have antitrust laws.

Like the problems of dual liability that involve U.S. law, the problems of dual liability under laws that are wholly foreign have not yet appeared in specific proceedings. Since the reasons are the same as for the other kind of dual liability—the recency of the foreign laws and the initial preoccupation of officials with domestic issues—this is not surprising. But the chances are that those who assert extraterritorial jurisdiction will eventually exert it. When they do, both kinds of dual liability are likely to create problems.

Such dual liabilities may become, in fact, considerably more than dual. With several foreign jurisdictions asserting extraterritorial authority, U.S. firms that do business in most of these countries probably will encounter, in time, several instances of dual liability, differing from country to country in the limits imposed by foreign law and hence in the points of difference between foreign and U.S. law, and between one foreign law and another.

The more numerous the dualities, the harder to cope with them. Yet the more numerous they are, the clearer it must become that the difficulties they create cannot be met by unilateral relaxation of the U.S. antitrust laws.

Multiplicity of Curbs

The problems of differences in policy toward trade restrictions between U.S. law and some foreign law, or between two (or more) foreign laws are likely to be enhanced as the number and diversity of laws increases. At some point in this growing complexity the problem changes character, at least for firms that do a far-flung international business. Such firms are no longer primarily concerned with particular differences in business opportunity traceable to the different application of antitrust laws. Instead, they are likely to find that antitrust legislation is so diverse that in the aggregate it creates obstacles to coherent management of international enterprises. Where activities involve possibilities of trade restriction, they may find that each of the more attractive lines of action is questioned by one or more countries, that no test of the legitimacy of action is valid in all countries and that efforts to make action acceptable under the different antitrust laws of the various countries entail truly impressive burdens of legal analysis, negotiation and delay.

Whether or not diversity has yet reached these forbidding dimensions is uncertain. It is clear that diversity is already formidable and that its effects upon international business are likely to increase as administration of the newer laws and the ones more laxly applied becomes more thorough.

Only by examples can one make vivid the extent to which the diverse provisions of the national laws and the international treaties are sources of multiple and partly inconsistent substantive requirements applied in a vexing variety of ways.

A firm that does business in each country in Europe, North America and Japan is obligated to report its restrictive agreements in seven different countries and, if it wishes to qualify them for exemption from the prohibitions of the EEC Treaty, also to the EEC Commission. The reporting requirements differ as to the meaning of "agreement" and of "restriction," the extent of the information that must be supplied, the kinds of agreements that are exempt from reporting, and the legal effect of failure to report.[9] In five of these countries the obligation to report extends beyond restrictive agreements if the firm has a dominant position or individually engages in restriction, but the definition of those who must report and the scope of what must be reported differ from country to country. Mergers and similar acquisitions must be reported in three countries—in one country in advance and regardless of size, in the others subsequently and only if the acquirer is large (by a definition that is different in each country). In two countries a firm is subject to special reporting requirements if it is foreign, and in one country, if it is large, it must report its stockholdings.

Substantive control over restrictive activities is equally dissimilar, with a different pattern of diversity for each kind of restriction. The status of exclusive dealing will serve as an example. A U.S. firm that desired to use exclusive distributors in selling its products in the United States, Canada, Japan and Western Europe (except Finland) would need to consider the bearing of the restrictive practice legislation of fifteen countries and of the EEC upon its proposed program. In one country, Canada, the law would seem to contain no relevant provisions. Conspiracies to restrain trade and monopolies, against which the most nearly relevant parts of the Canadian law are directed, are so defined that there is little likelihood of the law's use against exclusive dealing. In four countries, the United Kingdom, the Netherlands, Belgium and Switzerland, any curbs that might be relevant would be found only among provisions applicable to powerful business enterprises. In the other ten countries and in the EEC, controls applicable to agreement or to restriction by single firms would be such that they might apply to exclusive dealing even by a relatively small firm.

If the firm considering the program were sufficiently large that it needed to consider the laws of fourteen countries, it would find that in five of these countries the statutes and related official documents would make the legal status of exclusive dealing reasonably clear. In the other nine countries, the legality of its proposed program would depend upon the interpretation that might be given to diverse legal standards by the various official bodies charged with decision. These standards are concerned with the effect of the program upon the interests of other parties to the arrangement, upon the interests of firms excluded from the agreement, upon competition or upon the public interest. To assume that even similar and relatively specific statutory language might be differently interpreted by different official bodies would be reasonable, but in most of the nine countries the applicable legal standards are of a kind deliberately designed to convey considerable discretion to those who apply them, and the leeway for divergent interpretation is correspondingly wide.

Country Variants

Summarizing the situation as explicitly as it could, the firm might reach the following conclusions. No legal obstacle would be encountered in three countries: Canada, the Netherlands, Norway. The Netherlands and Norway have exempted exclusive dealing agreements from reporting requirements that are applicable to restrictive agreements generally. Nevertheles, Norway has statutory power to forbid an enterprise to refuse to deal with another if the effect upon the other would be unreasonable or contrary to the public interest. The Netherlands can order a dominant firm to make deliveries to designated customers if the dominance has consequences deemed contrary to the public interest.

In another country, France, the program would be lawful or unlawful, depending upon whether it had or lacked characteristics specifically set forth in official interpretations of the law. Exclusive dealing is permitted in France as an exception to a general prohibition of refusal to sell, but only if (a) both the supplier and the distributor are bound exclusively; (b) the area covered is precisely defined; (c) use of exclusive contracts by the supplier is general; and (d) the arrangement is not tainted by resale price control.

In one country, Spain, the program would be unlawful. Spain issued in 1966 a decree (Decree 3052/66) that prohibited refusal to sell. Under the Spanish Act Against Restraints of Competition, refusal to sell by a dominant firm might also be regarded as a forbidden abusive practice. A dictum to this effect was included, upon request by the Service for Protection of Competition, in a judgment by the Court for Protection of Competition.

In three countries, the United Kingdom, Belgium and Switzerland, the program would be lawful unless the firm had a dominant position, but in that case legality would be uncertain, since it would depend upon imputations by the authorities as to purpose, abuse of power or effect upon the public interest. In the United Kingdom, bilateral exclusive dealing agreements are explicitly exempted by Section 8(3) of the Restrictive Trade Practices Act. But under the Monopolies Act of 1948 (Sections 3 and 10) and the Monopolies and Mergers Act of 1965 (Section 3) such agreements may be terminated if undertaken as a result of or for the purpose of preserving control of one-third or more of the national supply and if they operate against the public interest. In Belgium, the law's general provisions about correction of abuses of economic power might be applicable to exclusive dealing by powerful firms. In Switzerland, prohibition by a dominant firm of the purchase or delivery of goods is unlawful if its purpose is to interfere appreciably with freedom to compete, unless it is held to be justified by overriding legitimate interests, particularly the establishment of an economic structure that is desirable in the general interest.

Legality would also be uncertain in the remaining seven countries. In five, Austria, Denmark, Sweden, Ireland and Japan, the test of legality would be the reasonableness of impediments imposed by exclusive dealing upon participants or third parties. Though Section 18 of the Austrian Cartel Act denies registration to agreements that provide for exclusive sale, the Austrian Supreme Court has interpreted the provision as inapplicable to an individual exclusive dealing contract in which the parties had no common restrictive purpose. Under the Austrian law of unfair competition, the legality of such a contract turns upon the question whether or not there is intent to damage competitors to an extent not justified by economic considerations. In Denmark and Sweden, refusal to sell is the subject of numerous proceedings under the broad provisions applicable to restrictions generally. In Sweden, the relevant question about exclusive dealing is whether or not the arrangement has, by impeding the trade of others, a harmful effect contrary to the public interest. In Denmark, the relevant question is whether or not the arrangement unreasonably restrains freedom of trade or is unreasonably discriminatory.

Irish law authorizes promulgation of rules and orders that establish fair trading conditions and sets forth a list of unfair trade practices, including: "without just cause prohibit or restrict the supply of goods to any person . . . or give preference in regard to the provision of, or the placing of orders for the supply of, goods, or restrict or are likely to restrict unjustly the exercise by any person of his freedom of choice as to what goods he will supply or distribute." In practice, the rules and orders have varied from trade to trade but have often included rules against discriminatory refusal to sell to traders at the same distributive level. In the motor fuel trade, exclusive distribution of gasoline has been permitted, subject to a five-year time limit for contracts, but exclusive distribution of lubrication oil has not.

Japanese law forbids unfair business practices as designated by the Fair Trade Commission. A generally applicable list of such practices issued by the Commission includes language that covers exclusive dealing and has been applied against it.

In one country, the United States, the test would be the probable effect on competition. Section 3 of the Clayton Act forbids sale on condition that the buyer shall not deal in the goods of the seller's competitors where the effect may be to lessen competition substantially. If the exclusive arrangement is one of a number by which a supplier's territory is allocated among his distributors, the arrangement may also violate Section 1 of the Sherman Act as a combination to restrain trade. In the White Motor case, the Supreme Court refused in 1966 to treat such a program as a per se violation but remanded the proceeding for the taking of evidence. Instead the defendant accepted a consent decree enjoining the practices named in the complaint. Subsequently, in the Schwinn case, the Court held that restrictions upon resale, including territorial restrictions, are unlawful if the supplier does not retain title to the goods.

In one country, Germany, tests of the effect on competition and of the effect on third parties would both be applicable, with illegality resulting from adverse decision as to either. Section 18 of the German Act Against Restraints of Competition authorizes the Cartel Authority to invalidate and prohibit agreements that restrain one party in obtaining goods from or delivering them to third parties where these agreements either unfairly restrict access by other enterprises to the market or substantially affect market competition. Exclusive dealing may also be subject to the provisions of Section 22, which authorizes corrective orders against abuse of power by dominant firms; and to Section 26, which forbids such firms and firms that fix resale prices to treat other firms differently without justification or to hinder the business activities of other firms unfairly.

The nine countries in which legality is uncertain present nine different problems, partly because of different statutory standards and partly because of different sources for interpretation of similar standards.

The EEC Approach

Instead of reducing the diversity that is evident in the foregoing summary, EEC's treatment of exclusive dealing has added one more variant. Simple two-party exclusive dealing contracts have been exempted from EEC's prohibition of restrictive agreements, provided that they impose no territorial restriction upon the distributor other than an obligation to refrain from sales effort and operation of branches or warehouses outside his territory, and provided that they contain no other significant restrictions. This exemption is subject, however, to a provision under which the EEC Commission may examine individually cases in which there is reason to presume that the products covered by exclusive contracts are not in competition with similar goods or in which the exclusive distributor sells at unreasonably high prices or refuses unreasonably to sell to certain buyers. Unless an exclusive arrangement is covered by the exemption, its validity is determined by applying the general rule against restrictive agreements, as modified by the general rule authorizing exemption of agreements that provide specified benefits. The Grundig-Consten case has made clear that exclusive dealing will be prohibited under these provisions if it prevents purchase of the relevant goods by buyers in one member state from the exclusive distributor in another member state. The effect obviously is to limit the power of exclusive distributors in each member state by exposing them to competition from imports of their own goods.

Antitrust policies are now in the process of being established, not only in the European Communities, but also in most of the 24 countries in which there are antitrust laws. To establish uniform trade regulation and uniform opportunity by removing the antitrust controls that apply to international business is no longer practical.

To remove dual, or multiple, liability for the same restriction is also not practicable—at least if the means employed is to consist of relaxation of the extraterritorial application of national laws without provision of other ways in which to curb restraints that have international effects. Yet for an international business multiple liability is a burden, and diversity of laws is probably a greater burden. As application of the newer laws becomes more systematic and as interpretations of each law harden into precedents, the burdens are likely to increase, even if no additional laws are passed in countries such as Italy and India, which have been considering antitrust legislation and may be the next to enact some regulations.

The time is ripe for the most antitrust-conscious segment of international business, that based in the United States, to reconsider its attitude toward the application of antitrust laws to restraints that affect international trade. Business opposition to extraterritorial applications of law has failed here and has not prevented enactment of laws elsewhere that provide for similar application. Business opposition was successful in blocking the two postwar U.S. efforts to bring about international cooperation in policy toward restrictive practices, but in doing so it did not block the growth of antitrust laws abroad. It merely assured that these laws would develop with no coordination (other than that provided in the two European Communities) and that the United States would lose its position as leader in this field of policy. In the interests of U.S. international business, as well as of reduced restriction in world trade, these negative attitudes should be replaced by a positive one. Since restrictions that have international effects will be curbed either by national acts devoid of coordinated standards and procedures or by some alternative means, U.S. business should recognize this fact and should encourage search for the alternative.

The alternative might be either an international agency concerned with restrictions that are international in scope—a larger EEC—or agreement among countries with antitrust legislation about the standards by which such restrictions are to be appraised under national laws, the methods to be used in detecting and curbing them by national action, and the extent to which countries should help each other in this work. Along either line, action today would be more difficult than in 1948, when continued U.S. support might have established the ITO Charter, or in 1953, when continued U.S. support might have brought into being the international effort that was considered by the United Nations Economic and Social Council. Further delay will make action more difficult still. Within a relatively short time, an increase in the number of national laws and further hardening of the peculiarities of each law may make diversity less tolerable, yet incapable of being harmonized.

NOTES

1. See Corwin D. Edwards, *Control of Cartels and Monopolies; an International Comparison,* Dobbs Ferry, New York: Oceana, 1967.

2. William Persen of *Business International* explained the lack of specific case material as follows: "One area where almost all companies are loath to talk even on an off-the-record basis . . . is that of antitrust. . . . It is because they simply are never certain what is and what is not an offense." *Foreign Trade and the Antitrust Laws,* hearings before the Antitrust Subcommittee of the Senate Judiciary Committee, Part I, 1964.

3. See decisions reproduced in *International Aspects of Antitrust,* hearings before the Antitrust Subcommittee of the Senate Judiciary Committee, Part 2, Appendix, 1967. Restraints that took effect within the United States or allocations of territory designed to keep foreign competitors out of the United States were central in all of these cases in which violations were found except the case involving coated abrasives. In the abrasives case, firms dominant in the U.S. market had undertaken joint production in other countries, with consequent reduction of exports from the United States by themselves and their U.S. competitors.

4. *Foreign Trade and the Antitrust Laws, op. cit.*

5. Report of Committee 11 of the White House Conference on Export Expansion.

6. Cartel practices were explicitly described and analyzed in George Stocking and Myron Watkins, *Cartels in Action,* New York: Twentieth Century Fund, 1946; Erwin Hexner, *International Cartels,* Chapel Hill: University of North Carolina Press, 1945; and Corwin D. Edwards, *Economic and Political Aspects of International Cartels,* Monograph No. 1, Subcommittee on War Mobilization, Senate Committee on Military Affairs, 78th Congress, Second Session, 1944.

7. Corwin D. Edwards, *Cartelization in Western Europe,* Washington: U.S. Department of State, 1964. The ensuing passage describes a case in which a U.S. firm that refused to join a price and quota cartel was sheltered by the cartel arrangement while it modernized its plant in preparation for an aggressive sales campaign.

8. The laws mentioned in this section appear in English translation in OECD's *Guide to Legislation on Restrictive Business Practices.*

9. See Edwards, *Control of Cartels and Monopolies, op. cit.*

CHAPTER 24

GEORGE W. BALL

*Needed: an international companies law that will
enable the world enterprise to pursue "the true logic of the
global economy" without ceaseless interference
from its puzzled parent, the sovereign nation.*

Cosmocorp:

The Importance of

Being Stateless

DURING THE several millennia of our history there have been long
periods when time seemed to stand still. Now in this last third of
the twentieth century it has not only caught up, but seems at times
to be moving ahead of us. Caught in a whirlwind of pervasive and
accelerating change, we have barely enough time to inquire as to
its larger implications, and where they may lead us a decade hence.

We recognize that we live in a world whose resources are finite
and whose demands are exploding. To avoid a Darwinian debacle

on a global scale we will have to use our resources with maximum efficiency and a minimum of waste.

In these twenty postwar years, we have come to recognize in action, though not always in words, that the political boundaries of nation-states are too narrow and constricted to define the scope and activities of modern business. This recognition has found some reflection, though not enough, in political action. Six countries of Western Europe have frontally attacked the stifling restrictions imposed on trade by shedding the ancient concept of nation-states. They have created a thriving common market.

In the summer of 1968 goods will move with full freedom throughout Western Europe to serve the needs of nearly two hundred million people. Nor is this the end of the process since, in spite of the counterwind of nationalism that is blowing with gale force from Paris, I have no doubt whatever that, within a few months or years, the European community will be expanded to include Great Britain.

The importance of common markets and free trade areas rests not only on their economic efficacy but also on the seeds of political unity they carry with them. Yet they by no means provide a full answer to the imperative need for efficiency in marshalling the world's resources; nor should we look for only one answer.

International trade, as everyone knows, is as old as time. Internationalized production is less familiar. Businessmen in the United Kingdom are old hands at making their living in world markets and exporting capital to produce goods abroad. This has not always been true of the United States. Except in extractive industries, most U.S. enterprises until recent times have concentrated their activities on producing for the national market, exporting only their surplus. Many still do. However this is no longer adequate for the requirements of the world we live in. In order to survive, man must use the world's resources in the most efficient manner. This can be achieved only when all the factors necessary for the production and use of goods—capital, labor, raw materials, plant facilities and distribution —are freely mobilized and deployed according to the most efficient pattern. And this in turn will be possible only when national boundaries no longer play a critical role in defining economic horizons.

It is a fact of great import, therefore, that, at a time when politicians have been moving to create regional markets to supersede national markets, businessmen have been making quiet progress on an even larger scale: The great industrial enterprises of the world are moving to recast their plans and design their activities according to the vision of a total world economy.

In this development, as is so often the case in history, commerce has been in advance of politics. In a thoroughly pragmatic spirit it has improvised the fictions needed to shake free from strangling political impediments. To make possible the global activities of modern business, it has extended the fiction of the corporation— that artificial person invented by lawyers to free entrepreneurs of personal liability in doing business and thus enable them to mobilize capital from diverse financial sources. The corporate form was originally conceived as a special privilege granted by states to some businessmen for attainment of the states' political purposes. But, over the years, the corporate form of business has become common everywhere and enabled business to roam the world with substantial freedom from political interference, producing and selling in a multiplicity of national markets and creating corporate offspring of various nationalities.

An Emancipated Personality

Today we recognize the immense potentials of this emancipated corporate person. For at least a half century a handful of great companies have bought, produced and sold goods around the world. Since the Second World War the original handful has multipled many fold. Today a large and rapidly expanding roster of companies is engaged in taking the raw materials produced in one group of countries, transforming these into manufactured goods with the labor and plant facilities of another group, and selling the products in still a third group. And, with the benefit of instant communications, quick transport, computers and modern managerial techniques, they are redeploying resources and altering patterns of production and distribution month to month in response to changes in price and availability of labor and materials.

This is an achievement of impressive magnitude and we are only beginning to know its implications. By no means all industries in the United States or elsewhere have comprehended the full meaning and opportunity of the world economy. But they will soon. Meanwhile we can detect the extent to which the concept shapes corporate thinking by the attitudes of management toward liberal trade.

By and large, those companies that have achieved a global vision of their operations tend to opt for a world in which not only goods but all of the factors of production can shift with maximum freedom. Other industries—some of great size and importance in the United States, such as steel and textiles—which have confined their production largely or entirely to domestic markets, anxiously demand protection whenever a substantial volume of imports begins to invade national markets.

Hold the Hailstones

At the moment, in the United States the free-trade movement is again threatened by protectionist storm clouds. I am confident that these clouds will blow by with more wind than hailstones. American businessmen have become involved in world trade to an extent where they can no longer turn their backs on it. But trouble will always arise in some places as business continues to expand its horizons. Conflict will increase between the world corporation, which is a modern concept evolved to meet the requirements of the modern age, and the nation-state, which is still rooted in archaic concepts unsympathetic to the needs of our complex world.

The lack of phasing between the development of our archaic political and modern business structures is sometimes abrasive. The abrasion has already surfaced in several places. The phenomenon is complex. It reflects not only honest business anxiety but a kind of neo-mercantilism. Even in economically advanced Western Europe the concern of local enterprises over the superior size and resources of the global company is being loudly voiced. European businessmen are worried because the measures taken to liberate the movement of goods have preceded adequate modernization of the structure of their own enterprises. They have not had time to build up their strength. They have not yet effected the across-boundary industrial concentration that is essential for European industry to stand on its feet and meet the competition of direct investment by the great global corporations.

The problem is perhaps even graver in Canada, where business and political leaders are deeply worried about how they can maintain their national integrity while living next to an economy fourteen times the size of their own, and yet not jeopardize the inflow of investment capital on which their prosperity depends.

We see comparable phenomena in the developing countries. Hypersensitive to anything that suggests colonialism, they are afraid their economies will fall under foreign domination and, to prevent this, they impose obstacles to the entry of foreign firms, thereby blocking the inflow of the capital they desperately need.

Yet, though the anxieties of local business cannot be ignored, I doubt that this is the most serious danger to worldwide corporate enterprise. A greater menace may come from the actions of governments addicted to a regime of planning, who see in the global corporation a foreign instrumentality that may frustrate their economic designs. The basis for their concern is easy to understand, especially in countries where a world company, if allowed in, would become the largest employer of national labor and consumer of national materials. The problem is something like this: how can a national government make an economic plan with any confidence if a board of directors meeting 5,000 miles away can by altering its pattern of purchasing and production affect in a major way the country's economic life?

Businessmen Better than Bureaucrats

Most managers of world corporations are, of course, thoroughly aware of this problem and may have achieved a commendable level of sophistication in dealing with it. Frequently, in fact, these global businessmen are more sensitive to possible abrasions than are the bureaucrats, who at times can be quite gauche. For example, the government of a major nation has exacerbated the conflict between corporation and country by loudly proclaiming its impotence to control the corporation without doing major harm to its economy.

The government of the United States is far from blameless in the corporation-state struggle. On more than one occasion it has sought to enforce its domestic legislation abroad by trying to extend its writ to actions of foreign subsidiaries of American companies. But, happily, there is a growing realization in the United States that we cannot use Amercan-based world corporations as vehicles to export our own national psyche—our prejudices, whether with respect to trading with China or other communist countries or to controlling monopolies or concerning restrictive practices—without diminishing the utility of the corporate institution itself. And if we are going to be consistent in our encouragement of the world economy and the global company that inhabits it, we shall have to change our ways.

On Shifting Sands

Not that changing our international perspectives would solve or even touch the fundamental problem, for it is in the nature of things that the world company should frequently tread on hostile ground. After all, it is a new concept and one that has not yet fully found its own rationale. Implicit in its operations is a troubling question of political philosophy not yet fully resolved: it is the central question of the legitimacy of power. On the one hand, the shareholders of corporations have a right to expect a reasonable rate of return on capital and a chance to earn income in relation to entrepreneurial risks. But, at the same time, a foreign government is quite validly concerned with the ability of corporate managements to influence the employment and indeed the prosperity of the country. The dilemma arises because neither the people nor the government of the country in question plays a part in selecting the directors or the management of world corporations. Since it is only through national legislation that managements can be made in any way responsible to the local people, there is bound to be frustration when the managements of world firms are out of reach of such legislation.

Thus there is an inherent conflict of interest between corporate managements that operate in the world economy and governments whose points of view are confined to the narrow national scene. We are going to have to ponder the problem far more in order to find the means to resolve the conflict.

One obvious solution is to modernize our political structures—to evolve units larger than nation-states and better suited to the present day. But that is going to take a long time. Meanwhile, many company managements, sensitive to the problem if not always to the full range of considerations that produce it, have developed corporate diplomacy to a high level of sophistication. Not only do they take great pains to ease pressures on national governments but many seek to attach a kind of national coloration to their local subsidiaries.

These commendable efforts take a variety of forms. For example, some world corporations associate themselves with local partners; others take only minority holdings in their local affiliates. In some cases they leave effective control of local subsidiaries to local managers while inserting only a minimum of direction.

While leaving control to the local managers sometimes works well, often it gives rise to additional problems. It is clear to me that national ownership in local subsidiaries impedes the fulfillment of the world corporation's full potential as the best means yet devised for utilizing world resources according to the criterion of profit: an objective standard of efficiency.

The obvious drawback of local ownership interests is that they necessarily think in national and not in world terms. Thus they are likely to impress their narrowly focused views on vital policies having to do with prices, dividends, employment, the use of plant facilities in one country rather than another, even to the source of component materials. In other words, once the central management of a global company is restricted to the divergent interests of national partners, it loses its ability to pursue the true logic of the global economy.

"Denationalization"

This leads me to suggest that we might do well to approach the problem at a different level, not by nationalizing local subsidiaries but by internationalizing or perhaps more accurately denationalizing the parent. Only in this way can we preserve the full economic promise of the world corporation as an institutional instrument of the world economy.

A solution in these terms represents a step well in advance of solutions that have been generally considered. Perhaps it may seem utopian and idealistic, but I would be prepared to wager that over the next decade or two we shall have to find a solution along this line if world companies are to avoid being increasingly hamstrung and emasculated by national restrictions.

The essence of this suggestion is that those artificial persons whom I have referred to as world corporations should become quite literally citizens of the world. What this implies is the establishment by treaty of an international companies law, administered by a supranational body, including representatives drawn from various countries, who would not only exercise normal domiciliary super-vision but would also enforce antimonopoly laws and administer guarantees with regard to uncompensated expropriation. An inter-national companies law could place limitations, for example, on the restrictions nation-states might be permitted to impose on com-panies established under its sanction. The operative standard de-fining those limitations might be the quantity of freedom needed to preserve the central principle of assuring the most economical and efficient use of world resources.

Obviously such an international company would have a central base of operations. It would not be like Mohammed's coffin, sus-pended in air. It is clearly unnecessary that there be a single profit center. The international company's operations in its home country would be subject to local laws to the extent that they do not infringe the overriding regulations of the organic treaty.

I recognize, of course, that a company will not become effectively a citizen of the world merely by a legal laying on of hands. It requires something more than an international companies law to validate a company's passport; the company must in fact become international. This means among other things that share ownership in the parent must be spread through the world so that the company cannot be regarded as the exclusive instrument of a particular na-tion. Of course, in view of the underdeveloped state of most national capital markets, even in economically advanced countries, this is not likely to occur very soon. But eventually, as savings are effectively mobilized for investment in more and more countries, companies will assume an increasingly international character. At the same time, we can expect a gradual internationalizing of boards of directors and parent company managements.

These suggestions are offered in tentative and speculative terms. They are not the only solution. One can envisage an international treaty, for example, directed at resolving jurisdictional conflicts and limiting national restrictions on trade and investment. Yet an international companies act, as I see it, has intrinsic merits. It offers the best means I can think of to preserve the great potential of the world corporation for all society.

Nor is this suggestion far beyond present contemplation. It is merely an adaptation in a larger arena of what is likely to be created within the next few years in Europe: a common companies law for the European Economic Community together with a body of regulations to be administered by the EEC.

But let me be quite clear on one point. This proposal does not rest on the notion of world government or anything resembling it. I have lived far too long on the exposed steppes of diplomacy and practical politics to believe in such an apocalyptic development within foreseeable time. Nonetheless what I am suggesting necessarily has its political implications. Freeing commerce from national interference through the creation of new world instrumentalities would inevitably, over time, stimulate mankind to close the gap between the archaic political structure of the world and visions of commerce vaulting beyond confining national boundaries to exploit the full promise of the world economy.